From Butcher's Boy to Beefeater

Geoffrey Abbott

Yeoman Warder (retd.)
H.M. Tower of London
Member of the Queen's Bodyguard
of the
Yeomen of the Guard Extraordinary

The right of Geoffrey Abbott to be identified as the
Author of the Work has been asserted by him in accordance
with the Copyright, Designs and Patents Act 1988.

FROM BUTCHER'S BOY TO BEEFEATER

Copyright © Geoffrey Abbott 2014

Published by
Candy Jar Books
113-116 Bute Street,
Cardiff Bay, CF10 5EQ
www.candyjarbooks.co.uk

A catalogue record of this book is available
from the British Library

Printed and bound in the UK by
CPI Group (UK) Ltd,
Croydon, CR0 4YY

ISBN: 978-0-9927548-7-7

ACKNOWLEDGEMENTS

The correspondence from Buckingham Palace included in the Appendix has been reproduced by permission of the Royal Household, and the illustration of H.M. The Queen and H.R.H. The Duke of Edinburgh with the Body of Yeoman Warders is a Crown photograph. The inclusion of my service with No. 291 Signals Unit has been sanctioned by the Ministry of Defence.

Acknowledgement for the large framed picture of the author in State Dress is made to Charles Torrington, for that of the Tony Robinson illustration to Spire Films, and to Christopher Holmes Photography for the one of Helen Skelton, the Blue Peter presenter.

Acknowledgement is also due to Ed Geldard for the Sword Bearer illustration, to the *Westmorland Gazette* for that of the Mace Bearer illustration, and to the publishers of the German *Zeit Magazin*. Not forgetting all my colleagues on foreign airfields and locations who, across the years, pointed their Box Brownies, squinted through the view-finders, and pressed the releases!

Whilst every effort has been made to trace copyright to material in this book, the author apologises if he has inadvertently failed to credit any ownership of copyright and this will be rectified in any future reprint.

Digital imaging and other photography by Chris Holmes of Christopher Holmes Photography, Kendal, Cumbria.

ABOUT THE AUTHOR

Geoffrey Abbott joined the Royal Air Force prior to World War II and became an aero-engine fitter on Spitfires, Hurricanes, and many other types of aircraft. He saw wartime service in North and East Africa, Somalia and India, post-war in the Suez Canal Campaign, the Hashemite Kingdom of Jordan, Cyprus, Malta and the Gulf States, and later served with NATO in France, Germany and Holland. After thirty-five years of service with the RAF he retired in 1974 with the rank of Warrant Officer and then, on becoming a Yeoman Warder ('Beefeater'), lived in the Tower of London and was sworn in at St James' Palace as a Member of the Queen's Body Guard of the Yeomen of the Guard Extraordinary, and by Justices of the Peace as a Special Constable of the Metropolitan Police.

Geoff now lives in the Lake District, where he has written more than twenty-four books on his specialised subjects of history, torture and execution, some being published in the USA, Canada, Australia and New Zealand, with others translated into Japanese, Italian and Greek. His qualifications for such subjects are unquestionable. He once experienced having a noose placed round his neck by a professional hangman – the late Syd Dernley, a man endowed with a great, if macabre sense of humour!

He has appeared as consultant or executioner in more than

twenty documentaries and historical programmes on UK, American and French television channels, 'beheading' such celebrities as Tony Robinson, Rory McGrath, Adam Hart-Davis, and Helen Skelton, and by invitation has written the entries on torture and execution (both for the latest edition and the forty million word database of the *Encyclopedia Britannica*).

His opinion was also sought by the *New York Times* and the international news agency, *Associated Press*, regarding the gruesome hangings of the Iraqi dictator Saddam Hussein and his half brother Barzan el-Tikriti.

Having flown non-operationally in many bombers and fighters during World War II, he now keeps his adrenaline flowing (copiously!) by piloting small temperamental helicopters.

To a girl I once danced with

FOREWORD

No one is quite sure what the real origin of the name 'Beefeater' is – the name popularly given to the Yeoman Warders in the Tower of London or, to give them their full title, Members of the Yeomen of the Guard Extraordinary. If anyone is qualified to hazard a guess then it is Geoffrey Abbott – a larger than life character who, among his many accomplishments, was one of those 'Beefeaters' for nearly a decade. In this book, his autobiography, Geoffrey Abbott unfolds a most varied and colourful career – or series of careers, to be more precise.

Saturdays out of school running errands for his local butcher during the Great Depression earned Geoffrey Abbott the name 'Butcher's Boy' and thirty-five years service in the Royal Air Force were just the opening chapters to this remarkable man's story, and laid the professional foundation for what was to come. Thereafter a series of adventures followed, all set out in this book, which is best described as a compendium of spellbinding, but tongue-in-cheek, stories. Prior to this autobiography Geoffrey Abbott has had published a small library of books and appeared in a score of television programmes highlighting many facets of his colourful life and experiences.

But I judge that it was his time from 1974 to 1982 living in the Tower of London as a Yeoman Warder that has furnished him with some of his most powerful moments.

Today the Tower of London receives over two and a half million visitors a year, but it is at six o'clock in the evening, when the visitors have left, that the Tower really comes alive and its timeless relationship to history feels almost palpable. As Geoffrey Abbott records, it was walking through the Tower in the moonlight with David Scott, one of the astronauts who had actually walked on the moon, that the American spaceman had to concede that the Flamsteed Crater had first been spotted and chronicled from the northeast turret of the White Tower in the early seventeenth century by the then Royal Astronomer, John Flamsteed.

The Tower of London stands as a living monument to a thousand years of British history. Those most deeply associated with that story are the Yeoman Warders and those who came into their care, be they kings, princes, prisoners or paupers.

Geoffrey Abbott's autobiography is a glorious march through a personal career against the backdrop of the turbulence of the principal events of the twentieth century, and all in the shadow of the Tower of London, with its hopes and fears, excitements and sorrows. In this book Geoffrey Abbott invites you into the secrets of his life and the mystery of the Tower of London. There is something here for the avid historian and the general reader alike. It is a long road from butcher's boy to beefeater, but Geoffrey Abbott is asking the reader to join him on the way. If you accept that invitation, you will not be disappointed.

Richard Dannatt
General the Lord Dannatt GCB CBE MC DL
Constable, Her Majesty's Palace and Fortress, The Tower of London

PREFACE

This story starts in a world in which pens had nibs, bicycles and police cars had bells, and automobiles had starting handles; where people went to work by tram, and to holiday resorts by steam train, read books by the light of soothingly hissing gas-mantles, and where worn socks weren't thrown away but darned; a world where a computer was a man who worked out mathematical problems, a mobile was a collection of small ornaments suspended by a length of string from the ceiling, TV stood for terminal velocity – the maximum speed at which you'd hit the ground if you fell out of a plane (120 mph), and frozen meals were those which had been left for too long out in the larder. Twitter was what birds did, and websites were where spiders lived.

But don't be too smug or disparaging towards the occupants of that world and their 'primitive' way of life. If *you* ever write *your* biography, years hence, your readers will be just as disparaging when you go on about iPods/BlackBerries/MP3s/emails/bytes; when you boast about taking as little as five hours to fly to the USA; are sceptical when scientists talk about living on the Moon; dismiss talk of robots as childish fiction; or many of the other new discoveries of *your* lifetime.

Now we've got that settled, I'll go on.

Chapter One
SATURDAY JOBS
AND TAKING THE KING'S SHILLING

I was born in Moss Side, Manchester, on 22nd August 1922, and was christened 'Gerald'. I hated the name and although I protested vehemently by going purple in the face and kicking wildly, splashing the vicar with the font water, it was no use. I soon chose the pen name 'Geoffrey' and, later on, acquired the nickname 'Bud'. Moss Side was a highly respectable locality in those days, my grandfather being not only an inspector in the Manchester Tramways Department but also warden of nearby St Clement's Church. It wasn't a good time to be born, only four years after the end of World War I and with the Great Depression looming, when living conditions for the less well-off were harsh. My father Frank – a soldier wounded in France in the trenches – and my mother were separated (divorce was rare among the working class) and so, in the 1930s, my younger sister Doreen, my mother and I had to cope as best we could. Children grow up rapidly when money is scarce. As the 'man' of the family it was up to me to supplement the minuscule family allowance as much as possible, welfare payments being nowhere near the magnitude of today's generous hand-outs. From about the age of twelve, I had to take on odd jobs. Like any other lad of my age, I would have much preferred to kick a football about in our local park, or go to the morning matinee at the cinema on Saturday mornings (where admission was by empty returnable lemonade bottles, halfpenny on each!). Instead, I did as my mother told me, looked in newsagents' shop windows for 'errand boy wanted' adverts, then applied. I got a job with a butcher in Didsbury, some distance away. I had to cycle there and 'report' to the shop, with its slippery, sawdust-strewn, tiled floor and gory carcases of sheep and cows hanging from hooks in the back room. Rabbits and game birds were on display in the shop where gruesome-looking cleavers and knives lay on the rough-surfaced wooden bench. The odour of blood pervading while I loaded the carrier of my bike with chunks of meat wrapped up in white sheets of paper to deliver them around the district.

Other, sometimes simultaneous jobs, were fitted in on weekday mornings and evenings before and after attending Ducie Avenue Elementary School. Delivering the *Manchester Evening News* and the *Evening Chronicle* brought in six shillings a week. When there was 'breaking news' I had to ride my bike round the neighbouring streets whatever the weather shouting, 'Special! Extra Edition Special!' and residents would come out of their houses to buy a copy. Although I didn't enjoy having to shout in public, the training proved invaluable in later years when, as an NCO, I had to drill airmen on RAF barrack squares.

In the early mornings I was a milkboy. My mother would wake me up at 6.00am for the rendezvous outside our house on Burnage Lane with the milkman employed by Dobson's Dairies, Levenshulme. He drove a horse-drawn milk float, a vehicle equipped with two front candle lamps, the small sections of red glass at the back of each lamp performing the duty of rear lights. Two metal crates filled with twelve heavy glass bottles of milk would be lowered into the deep frame over the front wheel of my delivery bike. This unwieldy load meant that my bike would often attempt to go straight on at a bend in the road – which was dodgy!

By this time I had a stepfather, Fred Lightburn. He had fought in the Great War with the Border Regiment in Burma and treated me as if I were his own son. He knew how interested I was in shooting (and how I loved those cowboy films!) and so, one Gunpowder Night, under cover of the noise of exploding fireworks, he allowed me to fire his shotgun a couple of times.

Eventually I succeeded in winning a scholarship and attended Burnage High School. I also went to night school and, under the impression that I was now a fully grown adult, started, and after some time succeeded, to smoke cigarettes without coughing too much. Limited by my meagre pocket money, they had to be Wills Woodbines, five in a small open-topped paper packet for 3 pence.

By 1938 adulthood overtook me in earnest. I left school and got a job at the factory of Fairey Aviation Company, Levenshulme, within bike-range of home. That firm manufactured single-engined Fairey Battle bombers, and I received the princely wage of 18 shillings and 3 pence (91p) a week, a sum which helped my mother to cope somewhat with the rent and bills.

All employees had to clock in and out using cards stamped with their personal clock number. On entering the factory one removed the card from the rack on the left-hand side of the clock, inserted it in the slot of the clock, and after pressing a brass lever, which recorded the time on it, removed the card and placed it in the right-hand rack. The routine was repeated in reverse at the end of the day. Should a workman be only a minute or so late, he would be 'quarter-houred', a quarter of an hour's pay being deducted from his total – as the average wage of a qualified fitter in those days was only £3.12.6, lateness was to be avoided.

I was initially employed in the component-ordering office with other would-be apprentices. We ate our packed lunches in the factory canteen, where the workforce diners were 'serenaded' by members of the world-renowned Fairey Aviation Brass Band practising for their next musical festival, its members all being full-time employees of the company.

When our boss Mr Knight was elsewhere and we had the office to ourselves, we discovered that we could considerably increase our knowledge of aerodynamics and powered flight by turning a chair upside down, holding it firmly on a table top and attaching the ends of a long length of bungee rubber cord to two of the legs. One could then fire a large wodge of folded paper-orders at high speed with sufficient force to strike one's opponent crouched behind *his* chair at the far end of the room. But such mind-improving activities had to stop when I was moved into the factory, on to the long production line where the aircraft neared completion. In addition to learning how to use basic tools – hammers, files, etc – my other task was to perch on the bench and hold the nose ring firmly on its 'dolly', a solid steel block, while the fitter worked on it with hammer and rivets.

The factory output was two aircraft a day, but this allowed plenty of time for other activities, one being the solemn ceremony performed when any of the hundreds of workers was to be married. The factory was a very long, very high glass-roofed building. Prior to the ceremony an extended ladder was positioned leading up to one of the iron girders supporting the roof. At the apex a large bunch of balloons would be tied, together with a china chamber-pot and strings of sausages, and then everyone would wait until the prospective groom arrived for work. On his appearance the entire workforce would commence beating on their work benches with hammers; the deafening noise increasing to an ear-splitting crescendo, a veritable cacophony, as he ascended the ladder and cut the 'trophies' down – verily, an ancient ritual, its origins lost in the industrial mists of time!

Although fascinated by aircraft – what sixteen-year-old lad wasn't – or isn't – I soon found that mind-numbing repetitive work making them wasn't for me. In the middle of 1939 I applied to join the Royal Air Force. I think my mother accepted that I wanted to leave the nest and see what life 'out there' was really like, and she didn't make any attempt to make me change my mind; I took and passed the required examination, which qualified me to become an Aircraft Apprentice. We were known as 'Trenchard's Brats' – Lord Trenchard having introduced the system in which youngsters aged between fifteen and seventeen were recruited and trained to be highly skilled fitters.

Now *you* know that World War II was declared on 3rd September 1939, but before then obviously no-one, much less youths of my age, the unsuspecting members of the cannon-fodder generation, knew that it was going to be, or whether there would be one at all. Similarly *you* know that we eventually won, but as the months and years passed by and one by one our allies surrendered and were occupied, we still didn't even know whether we would win or not. On my seventeenth birthday, 22nd August, just twelve days before that historic declaration (hankies at the ready) I bade my mother farewell and travelled south to the training school, RAF Halton, Buckinghamshire. There, together with scores of other would-be airmen, most of them fresh out of school, I was issued with a uniform and a bed-space in a barrack block. We were all raw material in a new and strange world but somehow we settled in and over the first few days slowly got used to the rules and regulations, the requirement for short haircuts and shiny boots being paramount. A week after arrival we 'took the King's Shilling', and were sworn in (apparently when the news reached Berlin, Hitler reputedly said that if England was that desperate, he would immediately invade Poland!). We were all given Service numbers. My number – 576660 – with its devilish connotations perhaps prefigured the books I was to write in later years.

I vividly recall the day on which war was declared. We assembled in the large dining room to hear the announcement, wearing uniform, of course, and carrying our gas masks, with rolled up gas capes tied across our shoulders ready for use, for rumours abounded that the German Air Force would launch indiscriminate bomb and gas attacks that very day. During the weeks that followed we were given practice in putting on our gas masks.

'Gas, gas, gas!' the sergeant would shout, and it was a case of headgear off and gripped between the knees, respirator cases opened, masks pulled out and donned – chin in first, straps over head – and headgear replaced (essential to remain properly dressed at all times!). Some RAF stations even had gas chambers through which we had to run without masks, emerging spluttering, our eyes watering at the exit. When air attacks finally started, some apprentices were selected to cycle around the countryside after classes, on the lookout for enemy troops landing by parachute. But as time went by we had more to worry about: learning our trade and generally keeping out of trouble.

The powers-that-be had two major and almost insurmountable tasks to fulfil: first, to curb the natural exuberance of high-spirited youths now freed from parental control, and train them to have questioning minds when considering whether an aircraft was fully fit to fly or not; second, deciding how to repair it, yet at the same time, as members of the Armed Forces, not questioning the need to obey seemingly pointless orders given by anyone superior in rank. One 'not far from the truth' joke concerned a Station Warrant Officer, the man in charge of overall discipline on the station, who ordered an airman to water the flower beds outside his office. When the man protested 'But it's raining, Sir!', our local martinet replied in his usual dulcet tones, 'Well, you've got an issue raincoat, haven't you?'

Failure to comply with such commands, or indeed any misbehaviour, resulted in being charged, marched in front of our squadron commander, and awarded a number of days 'Jankers'. Jankers consisted of drill on the barrack square after work, in best blue uniform with highly polished boots and gleaming buttons, plus full back and side packs, then an hour later, and now in working uniform, cleaning all the receptacles in the tin room of the cookhouse. After that it was back to drill in best uniform, and the routine continued all evening. Such was the discipline that Jankers was almost unavoidable; we were, after all, still teenagers.

Jankers drill came in addition to the routine weekly drill programme for all apprentices, marching and counter-marching on the square for what seemed like hours on end. It included having to stamp one foot when the squad turned left or right, and three stamps, knees high, on the about-turn. How they expected us to kick-start a Spitfire engine with dislocated ankles I never found out! 'Slow marching' was taught, as was 'Changing Arms on the March', i.e. switching the rifle across to the other shoulder during a long march without first coming to a standstill. This was a tricky manoeuvre, and the drill sergeant's picturesque comments regarding the physical inadequacies and doubtful parentage of those apprentices who happened to drop their weapons while attempting to reposition them, are not considered suitable to print.

We were taught how to salute when passing an officer: at a specified number of steps before drawing level to the gentleman, the right arm had to be stretched out to the fullest extent, then bent, with the fingers straight and together, touching the side of the head. Having passed the officer, the hand had to be returned straight down to the side, the slogan being 'the longest way up and the shortest way down'. The 'longest way up' could not be used as an excuse when court-martialled for striking the officer. Berets did not make their appearance for many years so, when saluting, care had also to be taken not to dislodge one's side-cap (aka forage cap or Glengarry). This headgear was worn fore-and-aft, with one side touching the right ear; if slanted too far over, one walked, not beneath it, but alongside it; if perched too centrally, one's silhouette resembled a well-sharpened pencil – not a pretty sight.

I had elected to become a FIIE, an aero-engine fitter, and a number of us were dispatched to RAF Cosford in Shropshire for training. Despite our vehement protests, we were transferred back to the more disciplined environment of Halton after a few months. Apprentice intakes were split up into squadrons and wings and housed in barrack blocks surrounding the square, about twenty apprentices to a room, with everyone allocated a bed, a mattress consisting of three biscuit-shaped squares, bedding, a bedside locker and a shelf above. Adjoining each room was a small room – a bunk – occupied by the corporal in charge. We had to keep the main room clean; weekly 'bull' jobs included the toilets, windows, and polishing the wooden floor with a long-handled, heavily weighted brush known as a 'bumper'. To keep the room in pristine condition for CO's inspection, whenever anyone crossed the room he slithered about the floor on squares of felt. Beds had to be made up each morning, with blankets and sheets folded up in the prescribed manner, boots displayed with polished soles uppermost, and locker doors left open to reveal one's meticulously lined-up issue kit, each item stamped with the owner's service number.

Parades and inspections became a way of life, and woe betide the apprentice with dirty buttons, hair longer than two inches, or slacks lacking sharp creases (these achieved by soaping the insides of the crease, placing the garments flat under the bottom blanket and sleeping on them. The soap did cause them to rot eventually, but...)

Reveille, sounded by an apprentice-band trumpeter outside the blocks, was at 6.30am. One apprentice from each room would then rush to the cookhouse, collect the 'Gunfire' – a large jug of tea and biscuits – serve them out, quickly get into PT kit – vest, shorts and plimsolls – and Physical Training would follow on the square. In bad weather, we wore greatcoats over the kit! Parades followed after ablutions and breakfast, marching us to the workshops, where we were first taught Basics – how to hammer and chisel, drill and saw, use micrometers and depth gauges – training in which my months at Fairey's proved a considerable advantage. At night 'Lights out!' was sounded by the 'Last Post' played on the trumpet and the corporal in charge of the room ensured that there was no talking after that.

We were paid the proverbial shilling (5p) a day, but actually only received three shillings a week, the increment being given to us when we went on leave, enriching us for the occasion with as much as three pounds! As food shortages became increasingly severe, going home on leave one was greeted, not by cries of welcome, but 'Did you bring a ration card?'

Smoking was strictly forbidden for those under eighteen, which affected just about everyone, most having joined at sixteen. Despite the regulation and our meagre pay, we bought cigarettes, rationing them by marking their lengths with pencil lines, then smoking them up to the next mark whenever we had the opportunity – so far at breaktime, so far in the evening. Most illicit smoking took place in the workshop latrines, standing astride the toilet so that one could drop the offending fag into the bowl as soon as the inevitable patrolling service policeman or 'snoop' approached. Threatened with more Jankers, we would try to look innocent, while unavoidably exhaling smoke!

My eighteenth birthday was a big event. Walking into the NAAFI canteen I sat down – and lit up. Scarcely had I taken my first drag than two corporals, swooping like voracious wolves on a helpless sheep, appeared from nowhere, demanding my smoking pass. Triumphantly I produced it and, thwarted of their prey, not even able to get me for dirty buttons, they slunk away.

Sometimes, to avoid the inevitable and mandatory Sunday church parade, some of us would sneak out of camp (one of the vertical iron railings could be swung to one side) and make our way to the nearest road. There we would hitchhike as far as possible until midday then, wherever we were, cross the road and hitchhike back; anything to taste freedom. Unfortunately the practice came to an abrupt end when one unfortunate apprentice thumbed a car to find that the driver was the officer in charge of his squadron! Although we all wore identical uniforms, anonymity was out of the question; our small brass arm badge, a four-bladed propeller within a ring, signified that we were aircraft apprentices, differently coloured hat bands denoted the wing to which we belonged, the colour of the plastic disc behind our cap badges distinguished the squadron number and, getting down to real detail, the waist strap coiled round our respirator cases bore our service numbers on a white background – we were instantly identifiable without even opening our mouths.

'Bull' was rife, and never more than when *very* senior officers came to inspect the station. Everything, but everything, had to be immaculate – roads swept, signs cleaned; even the stones bordering the pathways had to be painted, the unofficial mantra being, 'If it moves, salute it; if it doesn't, paint it white!'

One of my great friends among the apprentices was Les Regan, from Liverpool, whose ambition had always been to join the RAF. Indeed, he was so keen that from a young age he had collected and assembled small models of aircraft, then suspended them from his bedroom ceiling. On leave over Christmas 1940 I visited him and we celebrated the New Year in the city centre. Among the throng was a girl named Dora, with whom I quickly fell in love. She felt the same way, and we kept in touch as much as we could after I returned to camp. The 'Top of the Pops' at the time was *Begin the Beguine*, and so it became *our* tune. Alas, the romance didn't last long. A few months later I received a 'Dear John' letter. I couldn't bring myself even to hum *Begin the Beguine* for ages after that!

After we both left Halton I didn't see Les again until I was instructing at RAF Cosford and he happened to be in transit through the camp. His first words to me after several years were, 'As I was saying...!' We had a lot to catch up on. He had volunteered for aircrew, passed all the tests, and qualified as pilot, initially flying Lancaster bombers. He had flown one at such a low level over his home town that three policemen took the aircraft's number, and he was consequently grounded. However, some time later, while stationed with a non-flying unit, he was on parade being inspected by a very senior officer, who noticed that he wore pilot's wings and asked him why he wasn't still flying. Hearing the story, the officer took decisive action, and within a matter of weeks, Les was back in the cockpit, happy again – and no doubt keeping at a respectable altitude whenever in the vicinity of Liverpool!

Because of the war our training course at Halton had been shortened from three years to twenty months. As time went by we all became more proficient in our test pieces and advanced to more specialised trade training on the various types of aircraft engines. By far the best part of the course took place during our last few weeks at Halton, when each day we were marched, accompanied by the sounds and skirls of the Apprentice Pipe Band, to the airfield, to be instructed on how to install, remove and maintain engines installed in *real* aircraft. Some of them were WWI biplanes, but at last we were where we had dreamed of for all those months; after enduring the petty disciplines, the Jankers, the saluting, presenting arms, forming fours – we were actually going to make propellers go round!

At the end of the course, before Easter 1941, we sat the final exams. Like the vast majority of my colleagues, I passed out as an AC2 – Aircraftman Second Class. It was the lowest rank in the service, but at least I was not a pen-pushing clerk, a cook or a store basher, but in the RAF's top trade group, as a qualified aero-engine fitter. There'd be no more Jankers or petty bull, no more bumpering the floor or foot-drill on the square – heaven! After the results we were informed of our postings – our first unit out in the big wide wartime world; mine had the mysterious initials of PTS/CLE, RAF Ringway, Manchester. Burdened with full pack and kitbag, we were all marched down the hill to Wendover railway station to start out in our new careers.

Chapter Two
FLYING WITH THE PARATROOPERS

After a long rail journey with frequent changes, I arrived by civvy bus at the end of the country road leading to RAF Ringway (now Manchester Airport) on 19th May 1941, a hot and sunny day. Wearing a full backpack and carrying my kitbag over one shoulder, I trudged the mile or so to the airfield. It was a typical pre-war RAF station, with the domestic area on one side of the road, the airfield on the other. The latter was still grass, though the construction of runways had just started at the far side of the airfield. On arrival at any new posting as a mere 'other ranker' it was important to try to get a corner bed in the barrack room, which usually housed twenty airmen, thereby increasing one's privacy by 50 per cent. But with many more personnel than the peacetime domestic site could accommodate, many of us were billeted in empty council houses a few miles away at Crossacres estate, Wythenshawe, and were bussed in and out to work. So after booking in at the guard-room I was taken there. The only furniture in the houses was service-issue beds and lockers on wooden floor boards, and I was allocated a bed space in one of the rooms, where I unpacked and stacked my kit, also taking possession of the shelf above the bed.

I discovered that PTS/CLE, RAF Ringway, its full title not being divulged earlier for security reasons, were the initials of the

Parachute Training School, part of the Central Landing Establishment, the other unit there being DU, Development Unit, which concentrated on glider pilot training and troop transport. PTS was equipped with twin-engined bombers, Whitley II, having radial Tiger 8 engines and Whitley V's with Merlin engines. The Development Unit trained their Army glider pilots using Horsa and Hotspur wooden gliders towed by Hawker Hector biplanes and Westland Lysanders. Occasionally a Whitley V would tow two gliders at once. Ringway also had a Cierva Autogyro, a forerunner of the helicopter, which taxied around but rarely flew. Many years later I would actually learn to fly a helicopter, albeit one far more advanced than a Cierva.

The airfield side of the camp consisted of a few hangars grouped next to other buildings near the airfield entrance, and a control tower – at that time called the watch office – a small, two-storey, flat-roofed building some distance away. One hangar was used almost exclusively for parachutist training, in which harnesses were attached to the roof girders and the troops swung between walkways positioned high along the walls. I used to see them practising turning in the air, then releasing themselves, hopefully to land facing forward on the big coir mats spread on the stone floor. Their physical training and unarmed combat instruction also took place there.

RAF practice at that time was to park aircraft around the perimeter of an airfield, in marked contrast to that of peacetime and earlier in the war, when they were always formed up in one long precise line in front of the hangars with even their propellers at identical angles. The change occurred when it was discovered that this ceremonial alignment of parked planes offered enemy aircraft an excellent opportunity to strafe and destroy a complete squadron with one long sustained burst of machine-gun fire or a low-level bombing run. So while dispersal was strategically necessary – and also fortuitously allowed ground crews to relax well away from 'Chiefy's' eagle eyes in his office in the hangar ('Chiefy' being the traditional name given to all flight sergeants) – it had its disadvantages, involving as it did, a long hike round the perimeter track at meal times, and only tepid tea in the urn by the time the NAAFI wagon got out there.

Peacetime practice still applied in so far as I was allocated my 'own' aircraft, a Whitley II K7220, call sign 'Y' Yoke. The main task of an engine fitter was to give the engines and their component parts a daily inspection, run the engines while checking all the gauges, repair any faults found, and then sign Form 700 to certify that they were fully serviceable, that there was sufficient fuel and oil in the tanks, etc, etc. Throughout my career as ground crew I was always very proud of 'my' aircraft and always aware of the considerable responsibility I had; one error and not only the aircrew but eight understandably nervous-looking young soldiers could be killed. No matter how long I had been a fitter I always metaphorically held my breath every time 'my' aircraft took off, only relaxing when it had reached a safe altitude.

Such was the decrepitude of the Whitleys that the pilots appreciated having their engine fitters accompany them in the air – it gave them a certain amount of confidence! So I occasionally flew in the adjoining seat as second pilot, winding the flaps down on the final approach. Sometimes the pilot would let me operate the controls to start gently to bank the large lumbering aircraft. Since this appeared to have little or no effect, I could sometimes forget that I'd done so – only to feel a sudden lurch after a time lag of a few seconds as the Whitley eventually responded. More often than not, however, I would prefer to stay on the ground, relaxing in the long grass out on dispersal for a smoke until my aircraft returned, when I would run out, direct the pilot to park in the designated place using the appropriate arm signals, and after chocking the wheels, check with him for any engine problems.

Our Whitley II bombers had already seen war service, having been used in propaganda-leaflet dropping raids over the Continent. Now old, they were capable of flying at little more than 95 mph. Indeed when the Whitley serviced by my engine fitter friend Ronny Hall attained 100 mph, no one could speak to him for weeks! Their 'dustbin' gun turrets had been removed from the underside of the fuselage to provide an exit for parachutists and, their tail gun-turrets removed as deemed unnecessary, they flew day and night in a training role.

Each flight took fifteen minutes, when dropping the entire stick of eight to ten troops at once over the drop zone at the nearby country estate of Tatton Park, or thirty minutes if circling to drop one soldier at a time. Such short trips did not justify retracting the undercarriage which was only essential at higher speeds, so for para drops it was left down.

Most drops were from as low as 300ft so that, when involved in enemy action, the stick of troops could quickly regroup and defend themselves from attack or move as one unit towards their objective, rather than be scattered over many miles, as they would have been if dropped from a greater height. A drop from such a low altitude did not allow sufficient time to count the requisite number of seconds' delay between pulling the 'chute's ripcord and hitting the ground. Instead, each 'chute cover was connected by a static line to a rail inside the aircraft roof which pulled the cover off and allowed the 'chute to open when the parachutist was clear of the aircraft's fuselage or tail wheel. Speed of exit from the aircraft was essential for the same regrouping reason. Once, in a demonstration held during a visit by Sir Winston Churchill, four RAF and four Army instructors vacated the aircraft in seven seconds, their feet literally resting on the heads of their colleagues.

I have vivid memories of my flights in the tail of 'Y Yoke'. The removal of the rear gun turret left one standing in the open air almost from the waist upwards; a hand rail had been fitted athwart the aperture and, as one faced aft, the slipstream was diverted by a small visor fitted to the top of the fuselage immediately behind one's head. The exhilarating sensation at take-off was heightened by being airborne well before the rest of the aircraft – the design of the Whitley was such that, due to the angle of the wings, the aircraft took off in a pronounced nose-down attitude, so that within the first few yards the tail was already high in the air.

Flying in that position over the drop zone gave me a unique view of each exiting paratrooper. Only a few feet below the tail, the first man would suddenly appear, travelling backwards at speed, arms and legs flailing in the slipstream. Every facial expression was clearly visible and usually showed understandable fear or at least extreme apprehension, for the cover over his 'chute had not yet allowed it to open. One after the other, they would appear, hurtling backwards immediately beneath my feet, their 'chutes exploding into life after a few seconds. Then, in sequence, they would fall away, getting smaller and smaller, each man swinging like a pendulum as he descended, the 'chutes looking for all the world like a string of mushrooms arranged in order of size. Sadly, many of these young men lost their lives at Arnhem, Crete, and other multi-drop para operations.

On the occasion of the Churchill visit, I suggested to one of the many journalists present that a press photographer could capture some superb photos by joining me in the tail for a 'drop' (not whisky!) over the drop zone. I gripped the crossrail with one hand and held on to him with the other as he leant perilously out over the tail. It was a hazardous arrangement, but resulted in some spectacular pictures.

Not that training went as arranged, of course, 'Murphy' being an ever-present though invisible crew member. (Murphy's Law states that 'If a thing can go wrong, it will go wrong.') Tatton Park was mostly grass, but there were small clumps of trees into which the occasional hapless parachutist would descend, dangling, his 'chute entangled in the upper branches, unhurt but helpless, until the ground party could bring ladders out and rescue him.

One paratrooper fatality occurred during my time there. While dropping 'singles' (i.e. one at a time), a Polish officer, 2nd Lt Kalewski, instead of dropping upright through the exit hole as taught, bent forward as he exited and so struck his head on the opposite side of the aperture. Although the static line attached to the aircraft roof operated his parachute, his legs fouled the shrouds (the cords of the 'chute), preventing it from opening, and regrettably he fell to his death. However, the series of circuits were continued and the other troops had to drop so as not to destroy their confidence.

Exercises were frequently held to give the Home Guard some practice in dealing with an airborne invasion. Along with other aircraft and ground crew, I flew down in 'Y Yoke' to Gatwick (then a sleepy little civilian airfield outside London) and spent a few days dropping 'enemy' troops in the countryside. At night I recall sleeping under the reception counter in a Gatwick edifice known as the 'Beehive'. There was little point in protesting about our make-do accommodation – 'There's a war on' was the inevitable reply.

Because the twin-engined Whitleys were parked in the open, servicing was difficult, especially in bad weather. We fitters swayed on high, rickety moveable platforms, although in bad weather the ingeniously designed engine nacelle covers gave some protection. These consisted of an upper section formed by two large U-shaped inflatable tubes joined by thick canvas, which sat over the radial engine once the cowlings had been removed. The plugged ends of the tubes were then inserted into four long metal pipes, and these were then stuck in the ground, and a long length of canvas was wrapped around them to form a very tall, oval-topped tent. Within this stood the working platform, the prop protruding through the lace-up canvas at the upper front. It was primitive and, when working inside, dark and claustrophobic, and proved a real challenge to erect in a high wind!

We operated in shifts: day and night. Night flying was made possible by illuminating the landing path with 'goosenecks' flares, similar to large watering cans but filled with paraffin with wicks protruding from the spouts, positioned at frequent intervals. They were very effective, albeit dirty and smoky. Even now I recall with goose pimples being on flare-path duty one night, when the air-raid sirens sounded to signify the imminent approach of enemy aircraft; The order came to douse the flares as quickly as possible and I bounced at speed across the uneven ground from gooseneck to gooseneck in an open truck, listening to unknown aircraft engines droning overhead and wondering frantically whether we'd get all the flares extinguished before Jerry realised we were there.

Duty Crew involved a fitter and a rigger (responsible for the airframe of aircraft), plus a Verey (single cartridge) pistol, taking their ease on the flat roof of the Watch Office, to look out for and attend to any visiting aircraft. As the range of British and Allied aircraft types was extremely wide at that time, all one's expertise was called for, even when finding the plane's cockpit-hood release in order to speak to the pilot. The aircraft would be marshalled in, parked in front of the Watch Office, refuelled, serviced if necessary and later started up and despatched. It was not altogether straightforward, since with the number of foreign refugee pilots such as the Poles, French, Czechs serving with the RAF, only improvised sign language got the necessary faults identified and repaired. While on Watch Duty on one occasion, a Defiant night-fighter aircraft landed short of fuel. It had been camouflaged with a matte finish of sticky soot over all the surfaces in order to be as invisible as possible at night and it was a filthy job indeed, clambering on the mainplane and refilling its fuel tanks again.

There were some crashes. A Spitfire pilot, landing fast, running out of grass and about to join the scenery, locked his brakes and flipped right over, the rudder post keeping the cockpit hood clear of the ground. As nearby groundcrews rushed to get him out before the fire and explosion of ammo, the pilot kept his wits about him. Before the first rescuer instinctively attempted to release his harness, the pilot stopped him, and told him to take his weight first. If the quick release had opened the pilot would drop and break his neck, a not unknown hazard in such circumstances.

On another occasion a twin-engined Baltimore bomber landed with its brakes partially on, a technique used by tricycle undercarriage aircraft in those days. Again, wet grass provided insufficient friction and the plane skidded at high speed across the airfield, smashing into one of the buses used to transport the runway construction workers to the site. The aircrew member lying in the Perspex glass nose was killed outright and the aircraft was a complete write-off. I was detailed to stand 'crash guard' with tent and rifle that night, and with gory debris and human remains scattered around, it was a sad and eerie vigil for a nineteen-year-old airman. It was an experience that brought me face-to-face with what war was really about.

There was little entertainment locally for the troops, although to their credit, some of the good ladies of the neighbourhood organised dances in the 'Cedars', a large house nearby, where we foxtrotted and waltzed to music from a wind-up gramophone – war was hell! I always looked forward to leave, of course; at that time my mother and my stepfather Fred lived in a cottage on a small farm at Chisworth in Derbyshire, and I was allowed to use his shotgun and shoot rabbits for the pot. Rabbit pie and rabbit stew provided a luxury addition to our diets in those days of strict rationing. I also learned to swing a scythe which is especially tricky for left-handed people like me.

I had been at Ringway for about a month when I was summoned to the Flight Office and told that the pilot of a Tiger Moth, a two-seater open cockpit trainer bi-plane, had run out of fuel and made a forced landing in a field some ten miles away. I was to take a supply and refuel it. A truck was waiting, with a corporal driver, and eventually we found the place. The Tiger had landed in a very small field where the pilot was impatiently waiting, surrounded by a gaggle of local villagers. Having had to divert from his planned route and make a hasty landing, the pilot asked some of the spectators for directions to Ringway. I was keen for the opportunity to aviate so, with the blind confidence of a nineteen-year-old, offered to accompany him and show him the way.

Visibly relieved, the pilot enlisted help from the onlookers to drag the aircraft back as far as possible to the hedge, to give him the maximum take-off run, and faced it into wind. It was customary for a Tiger Moth pilot, with a trainee, to take the rear cockpit with the trainee in the front one in order to give him the impression of flying a single-seater aircraft. The small field had a line of trees at the far side, so dangerously close that the pilot decided to improve my chances of survival should we hit them, and told me to take the rear cockpit, while he took the front. We both strapped in; he started up, and with full revs plus, no doubt, both feet on the instrument panel, we hurtled towards the treetops. I might have imagined the leaves brushing the underside of the fuselage...

Airborne, we flew at about 250ft, while I leaned over the side frantically trying to pick up a landmark. I quickly realised, to my horror, that things look totally different from the air! What made it worse was that, in order to foil German parachutists, all signposts, railway-station signs, large factory advertisements and such like had long since been removed, so that one field, one lane, looked very much like another. We seemed to have been flying for ages, and the pilot's cries of 'Where are we? – where the h... are we?' over the Gosport tube connected to the helmet I'd donned became increasingly frantic. Desperately I searched the horizon. Would we run out of fuel again? What would my commanding officer say? Would I be court-martialled for volunteering stupidly in the first place? Suddenly, like an oasis in the desert, away in the distance, I saw a number of parked buses, those of the airfield contractors. I was saved! Waving my arm above my head, I pointed forwards and downwards over the pilot's shoulder, his gasp of relief audible above the roar of the engine. We made a perfect landing and taxied to the

Watch Office, where we clambered out of the cockpits. Either speechless with gratitude, or unable to find suitable epithets regarding my mentality or parentage, the pilot went to book in without a word. I returned to the flight office, to be greeted by the MT corporal who said he'd been back for ages, and where the hell had I been? I decided that from then on I would fill up the fuel tanks then walk back to camp if necessary.

Boffins were ever-present at Ringway; one devised a drop method employing a number of small platforms in the aircraft, each large enough for just one man with his weapons and equipment. The platforms were designed to slide along rails in the fuselage floor, exit via an aperture at the tail and descend by means of a blade mounted on a shaft at the top of the platform which would unfold and rotate as it left the aircraft in the same way as does a sycamore leaf, slowing the platform's descent until a safe landing was achieved. Whether it worked or not, I don't know – there was certainly no rush of volunteers to test it from the groundcrews.

Each week we received training in airfield defence. This was before the formation of the RAF Regiment (its guardian 'soldiers') and so we were trained to work 'with a spanner in one hand and a rifle in the other'. If under attack by enemy paratroops, we would abandon the aircraft we were working on and man the gun-pits surrounding the airfield. This training stood groundcrews in good stead elsewhere during the war.

Being young and impetuous, firm in the belief that it's always other people who die early, I was impatient to join the real war 'out there'. My mother and Fred understood my ambitions, so after a brief hankie session and many urgings to 'take care, and do write', I volunteered for overseas and left Ringway on 11 December 1941, heading for I knew not where.

Chapter Three
A TARGET OF THE U-BOATS

Following brief embarkation leave, shortly after Christmas I reported to No. 5 PDC (Personnel Despatch Centre) Wilmslow, to be kitted out with KD (khaki drill), inoculated against foreign creepy-crawlies, and given a draft number: 3669, convoy UWUW/Y12/L. Draft numbers were given to groups of airmen destined for different units in different parts of the world, and on arrival I met seventeen other airmen, from various units, also on draft 3669. I was the youngest, at nineteen and a half years old, and Jock McNulty was the oldest, at thirty-seven. As we introduced ourselves we realised that our various trades – twelve groundcrew and six back-ups, a clerk, storekeeper, instrument repairer, general help etc – could mean only one thing – we were an embryo, small flying unit, lacking only pilots. Wartime regulations meant that we were not told of our ultimate destination in case we were captured and interrogated, so we had no idea what sort of flying unit it would be or where we would end up.

The specified overseas tour length was four years for single men and three years for married men. I was single and no-one could foresee the duration – or the outcome – of the war, and so a long *unknown* lay ahead. I left Wilmslow by rail, on the night of 6th January 1942, together with hundreds of other airmen. The night rail journey crammed into blacked-out compartments, travelling through blacked-out towns, first led to Gourock, Scotland, where we were marched straight from the railway station to the harbour. Very few of the hundreds of thousands of troops transported overseas during World War II travelled in any sort of comfort, let alone luxury; the vast majority endured conditions which were little short of appalling. In retrospect, and in view of the sheer numbers of men to be moved, plus the urgent requirements of the various battlefronts, there was simply no alternative to the use of hastily adapted and inadequately equipped merchant ships. In particular, the 'other ranks', of which I was one, endured conditions, which nowadays would be condemned outright by the RSPCA.

There was little doubting our fitness, considering the amount of equipment with which we were all festooned. Over my uniform tunic, slacks (no battledress for years to come) and greatcoat was fastened a skeletal webbing harness consisting of braces and blue canvas belt. From the belt hung a full water bottle on one hip and a sidepack – containing necessities such as eating utensils, washing tackle, etc – on the other. From the back of the belt hung my mess-tin, its thin handle folded inward between the lid and the base. The shoulder strap braces supported my backpack, a double affair, one above the other, secured together by buckles. To prevent them 'bouncing' as I marched, the lower corner of the bottom pack had a short strap known as the kicking strap which, when pulled forward and hooked to the front of the skeletal webbing, held the whole harness locked tightly to my body.

Over my backpack a large horseshoe-shaped roll consisting of a blanket rolled up inside the issue waterproof groundsheet was secured. Finally, I had a respirator in its canvas case strapped to my chest, and a steel helmet was secured to that by its chin-strap. The issue wasn't only the encumbrance: it was vital to put on each item in the right sequence; doing so required dexterity, and suppleness was called for in securing each one to the body. Calls of nature were out of the question once one was fully harnessed! Nor was this the only baggage to cope with – there were also two kitbags, each stamped with one's service number, packed full of issue clothing and kit. One, with a single blue ring round it, was the 'deep sea' kitbag. Its contents were not wanted on voyage, and so it would eventually go into the baggage hold of the ship. The other, marked with two blue rings, contained things that we might need en voyage. On the march it was just possible for me to sling one kitbag over my shoulder, resting it diagonally across the top of the horseshoe roll, and carry the other under my unoccupied arm, hoping that I wouldn't need to adjust or replace my headgear (a side-cap, this being in the pre-beret era). Few personal belongings could be taken, if only because the total permitted weight of kit and baggage was 60 lbs.

At the docks we were faced with the vertical steel sides of what appeared to me, a landlubber, as little short of a maritime leviathan. We struggled like human pack mules, bowed and breathless, up the steep gangways on to its deck, then picked our way down a series of steel stairways into the bowels of the ship, taking care not to overbalance on the slippery steps.

Like most troopships, Bibby Line's *HMT Staffordshire* had been hastily converted from its peacetime role as a merchantman. Officers now occupied the relative comfort and fresh air of the upper decks and cabins; hundreds of troops were crammed down below in three levels of hold, great metal caverns connected by tortuous companion-ways and steep steel ladders, all well below porthole level. Mess tables with benches each side had been welded to the floors, with scarcely room to sidle between them. Rows of small lockers lined the white painted steel walls, and each man was allocated a hammock, plus two hooks in the ceiling from which to suspend it at the appropriate hour, and a cork life jacket, which was worn every minute of the day and served as a pillow at night – without a doubt one's best and closest friend was his personal Mae West!

Four long days later, on 11th January 1942, we finally manoeuvred out of the harbour and into the open sea. By that time I had discovered which steel ladder led to where and had become adept at getting into a hammock. I quickly learnt not to touch the ruddy thing but to grasp the girder above it and swing my body up and in, and then keep hold of the girder while I stilled the hammock's yawing motion before it tipped me out again. Once in, it was necessary to lie flat on my back, for the thick canvas sides were under too much tension to permit any other position. Of course these manoeuvres took place, not in some peaceful garden on a summer's afternoon, but in a ship bucking and heaving in the teeth of a winter's gale, so getting into bed unbruised was a considerable feat!

At night the occupied hammocks touched each other, row upon row of them, all swinging in unison and stretching away under the dim emergency lighting into the far recesses of the mess deck. It was eerily quiet save for the deep inexorable thudding of the ship's engines somewhere beneath us, and the creaking of the vessel as it ploughed through the heavy seas of the Atlantic. Immured in a steel chamber down below the waterline, with little sensation of any forward motion, it was as if we were suspended in space. The hammocks hung less than a yard above the mess tables, so if one had to get up in the night to visit the 'heads' (naval for toilets), it was only possible to move in a crouched position around the mess tables, lurching as the ship rolled. Any loss of balance caused contact with an abruptly awakened fellow passenger and evoked an abusive tirade.

Our boat was one of a large convoy of grey ships widely dispersed over a grey and storm-lashed sea. In order to present as many small and difficult targets as possible, the ships had to be separated, yet if the total area of the convoy was too great, the naval escort vessels couldn't get round to protecting them all. For the early part of the voyage, we had an aircraft carrier and the battleship *HMS Resolution* plus a swarm of destroyers and similar small warships (I recall one having the number 'H80' painted on its sides, believed to be *HMS Brazen*) nearby. These seemingly diminutive escorts steamed at speed continually up and down the lines of lumbering troopships and merchant vessels – an incredible and very reassuring sight. The weather was appalling. The Atlantic in January is never a tranquil lake, and members of the crew told us it was the worst weather in living memory, which we found hard to dispute. The U-boat packs hunting off the west coast of Ireland necessitated heading well out into mid Atlantic which exacerbated the storm's effect on the ships.

The convoy could not maintain a direct course to reach calmer waters sooner, or even sail into wind. It had to proceed in a series of constantly repeated zig-zags to divert the aim of any lurking U-boat commander with his eyes glued to the periscope. In order to coordinate these laborious changes of direction while radio silence was maintained, every few minutes, day and night, the commodore's ship would give one blast on its hooter to signal a turn to port by a pre-arranged number of degrees, and two blasts for a similar turn to starboard, each being a prolonged manoeuvre for a convoy as large as ours. The entire convoy had to proceed at the pace of the slowest ship and at this speed the full force of the Atlantic weather wreaked havoc with the human cargo below decks, the ships heaving and rolling day and night, waves breaking over the smaller vessels, some occasionally vanishing in clouds of spray for minutes on end.

The conditions we had to endure for the first ten nights were, without exaggeration, sheer and utter misery. Because of the weather and the number of troops, most of the time we had to stay below in a foetid atmosphere noisome with the heady scents of the last meal, the hot oil drifting up from the engine room and the inevitable and pungent odours associated with cooped up humanity. I contracted lobar pneumonia but fortunately recovered after a couple of days in the ship's sick bay. Some men, overcome by extreme sea sickness, gave up altogether. They could be found, at all hours of the day or night, huddled at the foot of steel ladders or in corners of the holds, limp and exhausted after repeated bouts of nausea and retching, not eating or drinking, literally past caring what was happening or could happen; under such cramped circumstances, with hundreds of men packed together, little could be done for them.

Under a veneer of servicemen's cynicism, we were bewildered by our unfamiliar surroundings. Few if any of us had ever been to sea before. In those days we holidayed in Blackpool and Brighton, not the Costa Brava, Florida and the Far East. To increase our disorientation, we didn't know where we were going, or how long the sea voyage would take, and we were only too aware that we were exchanging air raids in England for torpedo attacks by the U-boat packs in the Atlantic, which were at that time devastating

British shipping. Between January 1942 and the following June, it is on record that no fewer than one thousand ships were sunk by U-boats. Unknown to the Admiralty, the Germans had broken our naval codes and so knew exactly the size of the convoys and even the dates on which they would sail. On land, when bombs were falling, one always felt that there was a bolt-hole, a refuge somewhere, in which one could take cover. At sea, in a defenceless troopship, the feeling of helpless vulnerability was at times overwhelming – there would be no warning siren or sound of enemy engines overhead, just a sudden overwhelming explosion, at any time of the day or night. If we were torpedoed we would find ourselves trapped below decks or hurled into the sea (and the ability to swim was rare in those days, even if of any practical use in the Atlantic). The convoy would have no option but to sail on; to stop in order to rescue survivors would simply provide the U-boats with sitting targets.

Somehow I, like my new companions, fought against giving way to blind terror, running round and round the upper decks shouting, 'Let me off! I want to get off!' We developed a fatalistic mindset and tried not to dwell on the fact that hour after hour, day after day, the ship was nothing but a floating prize which, sent to the bottom, would merit an ambitious U-Boat Kapitan an Iron Cross. As there were far too many men to be allowed on deck at any one time during the day, fresh air and a chance to smoke (forbidden below decks) were strictly rationed to comparatively few at a time. When it was our mess-deck's turn, I, Jack Brockhurst and a few others would lean against the rails and stare out at the wave-lashed horizon, convinced that every seemingly unusual ripple had been caused by a just-retracted periscope or just-launched torpedo, and that the seaman up in the crow's nest would have seen it if he hadn't been looking in the opposite direction. Night time was the worst; with little to think about one's imagination took over and it was difficult to relax and slip into an uneasy doze.

Duties were handed out of course, such as the galleys, pouring tons of potatoes into the internally rough-sided cylinders of the rotating scraping machines or removing the grease and burnt fragments from the scores of cooking utensils in the pan room! 'Volunteer' mess orderlies in particular had a rotten job: three times a day having to clamber up and down slippery steel ladders while carrying large cauldrons of tea, soup, etc. in a rolling ship, a daunting duty, as was trying to dish out twenty or thirty equal mess-tin portions on arriving back at the mess table.

An easier duty, though one with more macabre undertones, was deep below decks – that of manning the watertight steel doors which divided the full-length holds into different compartments. If we were torpedoed the order was to shut and lock them immediately so that some buoyancy could be maintained in the vessel. This had to be done, even if there were troops confined on the other side of the massive doors – and as you never knew exactly where the torpedo had struck, you would not know whether you were condemning them to a watery death by locking them out or doing the same to yourself. Despite our strong escort, wolf-packs of U-boats were indeed operating in our area. We learned subsequently that two of our ships had been torpedoed but had managed to limp into the Azores. Thankfully we were unaware of that at the time. The attacks could have taken place at night, or on ships positioned on the outskirts of the convoy, hidden from us by the waves and the stormy conditions.

Weather conditions slowly improved, and fourteen days out, on 25th January 1942, we saw land. We had arrived at Freetown, on West Africa's Gold Coast. Anchored off-shore we were surrounded by a fleet of bumboats, local canoes manned by natives and filled to the gunwales with goodies we hadn't seen for years: bananas, pineapples, mangoes and other exotic fruit. Baskets on ropes were thrown up; we put money in, lowered them back to the canoes, and the ordered delicacies were sent up, while we shouted, 'One for Kingi Georgie!'

We spent four days in Freetown harbour, confined on board, before we sailed again, destination still unknown. Dockers and wharfingers at the various ports must have thought we were crazy as, pulling in to moorings at the docks, hundreds of troops would lean over the rails shouting, 'Where are we? What country is this?' For when you can't tell one star from another, when you have no idea of the speed of the ship or even the geographical distance between countries, when the repetitive zig-zags deprive you of all sense of general direction, and the ship's crew don't talk – even if they knew – the smudge of land on the horizon could turn out to be Canada, the USA or even Australia.

Leaving Freetown the weather stayed hot and got hotter. As we knew that the Med was by that time almost enemy territory and out of bounds to Allied shipping, we assumed we must be heading south again, and not north towards Gibraltar. Some of the capital ships escorting us departed to return to the UK and pick up another convoy. Life became rather more worthwhile, especially when sleeping on deck on a rota basis was allowed and one's turn came round. To lie on my back on the deck, watching the ship's masts and rigging swing in slow lazy arcs across the brilliant stars of the tropical night sky, was something never to be forgotten.

Two more water-borne weeks passed before we arrived at Durban, South Africa, on 13th February 1942, having unknowingly rounded the Cape of Good Hope. We were greeted by a reception which we all found emotional. There to welcome us were bands and cheering crowds, and singing led by the memorable Lady in White. It almost made up for the miseries of the voyage. The hospitality and loyal support of the South Africans earned them goodwill that even our dislike of their apartheid system could not entirely extinguish.

We disembarked, entrained and travelled to Clairwood transit camp just outside the city, where we were fed well and able to generally recuperate. South African families invited us to their homes for meals and made us more than welcome – which is a lot more than could be said for the Kenyan residents of Nairobi, the 'Happy Valley' clique of remittance men with whom we were later to come into contact and for whom 'common' soldiers and airmen were worth less than the dust.

On 2nd March 1942 we were taken back to the docks and embarked in *HMT Letitia*. Her cooling system below decks had broken down and we learnt later that a large number of Aussie troops had previously refused to stay on board and had defied their officers by walking off. So, naturally, the powers-that-be put we 'Imps' (Imperial troops) on board! Thankfully they relented, for we were soon taken off, to re-embark in another converted merchantman, *HMT Narkunda*.

We sailed north into the Indian Ocean, keeping well to the east of French Madagascar, doubtless due to its uncertain allegiance at that time. Skirting around it, we reached Mombasa, East Africa, on 9th March, only to sail again the next day, having slept on board. By this time, two months out from UK and with no end to our watery horizons in sight, only our traditional cynicism kept our morale up.

Now that we were well away from the Atlantic gales, life on board improved, though it was still a rough and ready life. We lived cheek-by-jowl with our companions in the makeshift living quarters below decks, and we answered the calls of nature in the same way – or more accurately, cheek-by-cheek! Our improvised toilets were on the open deck in the bows and consisted of two long planks, flat sides uppermost, placed horizontally side by side, with a critical distance of a few inches between them. Supported at intervals and at each end, these planks thus formed a single bench on which I would join my draft 3669 mates and others answering nature's call, and sit poised over the gap, feet resting on a lower ledge. Beneath the gap ran a full-length metal trough flowing with water – we never dared investigate where it led. As many as twenty of us men would be seated there at any one time, gazing out over the Indian Ocean, basking in the hot sun, smoking and chatting to our neighbours, for all the world like some rather indelicate gentleman's club. The tranquillity of the scene was at times broken by some latecomer in urgent need of a place on the bench who, seeing that there was no space would, with Machiavellian cunning, light a piece of paper and launch it at the inlet end of the trough, sending it on a fiery voyage beneath the bare hindquarters of the unsuspecting squatters.

We were now part of a small convoy and headed out to sea, the position of the rising sun indicated that we were steaming east, and so at least not heading for the Western Desert campaign. On deck I watched the flying fish leaping in and out of the waves and the dolphins at our bows, escorting us day after day. The florescent glow of plankton swirled with the waves along the sides of the ship at night. Many of us had been in the doldrums about where on earth we were heading, when suddenly we found ourselves in the *real* Doldrums, for we were sailing through a totally calm sea, not a ripple, not a swell, as if we were poised on a vast sheet of ice as far as the eye could see, an incredible sight to landlubbing servicemen.

For nine days we sailed on, until excitement mounted as land was sighted once again. It was India! There was no welcoming committee at Bombay's docks. We disembarked and marched, carrying our kitbags on unsteady legs, to a nearby transit camp for the night. The next day we were loaded into the holds of yet another troopship, *HMT Felix Roussel,* a huge French liner with two square funnels, one of which was reportedly a cabin for one of the ship's officers. As soon as we were on board, the ship set off westward, back the way we had just come! Some weeks later we realised that the soldiers on board had originally been destined for Singapore and, had we been any earlier, we would have gone straight 'into the bag' as prisoners of war of the Japanese. As it was, we sailed again, sprawled on deck in the scorching sun, resigned, like the Flying Dutchman, never to reach an ultimate destination.

By now we had long since changed into KD – khaki drill – our heavyweight uniforms stuffed into our deep-sea kitbags when changing ships. 'Get your knees brown!' was a regular jibe aimed at new boys by those who had been overseas for some time, so we 'sunbathed' on deck as much as we could. Regulations demanded that we always wore a topee for protection against the sun's rays, most of us adopting the flat-topped 'Bombay Bowler' type rather than the ghastly scuttle-shaped Imperial topee issued to us (and thrown overboard early in the voyage).

Although still aware of the threat posed by Jap submarines, the menace felt in the Atlantic no longer hung over us. The conditions aboard the *Felix Roussel* were as before with the hammocks and mess tables, although not as intolerable as earlier in our journey – we had simply got used to the conditions. This vessel also had unforgettable lavatories, as unique as were those on the *Narkunda*. Far from primitive, the French ship's toilets were below decks and consisted of open-fronted cubicles bereft of seats. Although the design prevented anyone settling down with a newspaper, it had many disadvantages, not least when the ship rolled, and in time one acquired the dexterity and skills demanded of a bomb-aimer – or else finished up in the proverbial!

Three days out of Bombay, Aden was sighted and we anchored in the docks, although no shore leave was allowed. Some of us considered ourselves lucky to be among the quota permitted to sleep on deck that night rather than in the stifling heat below. In the morning though, our luck ran out, for the ship was a coal-burner, Aden was a coaling station, and during the night tons of coal had been brought on board, much of it in baskets borne on the heads of long processions of locals. It had coated everything, including our near-naked, sweating bodies, with a thick black layer of coal dust. We all rushed off to the showers which, being salt water, did little to cleanse and refresh.

From Aden we sailed up the Red Sea and finally disembarked at Port Tewfik, Egypt. Here we were loaded, kit and all, into railway cattle trucks. It was not luxurious, but I was one of those lucky enough to sit at the open sliding doors, legs dangling over the edge, while we travelled parallel to the Suez Canal. I watched with amazement as the huge ships moved along the Canal, a hundred yards or so away, only their upper decks and funnels visible above the sands. The desert war was obviously prepared to wait for our arrival, for the hundred-mile train journey to Heliopolis took exactly ten hours!

At Heliopolis we were taken by trucks westwards into the desert and, after another long journey, ended up accommodated in tents.

At last the ground didn't roll. We became adept at scooping a hollow in the sand for our hips before spreading out the groundsheet (much more comfortable when sleeping on one's side), and I never overlooked the need to shake my desert boots thoroughly before putting them on for who wants to share their footwear with a family of scorpions? Water was strictly rationed, personal stand-up washing in the open had to be completed before about 8.00am – after that the tanks were empty. Our irons (knife, fork, spoon) were cleaned by thrusting them into the sand a few times after meals. These consisted mainly of bully beef subjected to as many heat treatments as the cooks could devise – fried, boiled, baked – and when all else failed, even straight from the can. I, along with two of my fellows, Laury Hanson and Arthur Pursglove, managed to scrounge a couple of days leave in Cairo, so we rode on camels and joined guided tours through the pyramid of Giza.

After three months servicing aircraft in the desert, it was decided that another ration of sea air would do wonders for us, and so we members of draft 3669 and a couple of hundred other troops were transported back to Port Tewfik, and on 7th June 1942 we embarked on a small merchantman *HMT Burma*. There was a large number of Italian POWs aboard who had been captured in the desert and were bound for POW camps, so we guessed we were heading south somewhere.

We chugged slowly down the Red Sea, calling at Port Sudan, Aden and Berbera, though at all these ports we had to stay on board. On 15th June we left Berbera and headed out again into the Indian Ocean. We were on our own, a solitary, unescorted ship, a fact that could have had disastrous results later on. Out of sight of land, we made slow time – it took thirteen days to cover the 1800 miles to Mombasa, an average speed of less than six knots.

Perhaps we could have got there sooner except that, somewhere off the coast of Italian Somaliland (now Somalia), in a dead calm sea, those of us on deck noticed the wake of our ship suddenly abeam, then ahead of us, as the vessel steamed in a complete circle. Later, as the wind freshened, we realised that the ship rolled much deeper to port than to starboard (we'd learnt the correct jargon by then), and in the canteen that night we saw that the steel plates forming the floor had parted across the width of the ship; the slight gap emphasised by the electric lamps held by seamen working below, and opening and closing as the ship yawed and wallowed. Something was evidently wrong, although no explanation was forthcoming from the crew, probably to avoid spreading panic. The prisoners of war were confined below, but most of us stayed on deck, spending much of our time scanning the horizon for other ships that could come to our aid should the *Burma* flounder. We saw nothing and limped into Mombasa on 28th June 1942 where my seventeen fellow draftees and I were only too pleased to be hustled down the gangways and off the docks, then taken up-country by rail to RAF Eastleigh, Nairobi.

By now we were all great friends. We'd come a long way together, spent twelve weeks at sea in each others' close company, struggled manfully up gangways, swung side-by-side in hammocks, competed in trying to identify the next country spotted on the distant horizon, shared mangoes and bananas while anchored off Freetown – and cigarettes when supplies ran low – slept in adjoining patches of sand in the North African desert, and kept up the spirits of those who were married or who had girlfriends by not commenting on the news reports concerning the vast numbers of American servicemen flooding into the UK. Together we shared the constant worry about when the war would end – and who would win it. And we never stopped hoping that our next troopship would be the one which would take us safely back to Blighty.

Years later, while living in the Tower of London, I visited the Memorial to the Merchant Navy at Tower Hill. Studying the bronze panels engraved with long lists of the names of the ships and those of their crews lost to enemy action, among the ship names I saw two of those in which I and my mess-mates had sailed – *HMT Staffordshire* and *HMT Narkunda* sunk with all hands. My friends and I were indeed very lucky.

Chapter Four
SAND, SPITFIRES,
AND BIG-GAME SAFARIS

R AF Eastleigh was a modern station complete with parade
ground, two-storey barrack blocks, a dining hall, stores,
cinema, etc. The airfield side was equally modern and up-to-date
with large hangars and good ground equipment on a par with any
found in UK at that time. When we arrived, the authorities wanted
to know where on earth – or sea – we had been, for those of us on
draft number 3669 had been destined to form a new unit, No. 1414
Meteorological Flight, and we should have been off-loaded from
HMT Narkunda when it moored overnight in Mombasa harbour,
months before, on 9th March, and gone into action. Ah well, better
late...

The Met. Flight's operational role was vital, so vital that later
detachments were formed further along the East African coast, at
RAF Port Reitz, Mombasa and RAF Mogadiscio in Italian
Somaliland. The three bases provided essential weather information
inland for the two OTUs (Operational Training Units) at Nanyuki
and Nakuru – equipped with twin-engined Bristol Blenheim
bombers – and also informed the flying boat squadrons at Kilindini,
Mombasa of conditions out over the Indian Ocean (209 Sqn. and
259 Sqn. with Catalinas, 230 Sqn. with Sunderlands, engaged on
'search and destroy' submarine patrols offshore). Even more
important were the forecasts for the benefit of the hundreds of

supply and troop convoys from the UK sailing along the coast and bound for the Middle East, India and Far East.

Our aircraft consisted of four single-seater Gladiator Mk II biplane 4-gun fighters fitted with Bristol Mercury VIIIA radial engines and one single-seater open-cockpit Gauntlet Mk I biplane 2-gun fighter having a Mercury VIs radial engine. These aircraft were 'hand-me-downs' from the operational Western Desert squadrons, who had been re-armed with more modern aircraft, and reached us in their 'sand and spinach' (brown and green) camouflage. We resprayed them silver for ease of location should they force-land out in the bush. Both types of aircraft had a forward-facing machine gun installed in a slot each side of the fuselage, firing through the propeller arc. In order to keep the wooden propeller blades their necessary length and not reduced to mere stubs on opening fire, a cleverly designed interrupter gear involving the use of cams prevented the guns operating for a split second when a blade was in the way – no mean feat considering the high rate of fire and the hundreds of propeller rotations per minute.

Peacetime practice still prevailed: three of the aircraft were allocated, one to each engine fitter (traditionally 'leader' of an aircraft team), two aircraft being held in reserve. When it was my day off, 'my' aircraft was not flown or even touched by any other ground crew. The system engendered a sense of pride and personal possession, allowing us to get to know and recognise every burp and hiccup of our engines and to diagnose and rectify problems accordingly.

We flew two flights a day, at 6.30am and 2.00pm, to an altitude of about 25000 feet, which was high for the time. The pilot had a large barometer strapped to one thigh, a writing pad to the other, and a psychrometer (with wet and dry bulbs) strapped to a wing strut visible from the cockpit. He took various readings from both instruments at various heights, each flight taking about an hour, and we achieved an admirable record of over 80 percent serviceability.

I was allotted the Gauntlet and was fascinated to note that its large hardback logbook stated that the original owner of the aircraft was the Finnish Air Ministry, Helsinki. Apparently the aircraft (one of many of its type) had been sold to the Finns to reinforce them in their fight against the Russians. Clearly it had never made it there, who knows, it might have made all the difference! It was never popular with our pilots: its open cockpit was most inclement at higher altitudes and would have been at any altitude further north.

The day eventually arrived when we were re-armed with ex-Desert Air Force Hurricane IIBs. Despite the obvious shortcomings of the elderly Gauntlet and Gladiators, it was with real regret that we saw our biplanes pushed down to the salvage yard to be ruthlessly demolished, despite being 100 per cent serviceable. It felt as though puppies were being shot. In their turn the Hurricanes were replaced by Spitfire Mk Is then Vs, which were not designed with engine fitters in mind, for the Rolls Royce Merlin was not the easiest of engines to work on.

For the benefit of more technically minded readers, I should explain that the Merlin engine had two cylinder blocks in a 'V' arrangement. Between the blocks was a wide fuel duct and, should the sparking plugs need to be changed between sorties when the engine was still hot, there was every likelihood that a plug dislodged from the spanner would vanish out of sight beneath the duct. If it was left there, it could slide around during manoeuvres and jam the controls, so it was essential to recover it. That was far from easy without the ability to turn the aircraft upside down and shake it well! The only solution was to tie a magnet on the end of a length of string, lower it down the side of the duct and hold one's breath, hoping that once captured the plug wouldn't drop off half way up. At that time we didn't regard the Spit with the halo of public adoration it later received. It was a good day fighter but not as good as the Hurricane for night landing because its undercarriage design brought its wheels comparatively close together which made landing more difficult.

Eastleigh was quite a busy airfield, with a wide variety of aircraft staging to and from North Africa. As well as 1414 Met Flt, the airfield housed No. 25 AACU (Anti-Aircraft Co-operation Unit), its two-seater Boulton and Paul Defiant fighters and Fairey Battles equipped with winches in their rear cockpits for drogue towing, which were used to train East African troops as anti-aircraft gunners. It was rumoured that on the range an army sergeant held a rope tied to the firing arm of the native gunner, in case in his excitement, the trainee fired at the aircraft by mistake. Pilot and winchman flew with fingers firmly crossed!

Our pilots, Flight Lieutenant Bogle, Flying Officers Johnny Grant, 'Dicky' Gorst, Barry Harrap, Flying Officer Blanchard, Flight Sergeant Woods and others were highly skilled, several being ex-Battle of Britain and Western Desert/Italian Campaign veterans. None of us suffered from triskaidekaphobia, so when the date happened to be Friday 13th, one of our pilots would usually come into the crewroom and say that it was *that* date, so let's go flying! I sometimes flew as crewman with 'Dickie' Gorst in one of 25 AACU's Defiants, when he would delight in low-level hedgehopping across the African plains, chasing herds of antelope and giraffe at below tree-top height. I recall asking him over the intercom whether I should put my arm out to indicate when we approached a crossroads. With a crew of two and a heavy winch, the single-engined Defiant was considerably under powered, its take-off usually requiring a run of twenty-five seconds before it would unstick from the runway – and sometimes even that was not enough. Pilots flying the Defiants had been warned against banking steeply to port at low altitudes, because the winch projected over that side of the aircraft and so altered the weight distribution. One day, while working on a Hurricane, I happened to notice a Defiant piloted by a Wing Commander in the distance over the other side of the airfield. As I watched, I saw it bank steeply, then fall out of the sky, followed by a cloud of dust rising from the ground. His death was instantaneous.

Eastleigh's climate, at 5,371 feet above sea level, was pleasantly temperate, though 3-foot-deep concrete ditches lined the camp roads to cope with the rainy season. Locust storms swept through the area at times, grounding all aircraft fitted with liquid-cooled engines, as flights could terminate abruptly in midair with clogged radiators and air intakes. After encountering a swarm, metal-skinned aircraft would land with the leading edges of their wings and tailplanes flattened by the impact of thousands of bony flying bodies. Walking through a swarm was like being repeatedly struck by hail. When fried, the insects were classed as a delicacy by the natives, but I never felt an overwhelming urge to indulge.

Mosquitoes were a constant menace, and nets were necessary items in the barrack blocks. At Eastleigh they were circular, designed to encompass the bed, tapering up to a 2-foot diameter ring which was attached to the high ceiling. When not in use, the net was twisted into a loose rope and knotted so that it hung a few feet above the bed. At night it was tucked in beneath the mattress by the intended sleeper once he was *in situ*.

The nets may have been effective in keeping out mozzies but failed miserably where bedbugs were concerned. Our beds were 'charpoys', which were wooden frames with sisal ropes strung across to support the three biscuit-shaped mattresses. Between rope and frame, and in the nets, the bugs multiplied and flourished, nourishing themselves and their families at night on the free meals involuntarily provided by their host: the sleeping occupant. Before retiring each night, I would stand up on the bed inside the unfurled net and squash as many bugs as I could find with my thumb nail. Within days of a new net being issued, they became blotched all over as kills were registered. It was a losing battle however, for the bugs thrived and multiplied in every crevice and joint of the bed.

World War II might have been going on all over the globe, but I had my own private conflicts too. In addition to an annual medical check-up, everyone had to have a dental one. One dental officer had a reputation for not being gentle in administering treatment; he seemingly accomplished it by pressing his knee on one's chest while gripping the pliers with both hands to extract the faulty molar. When we heard that he had been on the staff of a well-known London hospital, most of us suggested that it must have been as commissionaire. At my check up, he announced that I needed a tooth extracted. No way, I thought – so, getting the dental chair between him and myself, I told him I intended to refuse treatment. This was permissible under the regulations, although it would go on your record. Realising I doubted his capabilities, he asked whether I knew that to refuse to obey an officer in time of war was a court martial offence. I had a vision of standing in front of the Board, hearing the Prosecuting Council denouncing my wilful insubordination, seeing the bewigged Judge Advocate General nodding approvingly and donning the black cap. Luckily the officer calmed down and ordered me curtly to have the tooth removed elsewhere and report back in seven days time. I visited a civvy dentist in town, who simply filled the offending molar. When I returned to have the tooth inspected as ordered, the officer's silence said more than any tirade.

Apart from the camp cinema, recreation facilities were almost non-existent. Pleasures in Nairobi for other ranks were few, and those that existed were very expensive. Unlike the hospitable settlers up-country, the Nairobi whites – expatriates and 'remittance men' – simply ignored the Imperial troops. Perhaps to them the war seemed a long way from their society life at Happy Valley and the Muthaiga Club. They certainly didn't bother to show any hospitality to common soldiers and airmen. Excluded from their company, my Met mates and I would patronise Torrs Hotel or the New Stanley Hotel, making a glass of Tiger Beer last ages and not leaving until we'd devoured the contents of all the bowls of nuts on the tables. Rickshaws provided the transport back to the airfield, manned by one local native between the shafts, another pushing.

Assaults on servicemen were frequent (we were usually carrying money, didn't know the social mores of the country and were sometimes travelling alone after a night on the town), and so most of us carried some sort of defensive weapon. My personal favourite was a cosh, a short length of hosepipe with a long steel bolt inserted in one end, which could be carried doubled up in my tunic pocket. I christened it 'Percy', short for persuader. The need to use it never arose, for exhibiting it to the 'puller' and the 'pusher' prior to setting off guaranteed a safe arrival at my destination.

Servicemen fortunate enough to be invited to spend their leave on the farms of the hospitable settlers up-country were allowed to take a service .303 rifle and fifty rounds of ammunition with them, with which to shoot for the pot. When I was given the opportunity, I stayed in the house of an elderly lady who, although welcoming and patriotic, was decidedly 'old colonial', a feature I only discovered, to my embarrassment, at the dinner table on the first night. When one of her Kenyan servants placed a dish of food before me, I thanked him, causing my hostess to exclaim, 'Don't you dare thank any of my boys again! You'll have them thinking they're as good as we are!' Abashed, I apologised; after all, it was her house, and I was her guest. Despite these attitudes, she was a very brave lady. She lived there all alone, literally miles from anywhere – and in Africa that means a very long way indeed. Her only guardians were four Rhodesian Ridgeback dogs. At nightfall they slept one on each side of the house to fend off marauding leopards.

During that visit I met Andrew Holmberg, a pre-war big-game hunter and guide. On emigrating to that country from Sweden, his family had stayed with their friend Karen Blixen, celebrated author of *Out of Africa*, and Andrew was born in her house in 1918. He invited me to stay with him on my next leave, and I was thrilled at the thought of staying with a big game hunter. Over the following two years I went on many safaris with him in the Aberdare Hills.

Africa was truly wild in those days – without safari parks and their hordes of sightseers pointing cameras at herds of zebras or gawping at slumbering lions from the safety of a 4x4 safari bus. Andrew knew I loved shooting and would tell me to take one of his 'boys' and bring a deer or bush-buck back for the pot, warning me to watch out for dangerous animals, for the district abounded in lion, buffalo and even elephant.

On one occasion I almost had a run-in with some Maasai, the tribe who lived and hunted in the area. The *East African Standard* had recently reported that the Maasai youths, the 'Young Moran', had revived their tribal tradition of 'blooding their spears' as part of their initiation into adulthood, not by killing a lion as in bygone days, but by attacking and killing the teenage sons of white settlers. I had just shot a deer and, it being large and heavy, I told my 'boy' to go back and bring some assistance. As soon as he had gone, I looked up to find four or five Maasai facing me. Each one, sparsely clad and leaning on a long spear, just stood and looking at me, the expressions on their faces inscrutable. Unable to speak any Swahili – not even the word 'Help!' – I quickly slipped a cartridge into the breech of my rifle and held it threateningly, finger hovering over the trigger. They continued to stand there silently, and the impasse continued, with me not daring to move my eyes from them until my 'boy' plus a companion appeared, whereupon the Maasai simply moved away. I remember thinking at the time that the situation was more perilous than anything I'd ever read in my copies of *Boy's Own* or the *Hotspur*!

But it was joining Andrew on a safari that was the real experience. Before heading into the bush he would remind me that absolute silence was vital. I even had to swathe any loose change in my pocket with a handkerchief and empty all the matches out of the matchbox; a buffalo could pick up the slightest sound, and could charge at speed through the head-high undergrowth without warning – on the narrow path there would be little chance of avoiding it. Then Andrew asked me to raise my rifle to my shoulder. When I did so he told me to aim it from the other side. I explained that I was left-handed and always fired from my left shoulder. He asked me what I'd do if I was attacked from that side, pointing out that I wouldn't be able to swing round in time, so it was essential I learned to fire from either shoulder. He also told me never, ever to shoot at a moving animal, because I'd probably only wound it and it would die a slow death. Whenever a good aim was possible he said that it was important to target the heart or the head, but explained dryly that if the charging animal was a buffalo, its head protected its body, and the mass of bone between the raking horns protected its head.

We would set out with a couple of 'boys', me with my issue service .303, Andrew with a large calibre .475 elephant gun. Walking behind him – the safest place to be – and looking down the barrel of his gun as he sloped it over one shoulder was like looking down the Mersey Tunnel. As we moved silently along the narrow trail, he would suddenly hold his hand up and stop. Then he'd beckon me forward and point to some animal spoor or a pad mark on the ground. 'Lion' or 'leopard', he'd murmur. If it was dung, he'd break it up with his foot and whisper, 'Buffalo – three hours old!' This wasn't theatrical stuff designed to impress a young man who wouldn't recognise a wild animal unless it had vertical bars in front of its face – it was a life-saving necessity, for any misjudgement could prove fatal.

Once we went night-shooting, with torches strapped to our foreheads and two of his 'boys' bringing up the rear. The idea was to move quietly through the bush, swinging our heads slowly from left to right, and on seeing two glowing eyes, to aim between them. I facetiously suggested that two glowing eyes could be a monkey in a nearby bush, or a lion fifty yards away; it might even be two lions that had planned to escape being shot by standing side-by-side, each with one eye closed! Andrew shook his head slowly, but didn't answer.

One day, it so happened that two attractive young ladies from South Africa were visiting the locality, and I offered to escort them on a sightseeing walk through the bush. The impulse to impress the girls was irresistible, so I led the way, rifle in hand, ready to protect the defenceless females from any savage beast that had the temerity to charge us. But my big game hunter image suffered severe bruising when, as I splashed through a swampy bit of ground, I stepped into a five-foot-deep hole and all but vanished from sight! I instinctively raised my rifle above my head to keep the ammo dry, but then had to endure the indignity of being hoisted out by two giggling girls. Soaking wet, I squelched back to base, my pride shattered.

In the cool of the African evenings, Andrew and I sat on the stoep, (Afrikaan for veranda), and sipped Van der Hum liquor from small glasses while watching the moon come up over the veldt – this part of the war I didn't object to enduring. I will always be grateful to him for his hospitality and the fantastic experiences he provided. Many years later, when I was at the Tower, he visited England, and it gave me great satisfaction to show him around and introduce my colleagues to him, many of whom had served in East Africa against the Mau Mau and in other campaigns.

I served on various detachments between 1942 and 1945. One was at Port Reitz, Mombasa where I learnt, from Royal Navy seamen working in the dockyard, that *HMT Burma* had been struck in the rudder by a defective Japanese torpedo, while we'd been in Madagascan waters. Probably, after crippling the ship, they decided not to waste another torpedo on us. Had the torpedo not been a dud, the troopship would have gone to the bottom and taken us all down with her, since we had no vessels with us to help out. The Japanese submarine was subsequently accounted for by one of 230

Squadron's Sunderland flying boats based at Kilindini Harbour, Mombasa.

RAF Port Reitz was a small airfield that had been hacked out of the jungle and was buried among coconut palms and mango trees almost at sea level on the East African coast. The RAF detachment consisted of one or two aircraft, one pilot, one fitter and one rigger who between them serviced everything on the aircraft, including radio, instruments, oxygen, etc. We shared the airfield with the Fleet Air Arm and No. 41 Squadron South African Air Force. The latter, equipped with twin-engined Avro Anson training aircraft but armed with guns and bombs, maintained patrols inshore along the coast looking out for Japanese submarines, while the Fleet Air Arm serviced and repaired the wide variety of carrier-borne aircraft with which the Far East Fleet was equipped. All three services, RAF, FAA and the SAAFs, worked together as one, with no inter-service friction at all. In a hot and humid location thousands of miles from home, with common hardships and no immediate end to the war in sight, everyone mucked in and helped everyone else.

In those days the job of a fitter was to diagnose unserviceable components and, because of wartime shortages, repair them. Today, with all our technical advances in design, faulty components are diagnosed and simply replaced. We on the Meteorological Flight were always chronically short of spare parts – all I had was the issue tool box and a spare set of spark plugs! At one time I had two Gladiators with only one set of wheels between them, the other set having been urgently required at the Eastleigh base. The SAAFs recharged our oxygen bottles for us, and when we had Hurricanes the FAA actually gave me a 'gash' (spare) Merlin engine as the source of useful spare parts: carbs, magnetos, priming pipes, etc. But, to my disgust I had to return it with thanks, the RAF being unable to establish a bureaucratic way of adding it to our inventory.

Our Met Flt pilots naturally got on well with their FAA messmates. The naval pilots in their Seafires would sometimes 'bounce' (ambush) our Gladiator at the end of a met flight by lurking below cloud base and then making a mock attack. They didn't have it all their own way, for the biplane's ability to turn almost in its own length left the Seafire screaming round in a three-mile turn to get back into the attack mode. In North Africa earlier in the war, the Italian squadrons of biplane fighters Fiat CR42s caused so much havoc with our Hurricanes by using the same tactics that a squadron of Gladiators had to be drafted in to see the Ities off!

The airfield had no runways, just a grassy sand surface, the only concrete being the circular compass-swinging base, the floors of our huts and that of the one small hangar. Aircraft with wooden propellers, prevalent in those years, suffered. During ground running checks, the sand was whipped up into vortices, effectively sand blasting the ends of the blades until they were undynamically thin. The authorities decreed that used oil should be spread on the ground beneath the prop arc so that large oil cakes were whipped up and distributed at high speed, to the peril of anyone nearby.

An order with even more dire consequences required the exposed aircraft wheels and tyres to be protected from the scorching sun by canvas covers. It was found that the covers were being adopted as night shelters by black mambas, whose bites were reputed to be lethal within thirty seconds. The order was quickly rescinded.

Larger visitors to the airfield were equally unwelcome. Occasionally we had to evict an elephant who had wandered out from the surrounding palm trees on to the airfield. One guest always welcomed was Marie, a lame deer, who was more or less our mascot; for some reason she enjoyed eating any cigarettes offered to her. It was also fascinating to watch how the locals scaled the very tall palm trees in order to collect the coconuts. The man would stand facing the foot of the tree and bind his ankles together. Gripping the tree trunk with both hands, and with Herculean effort, he would double up and bring his feet further up the tree, then his hands, then his feet again until he reached the clusters of the fruit, where he would cut them down using the knife in his belt. They also trapped monkeys by tying a small bottle containing a few nuts to the base of a tree. The monkey would slide one paw into the bottle, seize one of the nuts, but then would be unable to withdraw its closed paw – and there it would remain until its captor arrived.

Creepy-crawlies there were aplenty, plus dung beetles – one variety of which would dig funnel-shaped hollows in the sand then bury itself at the bottom and wait for some unfortunate fly or ant to wander over the top of the slope. When one did, the beetles would use their heads to shovel sand above their victims, thereby rolling the helpless insect down to where hungry jaws awaited. We used to disturb the side of the slope with the end of a straw and watch the furious spray of sand projected by the occupant at the bottom!

Condensation was a continual enemy. It formed inside the fifty-gallon drums in which our petrol was supplied, and when we rolled the drums across to the aircraft before hand pumping the fuel into the tanks, the moisture mixed with the fuel making it potentially lethal. This was not suspected by the higher-ups until I lost an aircraft and almost its pilot. One morning my groundcrew friend, Jack Brockhurst, and I had pulled the chocks away and seen the aircraft get airborne at 6.30am. We had just moved back among the palm trees when I heard the sound that every engine fitter dreads more than anything – the spluttering of an engine failing just after take-off. When that happens, the pilot loses flying speed and needs to fly straight ahead and try to land. With nothing but palm trees in front of him, the pilot had no alternative but to bank round and try to land back on the airfield. Losing height rapidly, he was no more than fifty feet above the ground and getting lower every second. He was heading straight for us, as if he were aiming at us through the gunsight. It was a heart-stopping moment, and we stood momentarily rooted to the ground, then ran for our lives in opposite directions. At about twenty feet above the ground, the Gladiator crashed between the trees, shedding its wings as it did so, the fuselage skidding before grinding to a halt. Jack and I rushed back and wasted no time in hauling the pilot out of the cockpit. He was shaken but unhurt; luckily the aircraft's full tank of eighty-three gallons of petrol didn't catch fire or explode.

As the fitter involved I was not allowed to go near the engine, but the possibility of my being court-martialled for dereliction of duty, in not having seen and repaired a fault, vanished when the presence of water in the fuel was proved conclusively to blame. Following the court of enquiry, East Africa Command decreed that all refuelling was henceforth to be done using a filter consisting of a large chamois leather stretched across a funnel, a time-consuming but essential precaution (chamois permits petrol to pass through but not water). It's a good job it never rains petrol on chamois deer!

Khaki drill was worn full time by the RAF: shorts and sometimes shirts by day, slacks in the evening, when shirt sleeves were worn rolled down to defeat the mosquitoes. I was once issued with a short-sleeved khaki drill tunic which had a spine pad – a padded, cross-stitched area down the back – with a 'dog-collar' which buttoned right up to the neck. It was a relic of the North West Frontier, or even the Boer War.

Our accommodation was as makeshift as one would expect. There were no roads on camp, just narrow sandy tracks between the coconut palms connecting the huts. These were made of wood, single storey, with thatched roofs. For ventilation a 2-inch gap separated the top of the walls and the roof, and the windows were unglazed. Being so near the equator and only 186 feet above sea level, Port Reitz was tropically hot and humid. There were twenty men to a hut, each with their own bed, locker and shelf, with a communal table and two benches. Lighting was almost non-existent, just three unshaded bulbs, one at each end and one in the centre. Ants asserted their right-of-way through the huts, devouring any chai and wads (tea and buns) left for a moment, and we stood our bedlegs in circular cigarette tins filled with water, moat-like, to keep them from the beds. Sometimes they were the big soldier ants, columns of which would march in their thousands down one wall, along the length of the hut and up the other wall, an intimidating sight indeed – but after all, they were there first. There was never any shortage of the cigarette tins, for every serviceman in Africa was issued with fifty cigarettes a week, the usual brand known as 'C to C' (Cape to Cairo), though, because of the acrid flavour of the poor quality tobacco, they were better known as 'Camel to Consumption'.

Lizards would fall from the rafters with a sudden plop, shake their heads and scurry away. Coconuts thudded on the roof from the overhanging palms; this was not as romantic as it may seem – they weighed a ton, and to be struck on the head by one caused concussion if nothing worse. At night the local villagers would pound their drums incessantly, waking us up only when they stopped.

The sanitary arrangements were also primitive, to put it mildly. Taps and bowls were installed in long benches in the open air, and the lavatories were 'thunder boxes', wooden sentry-box closets erected over deep holes down into which one dared not look. They were not a place to linger. Malaria was rife; ten men a day succumbed to its scourge at one time. I escaped that hazard but instead contracted typhus (also known as gaol fever). It is a far from pleasant malady, its symptoms being a temperature of 102.2 degrees and sinister swellings in the armpits and groin – although it causes considerable loss of weight, it is not to be recommended as a cure for obesity. Colleagues said that I resembled a Jap POW! In order to trace the source of the typhus, the valiant Service Medical Officers on the camp experimented with every type of insect in the area, even allowing the creepy-crawlies lurking in the depths of the thunder boxes to bite or sting their arms, but it was eventually established that the disease had been transmitted by the Arab traders from the north, who plied the coast in their dhows.

The Kenya of those days was very different from that of today. No high-rise flats in its cities or towns, no white gleaming office blocks, cinemas or theatres; far from being a popular tourist country, it was still very much in the third world. There were few metalled roads and most native dwellings, known as shambas, were mud-brick houses with thatched roofs. The town of Mombasa consisted of not much more than bazaars and Indian shops, where we would occasionally purchase bracelets and necklaces carved from ivory, and similar exotic presents to send back via sea-mail to loved ones at home. Very often these never arrived and, although many losses were attributed to the large number of ships being torpedoed, we always bitterly suspected that many missing parcels had been 'acquired' by dockers when they arrived in Blighty. Communication with our families was severely limited. The occasional airgraph, consisting of but a few brief lines, was allowed. These and all seamail letters were understandably censored for any indiscreet disclosures regarding locations, units or military activities. Mobile phones still being in the realms of science fiction, one magical day occurred in our three or four year overseas tour of duty when we were given the opportunity to speak to our relatives 'over the wireless', a touching moment for all concerned.

Five minutes from the camp, down a gentle slope, the Indian Ocean provided recreation: swimming and boating in native dug-out canoes. Further fun was created when we obtained the wing-tip float from a scrapped Supermarine Walrus flying boat (thank you, Fleet Air Arm). Cutting an opening in the centre compartment, installing a wooden seat, weighting the fore-and-aft compartments with sand as ballast, we had a unique kayak. The seemingly endless beach was as good as Hawaii (albeit minus the bathing beauties; there were no white women for hundreds of miles, and many men risked contracting diseases by 'consorting' with the local native women). The white sands were edged with palm trees under which burrowed huge crabs the size of soup plates. Armed with one gigantic claw, they moved it from side to side as they scuttled along. I never felt any desire to walk along the beach after dark!

There was always lots of air activity at Port Reitz: Torpedo bomber Albacores and Swordfish biplanes, dive bomber Skuas, Fulmar and Seafire fighters, all coming in for servicing, test flying from the Fleet aircraft carriers arriving in the bay. There would be visiting aircraft from up-country, communication aircraft such as

five-seater DH Rapides and two-seater trainer Magisters as well as Catalina and Sunderland flying boats overflying the airfield from their base in the harbour. Naval pilots also practiced 'Daddles', dummy air-deck landings, the method of landing their aircraft within a marked area of the airfield, as if landing on a carrier deck. Occasionally there were hair-raising moments, as when three Albacores flew in from their aircraft carrier. Approaching one at a time, and being accustomed to having their tail hooks caught in the cable across a carrier deck, they came in nose-high and, touching down tail wheel first, pulled the stick back smartly – whereupon the main undercarriage legs hit the ground hard – and splayed apart, bringing the underside of the fuselage rapidly in contact with the earth and shortening the propeller considerably! One after the other came in and did exactly the same, while the spectators, working on their own aircraft – myself included – watched with sheer bewilderment.

At that time Blackburn Skua single-engined dive-bombers had a very bad reputation for losing their tails in a dive, with fatal results, and a few of them adorned the airfield perimeter, tail-less while undergoing modification. Always ready to scrounge a gash flight and firmly convinced that I would live forever, I jumped at the opportunity to go on a test flight in a Skua. The naval pilot was middle-aged and no dare-devil ace of the African skies; as I strapped on my parachute, he said gravely, 'If anything happens during the flight, don't wait for me to tell you – just bail out!' I thought at first he was putting the frighteners on me for a joke, but he definitely wasn't and the flight was one of the white-knuckle variety. Obviously, when flying Skuas, that was the only way to progress beyond middle age, bearing out the well-known RAF saying, 'There are old pilots and bold pilots, but there are no old, bold pilots!'

On another occasion I had a more than stimulating flight in a Fleet Air Arm two-seater single-engined Fairey Fulmar fighter aircraft equipped with eight wing-mounted Browning machine guns. We took off and I settled down in the rear cockpit, enjoying every minute in this fast and exhilarating aircraft, but, unbeknown to me, close mates of my navy pilot were returning to Mombasa by train after being on leave in Nairobi, and he intended to welcome them back with a memorable beat-up! In order to lose height down the escarpment en route from Nairobi, the railway almost crosses its own tracks, and this was where my pilot had planned to put on his display. He proceeded to 'dive bomb' the train repeatedly, wheels, flaps and dive brakes down before pulling out, then a short climb, a quick flick turn and down once again. Each time, I was aware of him climbing to gain some altitude then levelling off, but after that the horizon swung above my head. I could see little other than white-sleeved arms waving from the train windows and the expressions on upturned grinning faces; my senses were being scattered. Apart from the fact that only he knew what he was going to do next, it quickly became evident that the design of the Fulmar in such manoeuvres favoured the pilot, who was positioned more or less at the centre of gravity of the aircraft, rather than the crewman, who sat much further aft, and so was subjected to much greater 'G' forces. So when I wasn't blacking out in the climb, as the blood drained down from my brain, I was redding out in the dive as it poured back up again; when I wasn't hanging in the air against my straps, clear of the seat, I was jammed back as if about to exit via the tail. After that hectic and unforgettable experience, I almost felt admiration for the German 'Stuka' dive-bomber pilots.

There were times when I was the most popular man around the airfield because of being left-handed! Some light aircraft owned by settlers had been commandeered for the duration and were used by the Services in a communication role. A lot of these were powered by engines not fitted with an electric starter, and so they had to be started by hand-swinging the propeller which, in many cases, rotated anti-clockwise facing the aircraft. Now for a right hander to hand-swing one of those is the equivalent of asking a right-handed man to shave using his left hand, or similarly a woman to apply mascara – difficult and, not to mince matters, downright dangerous where a propeller was involved.

Hand-swinging is a straightforward procedure. The first thing to do is make sure that the man in the cockpit is completely trustworthy. The prop-swinger must force petrol into the cylinders by turning the propeller before the ignition is turned on. If when you call out to him, 'Switches off, throttle open!' you hear him reply, 'Which switches?' back away sharply and find someone who wouldn't benefit from your demise. If he is competent, he will reply in the same manner and act accordingly. You then rotate the propeller a few times, finally positioning it in about the twenty-minutes-to-two position. Having done that, you curl the fingers of your left hand one-third up the lower blade, brace yourself, and shout, 'Throttle closed, switches on – contact!' When your colleague replies, you pull hard on the propeller, twisting your body away like a demented ballet dancer as – hopefully – the propeller leaves your hand rapidly and the engine roars into life. If it doesn't, you go back to square one – 'switches off...' etc. until it does. Don't wear any rings on the fingers of your left hand. If the engine starts before you straighten your fingers and release your hold on the prop blade, you'll find that the edge of the blade has neatly removed your rings and taken all the flesh and some of the bone with it. And don't forget first to chock the wheels, or, when the engine fires, the aircraft will chase you back into the hangar.

Once one of these requisitioned light aircraft was undergoing repair in a hangar at the same time as we were being issued with our pay. Lined up in alphabetical order, we shuffled along while the airman working on the aircraft picked up the wooden propeller with the intention of replacing it. He slipped it back on to its shaft, waggling it as he did so to make sure it was in the correct position to slide on to the splines. What he didn't know was that someone had earlier been in the cockpit and had turned the two ignition switches on, so that when the fitter waggled the propeller the engine started up. The prop, not being bolted on, promptly shot off, hurtling over the head of the fitter and heading towards the queue at the pay table like a very unguided missile. Those in the queue up to 'J', luckily including myself, had already been paid, so we had a head start on the 'K' to 'Z's, who had to run for their lives. No one was injured, but many a hair-raising story was recounted over noggins of ale in the NAAFI that night.

The engines of larger aircraft were started up by other means, not all of which were without their own hazards. Twin-engined Ansons required the insertion of a long starting handle, similar to those used on older motor cars, into a socket in the side of the engine nacelle, which was cranked furiously until the engine fired. When removing the handle it was essential not to step inadvertently into the arc of the rapidly revolving propeller only inches away.

Normal naval routine was strictly observed at Port Reitz; procedures concerning eight bells and suchlike being full of wonder to us RAF types, though of course we were not involved. The messing arrangements were communal, all three services eating together. The food was standard wartime issue, augmented by local vegetables and fruit: mangoes, pawpaws, bananas, etc. Some RN

signallers occupied a cabin in the creek near the harbour, and those with friends among them had the opportunity to indulge in a gourmet meal of real white bread, courtesy of the Fleet bakeries – a veritable feast in those days of grey and almost tasteless loaves.

The locals performed the more menial tasks about the airfield, sweeping the huts, cleaning oily drip trays, and similar chores. Many had been recruited from their reserves upcountry and had had little or no contact with whites. Few had ever seen an aircraft before, and so they used the Swahili word for birds, *ndagi*. One of my 'boys' could not even be tempted to enter our flight hut while the radio was playing – for how, he reasoned, not illogically, could a man's voice come from such a little box? I found out I had been given a Swahili name by them, which sounded like *M'ramu N'chegi* and meant the 'tall thin warrior'. They were all friendly, simple and uncomplicated men. One man in particular, called M'Twinja, impressed me so much with his loyalty and hard work that I wangled a flight for him in a five-seater Rapide communication aircraft. His reactions on getting airborne and flying over herds of zebra and giraffe were a joy to watch, and it was very obviously a memorable experience for him.

Sometimes our huts were raided at night by local thieves, intent on stealing valuables left on bedside lockers. It was alarming to wake up suddenly knowing that an intruder was nearby, yet being unable to see out through the opaque mozzy net. As the net was tucked in securely beneath the mattress it was impossible to get out in a hurry but the thieves were impossible to catch anyway; they wore little or no clothing and oiled their bodies – they were truly slippery customers. Yet the occupants of one FAA hut solved the intruder problem with classic ingenuity. In the rafters they fixed a grotesque cut-out of a face and installed a dim light beneath it –

result, no thieves! A bit of superstition was better than Neighbourhood Watch – but it wouldn't work nowadays, unfortunately.

My career in the RAF made me realise that all airfields and camps had their own particular feel about them. Some stations were quite impersonal, cold and downright unfriendly, others warm and welcoming. Port Reitz belonged to the latter category, perhaps because of its primitive and impermanent location or because of the war years in which it existed. It was very far from being a base camp – a cushy number far behind the lines – despite its personnel having arrived there via dangerous convoy routes from North Africa or the Far East. The front line itself was the African coastline, where the Japanese subs, at one time operating out of the secluded inlets of Vichy-held Madagascar and later on long-range patrols from home or captured bases, preyed on the Allied convoys. This seemed to weld all the Port Reitz servicemen together into one friendly unit with a common aim, despite the onerous living and working conditions. 'Keep 'em flying' was very much the order of the day, so while Port Reitz occupied only a few acres of the vast African continent and warranted but a miniscule pin on naval war charts, it kept the Fleet supplied with serviceable aircraft and accurate weather reports, and played a small but strategic part in World War II. No parades, no 'bull' – it was just a question of getting on with the job in hand and I liked the place.

Conditions at Mogadiscio (now Mogadishu, Somalia) up-country were a complete contrast to those at Port Reitz. The camp had been designed for permanent occupation by the Italian Air Force and was strategically sited to command both the colony they had annexed and the Indian Ocean coastline. It had been custom-built for the tropical conditions. The living quarters on camp were superb compared to Mombasa – or, indeed, any other RAF overseas posting – consisting of single rooms fitted with ceiling fans and personal showers! The camp even had its own brothel, but the building had been demolished by the conquering British Army, leaving only an imposing flight of steps leading up to where the entrance once stood. The powers that be always did prefer their troops to risk their health and welfare in downtown disease-riddled shanties rather than in more clinically controlled establishments. The officers' mess was truly palatial in appearance not unlike a pre-war Odeon cinema but surrounded by gardens and fountains. It was shared by just two officers, our pilot and the officer commanding the signals unit. We were the only flying unit there; our pilot was also the Commanding Officer of the station, a convenient dual role when handling the complaints submitted by the female Italian residents regarding the met. aircraft flying low along the beach while they happened to be sun-bathing – what a coincidence! The signals unit of about thirty servicemen formed the rest of the station strength.

All round, 'Mog' was a good posting. Although totally bereft of entertainment and recreation, there was no bull nor parades and we, the half-dozen members of the ground crew, just concentrated on keeping the solitary aircraft serviceable and flying. That was not easy, bearing in mind its age and previous battlefield-flying service, but, as usual, that's what the job was all about.

By the time of the first detachment there, we had re-armed with Hurricane IIB aircraft, and two flights a day took place. A unit as small as this had to be totally self-supporting, and so we also manned the fire tender and ambulance during take-offs. F/O Dickie Gorst, mentioned earlier, occasionally beat up the airfield for fun, flying low-level passes so grass-cuttingly close that when standing on the fire tender's running board one could look down into the cockpit – now that's low flying!

There was no overland route from Kenya, because the intervening territory was inhospitable and almost impassable. It was inhabited by hostile 'Shifta' tribesmen who, it was reported, practised far from endearing intimate surgical operations on their victims. Pilots carried 'Goolie Chits' which promised a reward if on forced landing they were returned to the nearest military base with their private parts still intact!

Contact with our base at Eastleigh and the outside world in general was maintained by a Lockheed Hudson (twin-engined bomber/communications) which every Thursday brought in precious mail, fresh vegetables, spare parts for the aircraft, etc. Its arrival was indisputably the highlight of the week. Everyone, but everyone, turning out to watch it touch.

The town of 'Mog' held little for the serviceman, though it was clean and civilised, with wide streets, white buildings and a large triumphal arch erected in honour of the pre-war Italian capture of the territory. The small white population was Italian and as the colony had only very recently been liberated by the British forces, we were not exactly popular – there was no aggro, we were just ignored. Two Italians, the town barber and the wine shop owner, did befriend us, both with mercenary motives. When the former wielded the open razor at the back of my neck, I always hoped that he no longer bore a grudge against the Brits; meanwhile, the wine shop owner got his revenge by purveying his own homemade brand of gin, a seemingly innocuous brew which had no effect whatsoever until, hours later, one returned to camp and put the light out to get into bed – at which moment complete oblivion descended with the rapidity of a falling poleaxe. The native Somalis were understandably aggrieved at yet more invaders, and, while there was little open animosity, I always chose, on entering a café or hostelry, to sit facing the door with my back to a wall, a habit I maintained during future postings in the Middle East.

I was at RAF Port Reitz when the war ended in August 1945. Naturally, we were all exuberant and toasted the occasion in the usual service manner with a noggin or two of ale. In an emergency, when single-seater fighters had force-landed in the desert, sometimes colleagues would save the pilot from being captured by sitting him in the cockpit, then sitting himself on his knees to fly back to base. I suggested to my pilot that we celebrated by him taking me up in one of our Spitfires. My pilot, being more sensible than me, rightly said it was a dangerous thing to do, and that it would be silly to be killed when we'd just won the war.

However, just because victory had been declared, it didn't mean we all packed up and immediately returned to Blighty. There were tens of thousands of servicemen across the Middle and Far East to be repatriated, and the large numbers of ships returning with troops and equipment via the Indian Ocean still required weather forecasts. So, although many units ceased to operate, normal daily meteorological flying continued. Hearing the victory celebrations back home on the radio, we were, to put it mildly, frustrated – chokker was the word. A further four months dragged by until, in December 1945, the Met Flt was finally disbanded. I was the sole survivor of the original eighteen airmen, the others having been posted elsewhere in ones and twos and some – the married ones – having been repatriated after three years' service overseas.

In retrospect it had been a good unit on which to serve: small, compact, with a good gang of blokes, pilots as well as ground crew. Working out on the airfield and administering to the needs of one's 'own' aircraft is far more satisfying than being one of many in a workshop or maintenance unit on a production line. The Gladiators – not forgetting my Gauntlet – were characters in their own right, far removed from today's flying blowlamps – sorry, jet aircraft – and the Hurricanes and Spitfires with which we were re-armed had seen enough desert battles to give them personalities. Such are the complexities of today's aircraft that a team of specialists is required for each one. Long gone are the days when all that was required was a fitter and rigger per aircraft, with an instrument basher, an instrument wallah and a signals bod to cater for three or four planes. What a pity!

My 'great day' arrived when, at 7.00am on 10th December 1945, the other tour-ex airmen and I boarded a twin-engined transport Dakota aircraft. It had no seats, just metal benches running the length of the fuselage, and no heating – but so what, after take-off we just walked up and down the length of the aircraft to keep warm. Three hours or so later we landed at Juba in the Sudan, then after refuelling, got airborne again to Khartoum. Following four hours for a meal and replenishment, we took off again, landing at Cairo West Airfield at 7.30pm. From there we went by road, first to one tented camp in the desert, 22 PTC (Personnel Transit Camp), Asmara, Egypt, then on to another, 21 PTC El Hamra. From 11th December hundreds of us ate and slept under canvas, washed and shaved in the open, and spent only as much time as was necessary in the 'thunder boxes'. Each morning, we paraded in the scorching heat while lists of those due to depart for the UK that day were read out. Those not summoned trudged disconsolately back to their tents and waited, me among them, kicking our sandy heels, our spirits low, to await the following day's parade. Finally, on 20th December, my name appeared on the list – whoopee! – and, with others, I was transported to the Egyptian port of Port Said for the next stage home.

HMT Ascania awaited us, a large converted liner which took us across the Mediterranean (more hammocks, but no risk of torpedoes this time), during which we encountered storms worse than any we had had in the Atlantic. Christmas Eve found us in the war-scarred and battered Grand Harbour in Malta, but we were off again within hours on a three day run to Toulon, southern France, skirting the forlorn masts and funnels of the submerged French Fleet protruding from the waters of the outer harbour, the warships having been sunk by the Royal Navy to prevent the Germans from using them against us after France's capitulation.

During my further twenty-eight years of service with the RAF, overseas journeys were made by RAF transport aircraft, so no more troopships, thank heavens. But I will never forget my three months or so at sea, crossing the Equator five times in 'troopers'. Without wishing to be disparaging, the lads bound for the Falklands had a comfortable ride out, one which held little fear of enemy attack until the last few miles, a far cry indeed from the hazards and literal hard-ships of wartime troop travel. But then again, no doubt our military predecessors en route to the Crimea, Sudan and the Boer War would have considered we World War II types to have been on a pleasure cruise!

A week after leaving Egypt, at 7.30am of 27th December, we were offloaded from the *Ascania*, and 'welcomed' at a transit camp at Bram, near Toulon. Accommodation consisted of ancient bell-tents and the whole area was so deep in mud that even within the tents, duckboards formed walkways and 'mattresses'. Eight men slept in each tent, feet to the centre pole at night. We must have resembled a very soggy sliced cake, but we didn't care; we were Blighty bound.

29th December 1945 saw us packed like sardines into a decrepit steam train which chugged across war-devastated France for three days, six men with full kit shoe-horned into each compartment, one meal and a brief halt for a leg stretch each day. Eventually, we arrived at Dieppe and crossed the Channel to Newhaven. And there, unbelievably, were military police to greet us all with tea and English newspapers – an emotionally charged moment for all of us.

Four weeks' disembarkation leave followed, and this was spent at home in Manchester – more hankies and tears of delight from Mother, all the tales to tell Fred! At a local dance I met an attractive young lady named Win Sheldon. She had been in the ATS, manning an enemy aircraft locator unit on the East coast, and we became very close friends. After twenty-eight days my leave was up and I received a telegram to report to RAF Desborough, Northants. I was back in the machine again.

Chapter Five
DAKOTAS, DESKS AND
HEAVY BOMBERS

No. 1381 TCU (Transport Conversion Unit) Desborough was situated out in the country near Kettering, Northamptonshire, and was equipped with Douglas DC3 transport aircraft, known as Dakotas. Now that the war was over, there was a surplus of bomber pilots and a shortage of transport and communication pilots, so many of the former were being converted to a new role on this type of aircraft. Most of the conscripted ground-based airmen had been demobbed, and shortages of some tradesmen led to men being employed in less important tasks usually done by others, involving frequent postings between units. About that time thousands of servicemen were in transit between units or to their homes across the country, travelling by train, and most of the major railway junctions such as Crewe were inundated by members of the Forces lugging their kitbags from one platform to another or, with hours to wait for their next connection, asleep in the ancient waiting rooms. The good ladies of the WVS, Red Cross and other charities refreshed the weary travellers with much appreciated mugs of tea and sandwiches.

At Desborough the accommodation consisted of Nissen huts situated in fields a mile or so from the airfield. The huts were constructed from curved lengths of corrugated iron bolted together; they had no insulation whatsoever, and the only warmth was provided by a single coke-burning stove. Condensation formed rapidly and remained on the metal walls and ceiling, so the living conditions were primitive in the extreme.

I was surprised to find that I'd been detailed to work, not on the aircraft, but on the fuel delivery trucks. This involved travelling with other airmen in an RAF truck to the fuel dump at the local railway station, where we filled sacks with coke and then hoisted them on to the vehicle and distributed them around the huts. It was a filthy task; the smell of the coke impregnating our hair and clothing was seemingly ineradicable. As the weeks passed, my protests at having to refuel stoves instead of aircraft were ignored, so I took the exceptional step of applying for an interview with the Commanding Officer. Standing nervously at attention – he was a Group Captain after all, and I a mere airman of very minor rank – I diffidently pointed out that I was not a conscript with time to be filled while awaiting demob but a career airman fully qualified as an aero-engine fitter. The C.O. acted immediately, and the next day I found myself on another truck heading in the opposite direction – to the airfield where the Dakotas were in need of urgent repairs.

While at Desborough I visited Win as often as possible, and we were married in St Luke's Church, Benchill, on 20 April 1946. In that bleak post-war year, with long queues, strict rationing and shortages of food, clothing and just about everything else, the euphoria of victory had long since evaporated. We honeymooned in a hotel in Accrington – Florida it wasn't! There were no married quarters available at Desborough, so Win continued to live with her family in Wythenshawe. It was never much of a life to be married to a serviceman, always on the move and never sure of a permanent home, and I appreciated her for putting up with it all.

In July 1946 I was promoted Corporal (not before time either!). It wasn't only the authority or pay increase accompanying the rank that I appreciated but that I could move into a bunk, a room of my own – heaven! I was soon posted to RAF Cosford as an instructor, where at first I lived in a bunk in the barracks. Later, Win joined me in a 'hiring', a private accommodation hired by the RAF, on Molyneux Road, Wolverhampton. We were together at last.

The influx of National Service recruits at that time was high. Many were trained as flight mechanics, a degree less technical than fitters, and their training course lasted about eighteen weeks. Many of them understandably resented being torn from their civilian lives, subjected to military discipline and having to march daily to Cosford's workshops and listen to lectures about plugs and pistons, cams and carburettors. But the last two weeks of the course were spent on the airfield, working on the aircrafts they'd read about and seen flying over their houses. They couldn't wait to climb into the cockpits and sit at the controls.

Classes of between thirty-five and forty airmen were held in the hangars. They were not the best teaching conditions – the instructors having to vie with each other in order to be heard. The first week was spent disconnecting, then removing the Merlin engine from a Spitfire, only to re-install it, connecting everything up again and testing it. The tests involved pushing the aircraft out on to the tarmac, placing chocks in front of its wheels, then getting two airmen to lie across the tail, one each side, to prevent the tail lifting and the nose digging a hole in the tarmac when the throttle was opened wide. One at a time the trainees were allowed to sit in the cockpit, holding the control column back between their knees with their right hands, their left hands on the throttle, and feet on the rudder pedals. I stood on the wing, next to the fuselage, leaning into the cockpit, and with my hand over the trainee's, together we would open up the throttle to maximum revolutions in order to test the power output. With the deafening noise, the burbling of the exhausts, the shuddering vibrations of the airframe, the Spitfire straining to take-off, many trainees would freeze on the throttle and their hands had to be forcibly pulled back! Out in the slipstream and subjected to that ear-splitting noise so many times a week over many months, I eventually paid the price and developed tinnitus. At the time, the risk was unknown, and the need to use ear-muffs had not been realised.

Engine instruction and testing during the second week was more subdued. The trainees were taught on twin-engined Beaufighters, whose quieter though powerful radial engines had created havoc among the Japanese, earning them the name of 'Whispering Death'. Thankfully, the larger cockpit permitted me and the trainee to remain out of the slipstream.

The winter of 1946 was a particularly cold one, and heating fuel was in short supply. We felt the cold particularly in the hangars, the huge doors having to be left open to give us some light while instructing. All hangar doors were thick and strong in order to withstand any bomb-blast attacks; they were extremely heavy to push open and close, and whenever this had to be done the cry of 'Two Six, on the doors!' would go up. The reason for these particular numbers always puzzled me until, while researching other subjects many years later, I found them mentioned in a book about medieval wooden warships equipped with rows of cannon below decks. Each cannon was manned by six men, and sailors number two and six had the job of pushing the weapon back into the firing position again after it had recoiled. Military terms linger down the ages; phrases like 'clear the decks', 'pointblank', 'a flash in the pan' and 'pull your finger out' are all ancient. 'Pull your finger out' originated in the days when cannons were fired by igniting the gunpowder charge with a burning wick lowered into a hole on top of the barrel. In the wet, one of the gun crew would cover the hole by keeping his finger inserted until the wick was alight.

The conditions in the hangars were so arctic that a desperate remedy was attempted. A twin-engined Meteor jet aircraft was brought out and parked with its tail towards our hangar, and its engines were started up. We received hot air all right, accompanied by thick fumes which cleared the hangar in double-quick time. I suggested that we should all proceed to the sick quarters to be diagnosed as suffering from the fuel the Meteor used – paraffinalia!

In October 1947 I felt unusually off-colour. I didn't want to eat; I didn't want any company. To make matters worse, a posting came through for me to move to No. 3 School of Technical Training, RAF Weeton, near Blackpool, to be employed in the Records Section of the MT (Mechanical Transport) School there. Weeton was closer to where Win was living, so, rather than report sick at Cosford I decided to travel and report sick there.

I arrived on 25th October feeling ghastly, and, after a miserable night in an otherwise empty hut on a strange unit, I found my way to the Medical Inspection Room and gave my name to the airman clerk. 'Sorry corporal, you're too late,' he said, but I was past caring and sat down. The Medical Officer eventually arrived and walked through the waiting room, casting a professionally quick look round. He pointed at me, and after a short examination I felt myself led out to an ambulance. Within an hour I was in a bed in the nearest RAF hospital. There, in a daze, I watched as a nursing sister wheeled to my bedside a trolley laden with more scalpels, forceps and other shiny, sinister instruments than I ever imagined.

Eventually the doctor, Flight Lieutenant Rapinat, came in and said he was going to give me a lumbar puncture to extract some fluid from my spinal column for analysis. He explained exactly how he intended to insert the needle, and that I had to lie doubled up on my side so that the vertebrae would part sufficiently. The nurse clamped my neck and knees down so firmly that I wouldn't have been able to move even if I'd wanted to! After the doctor had filled the needle up, I was told to lie with my feet higher than my head for a few hours – apparently my toes didn't need the fluid as much as my brain did.

I was showing all the symptoms of poliomyelitis, an epidemic of which was sweeping the country, and the next morning the Flight Lieutenant – for whose solicitude and deft efficiency I shall always be grateful – confirmed that I was one of the many poliomyelitis casualties reported by the media over the last twenty-four hours. He explained that there was no cure; the disease would have to take its course, after which every effort would be made to repair the damage, depending on which muscles or organs had been affected.

Nationwide, there were some fatalities and hundreds of victims permanently crippled or disabled, but I was lucky; the disease only affected the muscles of one leg. I was put on a 'strengthening' diet (which included a bottle of Guinness a day!), and after a few weeks I was transported to the Medical Rehabilitation Centre at RAF Chessington in Surrey. There I was given, first moderate, then more extensive and concentrated exercises to repair the muscle wastage, before being allowed to return to RAF Weeton – in possession of a chit which every serviceman dreams of possessing: one saying 'excused marching'! For three months, while others obeyed the sergeants' not so gentle urgings to stop slouching and keep in step, I took my time and strolled to work.

The RAF station was not far from Blackpool, and buses were laid on each evening for servicemen to visit the many entertainments. As was usual on units built in wartime, there were no married quarters at Weeton, so my weekend passes were spent at Wythenshawe, where fortunately Win and I had been allocated a council flat. On 4th May 1949 we had a bonny bouncing baby boy, Stephen.

I remained at Weeton for two and a half years, and it was not until 31st March 1950 that I was posted again – this time to an operational station, RAF Scampton in Lincolnshire, the ex-home of 617 Squadron, the renowned 'Dambusters'. Wing Commander Guy Gibson's dog, Nigger, was killed crossing the main road outside the camp just before the squadron's take-off on that famous attack and lies buried in front of the offices near the perimeter track. I was allocated a married quarter near the hangars, one of a small number built before the intensive airfield expansion of 1938, when early war clouds loomed. It was of standard design, the inner walls painted light green below halfway, dark green above. We were not allowed to redecorate, and the very idea of even adding a shelf was quite out of the question. Everything was provided and was of standard design: furniture, kitchen equipment, bedding, the lot. We accepted all the restrictions – at last Win and I, and now Stephen, had a home together, and life was happier than ever.

Every time one vacated or was allocated a quarter in the Service, strict regimes had to be adhered to. These were, and doubtless still are, known as 'Marching In' and 'Marching Out'. On the morning of vacating the Families Officer appeared and visited every room in turn, clipboard in hand. The quarter had to be in an acceptable condition for the next occupant, so naturally he expected it to be spotlessly clean and most importantly wanted to see, laid in the appropriate room, *every* item that had been issued: all cutlery, pieces of crockery, every pot, pan, sheet, blanket, towel and brush, in accordance with his inventory. To avoid any arguments with the airman's wife over hardly discernible smears on a knife handle or a minuscule crack in a jug, only the airman occupant was allowed to be present. Any damage or deficiency had to be paid for.

When the next tenant moved in, the 'Marching In' took place, the routine repeated in reverse so that the newcomer was aware of everything for which he was responsible and its condition. The cynical saying used to be, 'Everyone leaves a clean quarter and takes over a dirty one!'

Ours was a comfy little house, and in the 1990s I returned on a memory trip. Although hardly expecting a blue plaque with my name on it above the door of our quarter, I was sad to find that all the houses on the site had long since been demolished, and it was now a car park for the Red Arrows aerobatic team.

My new aircraft at No. 230 OCU (Operational Conversion Unit) were Avro Lincolns, four-engined heavy bombers, successors to the Lancaster. They were used to train pilots in navigation and bombing roles and, because much of the flying took place during daylight hours, my colleagues and I were on night shift, not stopping work until all aircraft were serviceable for the following day's ops. I would complete all the repairs on the bomber for which I was responsible by the early hours of the morning, then clamber up the little ladder into the cockpit and test-run the engines. Starting with the port inner (that's the one that powers the generators and batteries), moving on to the other inner and the outers, I'd take them one at a time 'through the gate': maximum revs, check the magnetos, etc. After signing my life away on the Form 700, which confirmed that the aircraft was 100 percent ready to fly, I'd go back to my quarter, oil-stained and tired out, where Win would have the kettle on. Winter 1950 was bitterly cold, and fuel still in short supply, so the odd sack of coal would occasionally go missing from the camp's coal dump.

By now I had served eleven years and was still only a corporal. Although technical tradesmen, groundcrew on the front line as it were, were on a higher pay scale than other non-flying trades, promotions were very much slower than theirs. It was galling, to say the least, to have to take orders from physical-training instructors, clerks, cooks and education types who had been promoted to sergeant or higher ranks after much less service and training, many of them also enjoying better accommodation, status and conditions in the Sergeants' Mess. So when a new trade of Statistician was introduced, in which my technical knowledge would be invaluable, I volunteered to transfer for training.

My application was accepted, and in June 1950 I was posted to RAF Hereford, joining others to be taught advanced mathematics, charts and graphs, and statistical methods of analysis and interpretation. On my now relatively low pay, I could only afford to go back the 130 or so miles to Win and Stephen at Scampton for long weekends or leave by hitch-hiking. The war was still a recent memory, and motorists were generous in giving lifts to uniformed servicemen. It was best to stand still, facing oncoming vehicles, left arm outstretched, twirling the thumb clockwise; this usually worked and one eventually got home, albeit sometimes by a relay of two or more hitches. The intensive training course lasted eighteen months, and I achieved an A2 pass.

The RAF was divided into Commands – Bomber, Fighter, Signals, etc. – and these were further subdivided into Groups, usually on a geographical basis, which controlled each RAF station. My first posting in my new role, collecting, collating and analysing a huge range of statistics relating to the running of a fighting service, was to Headquarters No. 3 Group, Bomber Command, at RAF Mildenhall, Suffolk, where I arrived on 25th January 1952.

Chapter Six
IN THE SUEZ CAMPAIGN
THEN OFF TO IRAQ

No matter how long I had been in the Service, I always had a feeling of anticipation and excitement when joining a new unit. In the case of Mildenhall the excitement seemed justified by the discovery that unlike any of my previous postings Mildenhall was a 99.9 percent American Air Force Base, although registered under the auspices of the RAF. I became one of the 150 RAF personnel immersed among a population of 1500 US personnel. Win, Stephen and I moved into a prefab – one of the prefabricated houses built to provide short-term accommodation after so much housing had been destroyed by bombing during the war. It was compact and comfortable, and we got on very well with our American neighbours, shopping in the PX, the American NAAFI, and smoking Lucky Strike cigarettes, a bargain at two hundred for the equivalent of only fifty pence.

There was however a cultural difference between the two services. One day a tearful American wife came to our door very late at night seeking protection from her husband following a domestic shindig. There was of course only one British remedy – Win put the kettle on and gave her a cup of tea while she explained the circumstances. The family row had got violent – indeed she still held the weapon she had intended to use to protect herself from him, a vicious-looking garden implement like a trowel with three short, sharp, curved blades. She implored us to take her to the American guardroom, so we duly escorted her there.

It was an office environment the like of which I had never experienced before. I found myself facing a high counter over which a bebadged and beribboned US military police master-sergeant leaned, looking down at me, arms crossed. This arrangement was clearly designed to put the 'victim' at an immediate psychological disadvantage, so I hastily pointed out that I was an RAF serviceman and not one of his military minions. At that point the American lady emotionally explained what had happened, and the master-sergeant uttered a phrase so memorable that I recall it to this very day: 'You say the word, ma'am, and we'll bring him in and work him over.' To one accustomed to the conventions of the RAF, this blatant suggestion was astonishing, and I was further taken aback when, on the lady 'saying the word', we all piled into a jeep, three heavily armed military policemen clinging on to the sides, and charged at speed through the camp to our neighbour's house. There the vehicle screeched to a halt and the policemen rushed inside and hustled her husband, also a sergeant, out and into the jeep. I was no longer needed, so I retreated to my house, leaving the captive to be returned to the guardroom, no doubt to receive the promised 'working over'! Such US service habits were a revelation.

Eccentric behaviour was not confined solely to US Forces, of course; the RAF had a few of their own. Two of our Warrant Officers, one of whom had a glass eye, were stationed on a camp where each week new batches of airmen started their training as carpenters. The pair would visit the classroom, and the one with unimpaired vision would pick up a length of recently planed wood, look along the length of it, then pass it to his colleague and invite him to run his eye over it. Whereupon his colleague would remove his glass eye, slide it along the wood, replace it, and comment casually that it could do with a bit more off here or there.

On another station the Group Captain would habitually drive the wrong way round the roundabout outside station headquarters. After all, he was the Station Commander, so who would dare to correct him? And in one camp one airman had a medical condition which caused him to sleep with his eyes open – a disturbing experience for anyone, if not previously warned, who happened to walk past his bed in the middle of the night!

In the early 1950s turbulence in the service was widespread. Since the end of the war, thousands of men had been demobbed, yet with simmering unrest in the Middle East recruits were still required, and those still serving endured frequent disruption. On 21st October 1952 I was promoted sergeant and moved to a statistical post at Headquarters 43 Group, Maintenance Command, at RAF Hucknall, Nottinghamshire. Unfortunately no married quarters were available, so Win had to return to her family's home in Manchester. This separation was bad enough but was made infinitely worse when Egypt demanded the right to take over the control of the Suez Canal from Britain. I, along with other RAF reinforcements, had to report to No. 5 Personnel Dispatch Centre, RAF Lytham in Lancashire, for another overseas war-zone posting on 30th July 1953.

As was usual for all service personnel before being sent overseas, I was given a thorough medical inspection. Unfortunately the X-rays taken of my lungs revealed growths – polyps – caused by the pneumonia I had contracted on the troopship in 1942. Sent for by the Medical Officer, I sat shocked and unbelieving as, in sombre tones, he informed me that not only would I not be going overseas, it was even probable that I would be unable to remain in the service.

Leaving the RAF and becoming a civilian didn't bear thinking about! Seeing my reaction, he proposed that I should have a different type of X-ray, which would scan the core of the growths layer by layer, to see whether they were malignant or merely dried-up scars. In hospital I was placed on a mobile bed which moved slowly through a large tube while the X-rays did the checking. Later I heard with relief that the growths were harmless. I would be able to stay in the Service, but now I'd have to go overseas again and leave my little family once more.

On 22nd August 1953, my thirty-first birthday, I travelled to RAF Hendon and on to RAF Stanstead, where we were airborne at 7.00pm in a four-engined transport (Avro York) to Luqa, Malta. We landed at 1.35am the following morning, taking off again at 5.20am, and finally landed at RAF Fayid, Egypt five hours later. In sweltering heat we were bussed to El Hamra transit camp at Kasfareet and accommodated in tents in the sand for two days, which was quite long enough. A bus took us to our final destination, MEAF, the Headquarters of the Middle East Air Force at Abu Sueir, Egypt.

During 1953 and 1954 the Canal Zone was basically on a war footing; the Egyptians were actively encouraged by their President General Neguib and later Colonel Nasser, together with members of the government, to wage covert war on British bases in order to drive us out of the country. So we were 'piggy in the middle' of a siege situation. Conditions in the service establishments within the Canal Zone were almost identical to those in POW camps, except that the barbed wire was there to keep those outside from getting in. Most Army and RAF camps had double perimeters, an inner circuit of high fences and an outer circuit formed from rolls of barbed wire with a wide no-man's-land between. At night searchlights traversed this area, not illuminating it continuously but switching off, then pointing in another direction before switching on, in order to take the saboteurs/terrorists by surprise. Those of us on watch duty would open fire on any intruder seen. Some of those breaking in were not saboteurs but local thieves. Service camps, with their guns, stores and equipment, whether in Africa or the North-West Frontier, were always fair game.

Because of the complex political situation in the Middle East in the years preceding the Suez invasion, little was reported in the British press of the activities of those determined to drive us out by force, and there were few reports of servicemen and their dependents living overseas being killed or wounded. Coming so soon after the Second World War, the public had little appetite for another war. They'd had enough of battles, big and small, and were more concerned with rebuilding homes and industries, and increasing the amount of food and clothes available on ration. Because of this the casualties and the damage inflicted on the British bases were never fully reported in the newspapers of the day.

In later campaigns in 1991 and subsequently in Iraq and Afghanistan, the armed forces wore desert combats, camouflaged uniforms, steel helmets and body armour; in the Canal Zone in 1953, though, we wore just khaki shirts, shorts and berets, without any further protection. And while in Iraq many of the locals were friendly in the Zone, most Egyptians would be only too pleased to see us exit in body-bags. During the war the Egyptians had Nazi flags ready to wave and were fully prepared to welcome the Germans if we were defeated at El Alamein in 1942. Now, ten years on, they had ousted their King Farouk and were determined to emulate India and get the British out. Conditions for the troops were as hazardous as those pertaining during the recent past in

Northern Ireland, and worse in some respects. Off duty in Ulster, servicemen blended in with the local population – but we were always a white target in the Canal Zone, as are those who are fighting just as savage a war in Afghanistan. Once outside the heavily guarded camps, we were extremely vulnerable. Cairo and other cities were out of bounds, and those of us in the more outlying camps only left them by air or in armed convoys of ordinary vehicles. Because the camps had originally been sited for easy access to the social life of nearby cities, with their bars, restaurants and general nightlife, the camps themselves were sparse and utilitarian. To be locked up in them for months on end, with one night in three on armed perimeter patrols, was soul destroying. Here, as everywhere, the military bases relied on local businesses for fresh fruit and vegetables, meat, beer, and local labourers, but all interaction was stopped by the Egyptian government, forcing us to rely on food supplies by road or air.

We were given much practice in airfield defence, including bayonet practice, which involved the use of filled sandbags suspended about waist height from a series of timber frames. Our bayonets were the standard 'long blade' type, not the shorter 'spike' variety used with such deadly effect by our commandos during World War II. Levelling our bayonet-attached rifles, we would charge at the sandbags, reinforcing our murderous intentions by shouting loudly, and plunge the weapons as deep as possible into the semi-yielding targets. As it was assumed that more foes ready to repel our attack were lined up behind our casualty; the bayonets had to be withdrawn as quickly as possible, the order being 'In-Out-On guard!' This bloodthirsty – or rather sand-thirsty – drill continued until we'd run out of leaking sandy enemies or until the arrival of the NAAFI tea wagon. One couldn't really imagine what it would actually be like to plunge the sharp-pointed blade into an enemy's chest or stomach, and I always hoped that the practice would not be needed. If attacked at close quarters when on airfield defence sentry duty, any hesitation would be suicidal.

Much time was also spent on the rifle range using the issue .303 weapon, and we were also instructed in the use of the Sten gun. This was a light machine gun consisting of lengths of plumbing roughly welded together, and, though no AK47, it was capable of delivering withering bursts of rapid fire. The first time I held one to my shoulder, peremptory shouts by the NCO in charge echoed round the range, warning me not to fire. It seemed that the Sten had been designed for use by right-handed servicemen, with the empty shell cases ejected from the chamber at high speed from the right hand side of the weapon. Being left-handed, I ran the risk of having my right forearm painfully perforated. Despite this I was determined to learn how to use the gun, so I adapted my stance, keeping my right arm down below the path of the exiting shell cases. I always thoroughly enjoyed shooting – a vital requisite for a serviceman. We were also taught how to wear our steel helmets when on sentry duty, with the strap at the back of the head; if the strap was worn under the chin, an attacker creeping up behind could grip the helmet, pull it vigorously backwards and strangle the wearer.

Officers visiting other RAF stations within the Zone travelled in civilian-type Standard Vanguard saloons, rather than in armoured personnel carriers. They were escorted by pick-up trucks, in the open backs of which perched armed airmen, but such measures provided little protection against a trigger-happy Egyptian. Out of sheer boredom and claustrophobia, I occasionally volunteered as armed escort and would be issued with a Sten gun and forty rounds of ammunition and clamber into the back of the escort vehicle detailed to follow the staff car, taking my place on its metal bench with my colleagues. Every time I wondered whether or not, having survived the war, I was now pushing my luck.

The tactics of the convoys were to drive as fast as possible in order to make a more difficult target. Arab snipers would fire from the cover of the palm trees on the far side of the Sweetwater Canal bordering the main road, this stretch was known ominously as 'Sten Gun Alley'. I can't deny that my palms got somewhat moist, and my mouth was dry at the expectation of a sudden burst of enemy gunfire erupting at any second. With a magazine full of ammo in readiness, the sun beating down and the adrenalin flowing, I would grasp the Sten tightly. Although it would have been highly desirable to leave the safety catch off in order to return fire instantly, one dared not; it was a proven fact that an extra heavy bounce of the truck would cause the weapon to fire unexpectedly of its own accord – hardly good for one's nerves or continued existence. The speed of the vehicle, the enemy's invisibility, and the notoriously temperamental Sten made retaliation impossible. There wasn't a hope in hell of getting a shot off at the Arab crouching on the opposite bank before he opened fire, and at the end of each journey one could only feel relief at not having been hit.

Approaching other Army or RAF service camps along the road was, oddly enough, far from reassuring. They too were fenced and barb-wired, with high-mounted watch towers twenty feet high at frequent intervals along the lengths of their perimeter boundaries. Because the Arabs occasionally ambushed service vehicles, disposing of the bodies but retaining the vehicles and uniforms, all service vehicles were suspect. Frequently, such terrorists would drive along the road bordering the camps and open fire with automatic weapons without stopping, so as a legitimate convoy approached, the guns in the watch towers would 'lock on' to us as we drove past, each tower literally keeping us in their gun sights until we were out of range, an eerie and unpleasant experience. We just had to hope that we were recognised as genuine British troops despite our suntans.

Similarly disguised attackers would attempt to drive at speed straight into a camp and hurl explosives or open fire at guardrooms and other buildings, so all visiting vehicles were halted at a road block outside the closed gates. The 'gateman' checked the identities of the driver and passengers before signalling to the man on duty within to open the gates. I always admired their bravery, for if the occupants were disguised Egyptians, he died quickly and the camp gates remained locked.

Even going past a slow-moving car or bus along the metalled Treaty Road was hazardous; whilst overtaking, the driver might suddenly pull out and force you off the road into the soft sand. Thus, immobilised and probably injured, you made an easy target for the terrorists. We even lost an RAF coach. The driver left HQ MEAF Abu Sueir without an escort and when his ETA at RAF Deversoir had passed, the alarm was raised. Within ten minutes a Meteor jet was airborne, low level searching along the Zone, but the vehicle had vanished in a countryside that contained nothing larger than small mud huts. It was common knowledge that some Arabs were expert thieves but that was a classic; as far as I know, the bus and its driver were never found.

Despite night guards, wire and searchlights, the Arabs were undeterred in their efforts to steal anything they could. They were particularly adept at cutting lengths of cable buried near the perimeters, thereby severing all communications and daily replacement by the Army Signals unit was routine. One counter measure which had some success was the use of two track-driven Bren-gun carriers. One, old and noisy, would rattle along outside the camp in low gear; having allowed a decent interval to elapse, in which the thieves would resume their nefarious activities, an almost silent carrier would then approach at speed, catching them unawares and opening fire on them with their heavy machine-guns.

Many of the night guards were clerks, store men and the like – from the administrative staff which made up the bulk of the HQ. As few of them had ever fired a gun at a human being, even an Arab with murderous intent, their understandable reluctance and lack of accuracy was overcome by issuing them with Greener scatter guns, similar to shotguns instead of rifles. The Greeners, though not exactly lethal at a distance, did at least have a deterrent effect.

Shopping trips to the services' Fayid Shopping Centre, within the military zone, were frequently arranged. It was an area containing several shops situated near a clutch of service camps, its entrances checkpointed by armed troops. One could not entirely relax even there, for the centre swarmed with Arab employees, not all of them imbued with brotherly love for us, and many a BOR (British Other Ranks) or dependent was attacked, injured and robbed, even within the checkpoints. It was not until fifty years later, in 2003, that the authorities agreed that the servicemen involved in this campaign deserved recognition. We were awarded the General Service Medal, its bar bearing the words 'Canal Zone', while the rim of the medal was engraved with the medallist's Service number, rank and name. In March 1954 it was with a sense of relief that I received a posting to RAF Habbaniyah, to take up a staff position as Command Statistics Officer at Air Headquarters Iraq, later retitled AHQ Levant.

Our flight this time was in an RAF Vickers Valetta, nicknamed the 'Pig' because of its rotund shape. It was a sound and dependable transport aircraft most of the time, although when flying in one the previous year one of the two engines failed just after take-off, resulting in a white-knuckled circuit and hasty landing – followed by long sighs of relief from all on board. From RAF Fayid we refuelled at RAF Mafraq, Jordan then we were airborne again en route for Habb. Below, there was nothing but rocks and sand as far as the eye could see; the vista broken only by the trans-desert oil pipelines with their pumping stations at intervals every few score miles. The further east we flew across the Iraqi border, the more desolate the landscape became until, two hours out from Mafraq, an incredible, almost unbelievable area of green appeared. As we lined up on final approach at 12.35pm, we saw lawns and trees stretching ahead of us. This was RAF Habbaniyah.

It was a unique RAF station, vast in its acreage, reputedly the biggest British service camp in the world, not including the airfield, which was some distance away. Metalled roads were lined with eucalyptus trees (lethal to mosquitoes), and everywhere were green and luxuriant lawns – in the middle of the arid Iraqi desert! I soon found out that the whole station was criss-crossed with a multiplicity of narrow ditches broken up at intervals by small wooden sluice gates, and that throughout the night Arabs carrying lanterns would go round, opening some sluices, closing others, to a plan – to the unversed – of utter complexity, which controlled the flow of water from the nearby River Euphrates, so that every lawn and field received the irrigation it required over a certain number of days. So lush was the grass that we even had a herd of English dairy cows, which was milked for the benefit of the babies in married quarters.

Russia was our uncomfortable and unfriendly neighbour at that time, and all new arrivals had to sit a written examination to assess how much we knew about NBC (Nuclear, Biological, Chemical) warfare. Having just come from the Canal Zone I knew I was conversant with the subjects, but on reading the questions I was astounded to find I knew every answer! Accordingly, I completed the test quickly and left the room. A few days later, I was sent for by a senior officer of the RAF Regiment, a body of men more akin to the Army than the RAF, their function being to guard airfields and similar installations at risk from NBC attack. The officer had my answer paper in front of him and was so impressed by my knowledge of the subjects that he asked me whether I had ever considered applying for a commission in the RAF Regiment. For a moment the glowing prospect of being an RAF officer, even a very junior one, had immense appeal to me as still just a sergeant. But, thinking of the constant parades and interminable rifle drills performed by the Regiment, I politely rejected the proposition, saying that I wanted to remain in the non-commissioned ranks in the hopes that one day I might achieve the rank of Warrant Officer. It seemed better to be at the top of one heap rather than the bottom of another, and looking back I am glad I made the decision which led to so much in my future life.

The Air Headquarters building was very impressive, two storey, white and planned as a squared figure eight with two squares touching along one side. The inner quadrangles were open to the sky and contained gardens and trees. The offices had verandas and balconies looking out on to these quadrangles, compensating for the dazzling glare of the sun through the windows on the outside of the building. Immediately in front of AHQ was the flag staff, and as Orderly Sergeant I raised and lowered the RAF Ensign there many times. One occasion stands out, for I was the one who lowered it for the last time before nominal overall control of all RAF bases was handed over to the Iraqi Government in May 1955, the end of Imperial British Rule in Iraq. We weren't withdrawing of course, nor abandoning the flag tradition. It was a political ploy, and we noticed little difference except that afterwards the camp gates were manned by soldiers of the Iraqi Army, small smart men who were as friendly and respectful as we could have wished.

Habbaniyah had service police, of course, and they too were unique in that they were the only ones in the Service mounted on horseback, their saddle cloths decorated with the RAF Crest. Horses could travel over the sand where tyres couldn't, so it was a logical way of patrolling the sprawling camp. Incredible and exotic plants and trees were cultivated in the Command Gardens, thriving in the sunshine with the ingenious irrigation system.

The place was so immense that one never walked very far but instead phoned for one of the scores of taxis which plied for hire within the station bounds. The drivers were locals, the cars large American sedans, the fares standard throughout the camp. There were no fewer than five Sergeants' Messes and as many again for those of other ranks in similar proportion. Not far from the camp was Lake Habbaniyah, almost an inland sea and a pre-war staging post for the flying boats of Imperial Airways on their route to India and all points east. We had a flourishing yacht club there, which was very popular in the summer season.

I was in AHQ Sgts Mess; the quarters were good, single rooms, single storey, sparsely furnished, with verandas outside to keep the glare of the sun away from the windows. The latter had shutters against the sandstorms, but these afforded totally inadequate protection – not that anything could be adequate, for, batten down the hatches as one might, the wind would howl and the sand would penetrate through every minute crevice, getting into cupboards, drawers, bedsheets, even gritting in one's teeth. Outside each room, on the veranda, stood a large *chatti*, a porous pot or urn filled with water, its contents kept more or less cool as the water oozed out through the sides and evaporated. The food was excellent, fresh and well-cooked. Salt tablets were an essential part of the diet, and we had plenty of vegetables and water melon. We also had our native 'boys', men dedicated to their charges, who did our laundry and room cleaning and were loyal workers indeed. Mine was Mohammed, an Assyrian, and he was always there when needed.

The overwhelming heat was the great enemy, summer temperatures hovering around 120 degrees Fahrenheit in the shade – yet frost appeared on the grass in winter! Summer uniform consisted of the ubiquitous khaki drill in the summer: shirts and shorts with berets, slacks and sleeves rolled down after 6.00pm. In winter we wore blue uniforms, with greatcoats in the cold evenings. Working hours in summer finished at 1.00pm, and after tiffin (lunch) I would collapse on the bed in my room in the mess, all shades drawn, ceiling fan full on and try to keep as still as possible. Rising at about 4.00pm or so, I would try to refresh with a cold shower, clean clothes then go to dinner, which included the necessary intake of salt, sprinkled on water melon.

On camp we had our own shopping centre, with small shops owned and run by Indians and Pakistanis. Plenty of souvenirs – leather goods, watches, etc. – were on sale, and there were several good tailors capable of making excellent, smarter-than-issue KD uniforms and light-weight 'sharkskin' suits for mess wear. For gentle exercise one could stroll along the bund, the high bank bordering the wide Euphrates alongside the camp, and I used to watch primitive small ferry boats crossing from bank to bank, and marvel at the fishermen who were so adept at their craft. They used a circular net, about 8 feet across with weights around the circumference, and would spin it round their heads to gain momentum; then, thrown into the river, it would sink like a huge woven bag, open end downwards, and close as they pulled on the attached ropes, its contents threshing as they were pulled from the water.

We started an archery club, initially using Slazenger wooden bows, but lost quite a few of the arrows which, missing the target, slithered out of sight under the sparse grass (perhaps they will be discovered by future archaeologists and identified as weapons fashioned by early Palaeolithic tribes). It soon became evident that in the extreme dryness the heart of the wooden bows turned brittle, causing them to snap disastrously on 'full pull'. So we re-armed with Accles and Pollock steel bows purchased via the PSI (President of the Services Institute funds) and avoided concussion. By way of a change from repetitive target shooting, I introduced the sport of bow-fishing. The arrow was attached to the bow by a long length of fishing line and, provided one's aim was true, and the fish not too deep in the water, one hauled in the line, the arrow and the catch. We had a refraction problem, and often the target appeared to be where it wasn't. However, I once speared two at the same time – I don't know who was more surprised, me or the fish swimming deeper than its companion! Euphrates fish, the size of mackerel, were rather scaly, full of bones and not very palatable, though the sergeant mess cooks did their best.

One year a floodlit carnival was held. Floats representing each of the various sports and activities on the station processed around the camp. The Archery Club presented a tableau on one float, re-enacting the story of William Tell shooting an apple from his son's head, though rearranging it slightly to show what *might* have happened. William Tell stood at one end of a long float normally used to transport aircraft and called the 'Queen Mary'. His hand held the bow down by his side, and there was a look of consternation on his face. At the other end of the float stood the 'son', an apple secured on top of his cap, his mouth open wide, his arms spread and the feathered end of an arrow projecting from his chest, the barbed point protruding from between his shoulder-blades. The roads were lined with hundreds of Arab employees and their families, and the gasps, pointing fingers and expressions of disbelief on their faces were indescribable!

We created our realistic effect by breaking a wooden arrow in two and driving the broken end of the feathered section of the arrow against the fabric of the son's khaki shirt and into a matchbox secured inside. The tension provided by the fabric and box held the arrow near-horizontal. Another matchbox was placed in the back of his shirt and the broken end of the barbed section, its point liberally smeared with red paint, lined up with the arrow at the end and *voila* – William Tell had dropped a real clanger!

On another occasion a number of heavy Centurion tanks gave a demonstration of their fire power to members of the headquarters staff, and we all drove out into the desert and watched the awesome spectacle as the guns fired, the shell bursts clearly visible in the sand thousands of yards away.

As there was nothing outside the camp except the desert – and one can rapidly go off building sandcastles – the camp cinema was popular. It was a very large rectangular building, one half enclosed for winter use, the other half roofless. And it was bliss to sit in the cool of the evening beneath the dark sky and brilliant stars while watching a film. I also used to spend many hours in the Mess' snooker room, a game I thoroughly enjoyed, and I was never short of opponents. Snooker became much more of a gamble when one mess member somehow obtained a red ball which had been weighted 'off centre', so that when struck it would travel in a straight line and as it slowed roll away at an angle. The saboteur would casually stroll past the table and surreptitiously roll it gently among the others, thereby shattering the players' nerves for the rest of the game, for we never knew which one had been vandalised, if indeed, any had.

Camel trains travelled through the vast desert which surrounded the RAF station, en route between Jordan, Syria and the Iraqi towns further east. The drovers would camp nearby to rest and water their charges then move on. It made for a Biblical spectacle as the hundreds of animals were herded along in slow straggling processions at least half a mile in length. Equally spectacular were the desert thunder storms; at night, the lightning flickered around the horizon for hours, luridly brilliant forks blasting downwards in the clear atmosphere. Leave a camera, shutter open, on a tripod, pointing in any direction, and an hour later one would be rewarded with quite outstanding photographs.

Adjacent to the camp was the Civil Cantonment, in which lived the uncounted hundreds, probably thousands of locals and their families who worked on the RAF station. It was reputedly the third largest town in Iraq after Baghdad and Mosul. The rows and rows of shacks were mostly clay, others rather less primitive being made of wood. There were no roads, just sandy tracks lined with open drains in which flowed unmentionable liquids and partial solids. It was strictly out of bounds to all servicemen except those granted a special pass. I was issued with one for the purpose of teaching English to a polyglot assortment of Iraqis, Kurds, Indians and Syrians. As I spoke no Arabic, the curriculum was very basic but my pupils seemed to benefit from the sign language we employed and from imitating the word sounds I made, and we all enjoyed the sessions, for, unlike in Egypt, servicemen were accepted as friends in Iraq at that time. Two of my students were the local schoolmaster and his wife, with whom I spent hours chatting in their house; as the years went by, I often wondered what became of them. I gave up the teaching with regret when my meagre fees were subjected to income tax – all I wanted was a little baksheesh!

Baghdad lay fifty-five miles to the east of the base. The journey was made by taxi, travelling on desert tracks as there were no roads. Any vehicle ahead created such an enveloping pall of sand that one's own taxi would need to travel on its left or right, driving parallel but not behind. The rocky terrain and swirling sand made it a very bumpy and dusty safari. It was fatally easy to miss Baghdad altogether in the featureless desert; a disorientated driver could continue further east until fuel ran out and there was little hope of rescue, for one wouldn't be missed until overdue for work the following day – which would be too late.

Like other Arab cities in those days, from Bahrain to Mogadishu, Amman to Mombasa, Baghdad had no high-rise blocks or modern, western-style buildings; the tourist boom was in the distant future. I vividly remember the blistering heat, the completely shrouded women, the Arab boys pestering to clean one's shoes, and the literate letter-writers seated at their little tables in the streets, charging a small fee for writing letters for their less educated brethren. Actually, there was very little to do once one had found a hotel, showered and smartened up, other than drink in the night clubs and drool lasciviously over the belly-dancers. Those ladies had perfected the art of standing perfectly still and just flexing their stomach muscles rhythmically – hence their name – unlike their Western imitators, who merely sway their hips.

Staff visits to check on statistical data-collection systems and procedures in the units under our control afforded some welcome variety and a chance to get away from Habbaniyah and explore different surroundings, so I took the opportunity to fly by Valetta, York and Eagle Viking transport aircraft on various occasions to Malta, Cyprus, Amman, and our Persian Gulf outposts at RAF Basrah, Shaibah, Sharjah and Bahrain. In Bahrain the only 'other ranks' room to be air conditioned was the Sergeants' Mess Bar, and the results of drinking in the cool then stepping out into the furnace-like heat of the Gulf were quite shattering.

Generally, Habbaniyah was a boring posting with little social life, but it was preferable to the ever-present risk of being shot at in the Canal Zone. The overriding longing for married men like me on most overseas postings was to be joined by one's wife and children. The tour at Habbaniyah lasted two and a half years. If one did not qualify for a married quarter within eighteen months, one was struck off the waiting list, as Air Ministry Regulations did not allow anyone to occupy a married quarter for less than a year. So the first eighteen months were a worrying time for anyone married and for their wives back in the UK. As the deadline approached, minds were inevitably occupied with one's position on the roster. One's total entitlement points (so many for each child, so many for each month overseas) would increase as the time went by, but it was always uncertain whether enough married quarters would be vacated in time. And there was always the risk of being pipped at the post by some later arrival with more points (e.g. having many children, which would push one irretrievably down the list. I was thwarted in this way, and for some of the other unlucky, demoralised and disheartened 'eighteen-month-plus' men, alcohol provided the only solace, and many marriages suffered under the strain of the waiting and the ultimate disappointment.

My tour of overseas duty in Iraq expired on 9th October 1955, and so I departed without much regret by RAF Hastings, staging through RAF Idris (Castel Benito, North Africa) for a night stop there. Off again the next day, I reached RAF Lyneham on 10th October 1955.

Chapter Seven
INTELLIGENCE GATHERING ON THE EAST GERMAN BORDER DURING THE COLD WAR

B ack in Blighty I was given disembarkation leave until my next posting to CEE (Controller of Engineering and Equipment) Statistics Department of the Air Ministry. On 28th November 1955 I reported to the offices at Princes House on Kingsway in London, opposite the now long-gone Stoll Theatre. From here, my fellow sergeant, Eric Shipton, and I would sometimes be 'called to the Bar' at the Royal Courts of Justice. Though, in our case, the call was to have a beer at the bar in the basement (this judicial drinking hole has long since closed).

I was allocated a hiring in Northwood but found it hard to adapt to my new surroundings. My office work involved the collection and analysis of data gathered worldwide, and it was absorbing and challenging, but the sudden transition from being overseas in the desert to wearing civvies and travelling to work via two changes on the crowded Underground into central London was too much like being demobbed. In less than a year the novelty had worn off. Win and I discussed the situation, of course, and we decided that I should take a chance on getting a married quarter on the next station; so I volunteered for overseas again, and she vacated the hiring and returned to Manchester (Stephen was doing well at boarding school).

My new unit was to be No. 291 Signals Unit, 5 Signals Wing,

West Germany, and, without knowing what to expect – one never does in the Services – I left on 5th October 1956, travelling by rail and ferry via the Hook of Holland to RAF Goch, Germany and from thence to Hamelin. Motor transport then took me to where the unit was located, near Scharfoldendorf, a tiny village up in the Ith Hills only a few miles from the then hostile Russian-occupied East Germany.

The RAF station was perched near the top of a heavily wooded hill and approached by a circuitous route which included a complete 'U' turn in the steeply ascending road. Most of the camp was occupied by the signals area itself: wooden huts enclosed within two perimeters of barbed wire, the area between being no-man's land, constantly patrolled by service police with dogs. There was also a small domestic area, with stores, a single short road and a cul-de-sac, bordered by between thirty and forty married quarters, one of which I was only too delighted to be allocated. Such was our unenviable proximity to the border under the ever-present threat of a Russian invasion that our private cars had to be parked facing the open end of the road, and we were also advised to keep spare blankets and a small supply of tinned food in the cars, just in case we had to abandon the site in haste. Occasionally, very early in the morning, and often just as one began to shave, one or two Russian Mig fighters would fly very low and very fast over the camp, then quickly scuttle back across the border. This was presumably a ruse designed to check how quickly we could get our Meteors airborne from nearby airfields to intercept them. Playing cat and mouse could be amusing if one wasn't too conscious of being the cheese! Of course we could never be sure that these aerial intruders were not the precursors of an all-out surprise attack, and that the next thing we'd hear would be the rumble of the first wave of Russian tanks!

So isolated was the camp that domestic life was very circumscribed. Win enjoyed shopping trips, involving a long run to Hamelin, a quaint and picturesque little town. Local entertainment was found in nearby taverns, where we could try to improve our smattering of the German language ('*Noch ein Bier, bitte!*'). Few servicemen bothered to learn much of the language of the country in which they were stationed, for their next foreign posting could well be in another country altogether.

On arrival the role of the unit was totally unknown to me, and I was surprised at the tight security. All personnel working in the inner sanctum, where I would be employed, had to be P.V.'d, i.e. personally vetted, before being permitted to work inside the barbed wire. Personal vetting involves one's activities, proclivities, relatives, background, associates, hobbies, personal history and service record being closely investigated, so I was asked where I would like to work until security cleared.

Although by now I was thirty-four years old, I had not learnt to drive. At the age when most young men impressed the local girls as they drove second-hand Ford and Morris cars, I had been in the Middle East for four years. When I returned in January 1946, petrol rationing and a sheer lack of cars made the situation hopelessly difficult. The old cars were mostly clapped out, and almost all newly manufactured models were exported to earn foreign currency with which to replenish the country's depleted cash. I had planned to buy one of the much vaunted and, at that time, revolutionary VW Beetles while in Germany, so now I naturally elected to work in the Motor Transport Section, since all British Forces in Germany at that time were equipped with these cars as part of German reparations.

As it happened, all personnel at Scharfoldendorf were encouraged to learn to drive in order to be available in any hurried evacuation, so as the weeks and months went by I was taught by a MT corporal, who insisted on the highest proficiency. The first lessons were carried out in five-ton Magirus service lorries on the Autobahns – years before motorways were introduced into the UK. The lorries were not the easiest of vehicles to control, and ever since then I've had the greatest respect for the drivers of heavy-goods vehicles. I was given the same meticulous training when I graduated on to service Beetles, my instructor insisting that I 'should drive as if the Queen was sitting in the back seat... sipping a cup of tea.'

My time in the MT Section also gave me the opportunity to learn the mechanics of the VW Beetle, which proved an advantage when I bought my first one in December 1956, using the bonus £100 I received for extending my service to the age of fifty-five. The car was a 1954 LHD deluxe model from Autohaus Henschel in Hanover and had a VHF radio, something not introduced into British cars for many years. However, instead of a petrol gauge, it had only a dipstick. Older models even lacked windscreen washers, though owners easily overcame this lack by keeping a plastic bottle of water in the glove compartment to squirt from the side window when necessary. More technical owners purchased a suitable nozzle, drilled and fitted it in position in the bonnet and connected it with a length of tubing to the bottle in the glove box, thereby obviating the need to lower the window – though the driver still had to reach across the car, open the glove box lid, and squeeze.

After six months my PV finally came through, and I was sent for by the Commanding Officer, who asked me whether I was aware of the role of the unit. Amazingly, despite spending six months on such a very small unit, mixing nightly with other SNCOs in the

Mess and chatting socially, I had to admit that personal security was so tight that I hadn't the faintest idea, an admission which of course was highly gratifying to the CO.

At that time the Cold War was at its height, and many 'enemy' airfields operated along the other side of the border. Their operational aircraft, flown by Russian aircrews, were in constant training, ready to attack the West should Moscow give the go-ahead, so we in West Germany could not afford to relax. Obviously, the Allies' battle plan had to take the enemy's actions into consideration. If more up-to-date bombers suddenly appeared along the border, if air activity increased or if training tactics changed, our forces had to be correspondingly geared up. Strategically situated intelligence-gathering units along the border performed a vital role, monitoring the air movements and possible intentions of the Russian aircraft on the other side by deciphering and interpreting radio messages or 'intercepts' transmitted between aircraft and ground control and between individual aircraft. Chatter mentioning, for instance, the 'port outer' would confirm that that squadron was operating four-engined aircraft; and sometimes more off-the-cuff comments such as 'going home soon' passed between individual crew members, revealing that their unit would shortly be relocating back to Russia.

The listening-in and interpretation was done by Russian-speaking RAF personnel, mainly officers, with a clerical and support staff of NCOs of whom I was one. Each month the call-signs used by each 'enemy' squadron were routinely changed, and detective work had to be carried out to identify which squadron was which, whether some squadrons had been replaced, re-armed with a different type of aircraft, or additional squadrons flown in.

Security on the unit was obviously essential; it was so important that when it was discovered that, even when on their cradles, the diaphragms in standard office telephones could be adapted to act as transmitters and be used to relay all the office conversation to enemy agents in the vicinity, all phones were moved out into the corridors. The best form of security was to ensure that everyone working there knew and recognised everyone they met within the buildings, regardless of the fact that everyone must have had the necessary authority to enter the compound. Upon starting work there I was constantly challenged wherever I went, until everyone had got to know me.

Results of intercept analysis from all such units as ours were routinely passed to our military headquarters in Munchen-Gladbach, near Cologne, to NATO HQ and of course to London. Some of the gleaned information destined for the UK travelled by diplomatic bag, which was sacrosanct and inviolable, untouchable by Customs or any other authority of the foreign country in which one was serving. It was a heavily sealed white canvas bag and was handed over to the day's Orderly Sergeant against signature. When it was my turn to collect the dipbag, I was escorted everywhere from the moment of receipt by two armed service policemen – and I mean everywhere, even in the loo! I sat in the back seat of the two-door Service Beetle, they in the front seats, so that it was impossible to get at me without first overpowering them. Our route to Hanover took us through the countryside, and on the quiet roads there was always a certain amount of tension when cars followed or approached to overtake. At Hanover we would drive directly to the airport, where we waited in the lounge until I could hand the dipbag over personally to the pilot of the British airliner ferrying through to Cologne – first obtaining a signature, of course.

The efficiency of the Communist intelligence services was not to be under-estimated. We were aware that our identities were known to the Russians, and so, unlike members of Allied Forces serving in more orthodox units, we were forbidden to go on leave to West Berlin, as this carried the risk of suddenly disappearing and subsequently being 'persuaded' to divulge our methods of operation; this ruling continued long after being posted elsewhere. It was a disappointment, because I always wanted to see how thoroughly the RAF had bombed Berlin, where at that time, and for some years to come, little rebuilding had taken place, especially in the Russian Zone of that city.

After some time I was asked by the CO if I was prepared to go on a language course to learn Russian, a move which would have committed me to a service future spent on units similar to 291 Signals Unit. I wanted to keep some variety in the postings I was offered, so I declined, and in September 1957 I was posted to HQ 2nd TAF (Tactical Air Force) Munchen-Gladbach, a vast Army/RAF station west of Dusseldorf near the Dutch border. This camp, built as reparation by the Germans, sprawled over many acres and was criss-crossed by civilian roads. The 'Big House' was the Joint Headquarters for the control of all Army and RAF units in West Germany, and the service staff numbered many hundreds. The domestic accommodation was excellent, both for unaccompanied personnel and those who lived in the married quarters, and life was complete when one of them was allocated to us. The married patch was well laid out. Each house had a small garden in which was planted one apple, one pear and one plum tree. They were all attractive when in bloom, although they remained fruitless. We were well served by the local tradesmen. Milk and other necessities were delivered to the door and 'curry-wagens', which sold chips with mayonnaise, curry *wurst* and similar delicacies plied their wares throughout the married patch.

There were two cinemas, a large NAAFI, a 'WOs and Joes Club' for Warrant Officers and SNCOs, a civilian-type shopping centre, a post office and all modern facilities. Dusseldorf and Cologne were within easy reach, as were many smaller local towns. At Erkelenz, instead of traffic lights, a large four-sided 'clock face' was suspended above the crossroads, its single hand slowly moving between the 'stop' and 'go' positions. Nearby was the village of Wegberg, which was situated in the middle of the Wegberg Ring, a miniature version of Nurburgring, too small in area for modern racing cars. It had been used by the German High Command in 1939 to mass their squadrons of tanks in preparation for their invasion of neighbouring Holland.

So that Win could visit her family, I made many trips home on leave in the Beetle, via Belgium and France, and having joined the AA, on arrival at Calais I was always greeted personally by the AA man, whose role was to shepherd the member through the Customs, a much appreciated service that they provided in those days. On one occasion, while returning from the UK alone, I got hopelessly lost in Belgium and drove for miles in the dark with never a soul in sight. Eventually, I saw a pedestrian and stopped to ask him the way. Knowing no Flemish or French, I asked in German, '*Welche weg nach Munchen-Gladbach?*' (Which way to Munich-Gladbach?). He replied in some ghastly gibberish, so I asked again, this time including the words '*militarische hauptquartier*' (military HQ). Again he babbled unintelligibly, so assuming he was the local village idiot, I got exasperated and said in English something like, 'Oh, forget it, you idiot!' whereupon he exclaimed, 'Are you British?' It turned out that he was also in the RAF and was hitch-hiking back to his unit in West Germany. In the darkness he hadn't seen the Beetle's BFG (British Forces Germany) number plates and, knowing no German, naturally assumed that I was a Belgian speaking to him in Flemish. The spectacle of two Englishmen trying to make themselves understood in the wrong languages in the middle of the night on a country road in Belgium would have been hilarious to anyone watching! He climbed aboard, of course, and somehow we found our way to the German border.

As servicemen, we were always aware that, since the war was not long over, we were not exactly flavour of the month with many of the Germans, who perhaps understandably still harboured grudges against the occupying forces, especially the RAF, which had inflicted so much damage with air-raids. On the road we were instantly identifiable, for not only did our private cars have to bear BFG number plates, we also had to have separate GB plates fitted, which were interpreted by the Germans as '*Grosse Bruder*' (Big Brother).

It was also essential to watch out for the German *Autobahn* police. They drove white convertible Porsches and wore white overalls with matching helmets, and were empowered to fine offenders on the spot. This caused difficulties with servicemen because we were not paid in Deutschmarks but in BAFVs, British Armed Forces Vouchers, which were only valid in the NAAFI and other service institutes, in order to prevent unscrupulous types from dealing in the black market, selling tyres, batteries and luxury goods only available to the Allies. Petrol was rationed, and we could only use our vouchers at Aral petrol stations. Seeing a police Porsche in the rear-view mirror, we learned to disguise the fact that we were speeding by using the handbrake to slow down, rather than the footbrake, thereby not activating the brake lights! If pulled up by them and told to get out of the car, we knew never, ever, to lean on the open door or one would be charged with 'being so drunk as to be unable to stand upright unless supported'.

Despite all this Win and I made friends with many local Germans. Rather than affecting our friendship adversely by admitting they had fought against us, most of our German acquaintances said they had fought against the Russians on the Eastern Front. One family, that of Helmut and Friedl Wittwer, was particularly hospitable, and visits to their home were spent discussing life over many a cheese fondue or glass of *gluewein* (mulled wine). We enjoyed ourselves attending *Blumenfests,* with their parades of floats splendidly decorated with flowers, and *Schutzenfests*, involving appropriately lubricated local residents, clad in hunting green, attempting to shoot down targets fixed on top of tall poles. We also explored the local countryside, visiting such places as Schloss Dyck, a castle renowned for its large geese who greeted visitors with menacing noises and gaping beaks! Its lake had obviously been used as a dumping ground for weapons discarded after the German defeat. On one occasion we watched divers at work, rifles and other armaments appearing, held high above the surface, Excalibur-like, as they retrieved them from the muddy depths.

Service life there was very comfortable, the analysis and presentation of aircraft statistics absorbing, and it was with some regret that I had to leave when my tour expired in April 1959. That wasn't the last I saw of Munchen-Gladbach, however, for I was destined to be posted there again some nine years later, by then having finally achieved my ultimate goal, the exalted rank of Warrant Officer.

Chapter Eight
A WEDDING IN PARIS

After disembarkation leave I was posted to No. 3 Radio School, RAF Compton Bassett, Wilts, arriving there on 11th May 1959, to fill an office post maintaining trainee records. Regrettably, by 1961 things had gone drastically wrong between Win and me, and eventually the marriage irretrievably broke down. Marital difficulties in the service always pose a problem. Unlike in Civvy Street, the serviceman can't just walk out; if he does he's classed as a deserter, and unless his wife agrees to leave the married quarter the unhappy situation continues and invariably festers. We eventually divorced, and although I could have claimed custody of Stephen, I considered that generally a child was better off with his mother, and it would not have been fair to him to drag him round the world every time I was posted, so he stayed with Win, who shortly afterwards emigrated to Canada with her new husband. I found out much later that Stephen eventually became a proficient helicopter pilot, a skill which I was to acquire years later. Now he lives in Kenya, where I am proud to say, he thoroughly deserves his successes as a prosperous businessman and – like his dad – as an accomplished author.

Compton Bassett was an unexciting posting. On 30th November 1960 I was sent on a three-week instructors' course at RAF Uxbridge, Buckinghamshire. There were twenty-one other NCOs in the class, and we received intensive training in the art of public speaking, lessons which were to prove invaluable to me years later when conducting tours at the Tower of London. We received tips such as not to talk to one person in the group – it embarrasses them – but to keep casting one's gaze around. More specific maxims were given for the instruction of trainees; we were taught not to go on too long about a subject before getting it on the blackboard and having them copy it into their notebooks – 'A little bit of talk, a little bit of chalk'. Other hints were 'While writing on the blackboard, don't continue talking to it' and 'Introduce a new subject by going from the known to the unknown'. Throwing a piece of chalk at an inattentive student was strictly discouraged! Near the end of the course each student had to give a twenty-minute talk on a subject of his choice – not easy when delivering it to a group of one's colleagues, but good preparation for when one had to face a class of trainees – or a large group of tourists. On completion of the course I came second in the class in merit and performance, with an A2 Pass (no doubt because I had the 'gift of the gab'), and was subsequently posted to No. 7 School of Technical Training at RAF Kirton in Lindsey, Lincolnshire, as a statistics instructor, arriving there on 21 December 1960 – just in time for Christmas leave.

The camp was isolated many miles from Scunthorpe, the nearest town. The hundreds of young trainees were away from their home bases and families and had few recreational facilities, so I applied for permission to set up a closed-circuit radio station in a disused block of buildings. A local electrical firm installed the wiring connecting all the barrack blocks and the necessary studio equipment: microphones, twin turntables, high-lift needles, VU meters. A number of airmen volunteered to be staff members.

Corporal 'Chalky' White, Don Lowrie, John Enderby, Alan Cheal, Doc Wright and Geoff Wills all gave up their spare time in the evenings to keep KLN – Kirton Lindsey Network – on the air.

We visited sundry grocers in Scunthorpe and scrounged egg boxes by the score, sticking them everywhere, including the ceilings, and spraying them black. They made an eccentric but very effective and professional looking soundproofing system. We built up a library of records appealing to various tastes, most purchased by donations from the Station Institute funds. To improve my studio technique I visited the BBC Manchester studios. The staff there were very helpful, and I learned a lot. For instance: always have a stand-by record ready on a turntable, in case of a break in transmission. Programmes covering pop to classics to quizzes went on the air each evening at 6.30pm, starting with the popular 'Your Requests', which consisted of choices sent in by the girlfriends and families of the trainees and included transmissions from popular BBC Light programmes. Broadcasting continued until 11.00pm, when we closed down with a recording of the 'Last Post'.

We were lucky to have a top-of-the-range professional tape recorder, a Ferrograph, and, as the station did not have a band, I was 'persuaded' by the top brass to get a recording of marching music to accompany the morning parades on the barrack square. I obtained suitable music from the RAF Central Band, an eyrie was found for me in a barrack block overlooking the square, and loudspeakers were put in place around the parade ground.

The timings were tricky to say the least. The second the parade came into view round the corner of the building at the far side of the square, I had to press the 'start' button to coincide with the left feet of the men hitting the ground – taking into consideration, of course, the time it took for the sound to reach them. When the parade had halted on the square, the CO would inspect the men, moving slowly along the ranks to the melody reputedly composed by Henry VIII, *Greensleeves*. This was followed by the marching off to more martial music, in order to keep the hundreds of airmen precisely in step.

Every time, my nerves were stretched to breaking point, until the last squad was out of sight, for had the tape snapped (as they were prone to) while the marching was in progress, the prospect of the far-from-comical havoc which would have ensued – squads in total disarray, with men losing the step, tripping up and bumping into each other, NCOs shouting orders hysterically, officers going puce in the face... it didn't bear thinking about. Fortunately, it never happened during my stay there, but it was always a shambles threatening to happen.

Running the radio station sometimes required sensitivity, too. In November 1963, following the assassination of President Kennedy, I quickly had to replace the evening's light programming with more sombre music. For my efforts in brightening up camp life for the trainees by creating KLN (though I couldn't have done it without my ever-helpful staffers) I was awarded an Air Officer's Commendation – a recognition I certainly *wouldn't* have received had the tape ever broken!

Having completed the instructor course at Uxbridge successfully, instructing for real held no qualms for me. When the Canadian Air Force decided to introduce a Statistics Branch, they sent detachments to Kirton Lindsey and I found myself teaching batches of eager and attentive students. One trick I acquired to gain their attention when they entered the room was to write a sentence or two (usually 'Sit down and keep quiet!') either upside down or in mirror-fashion on the blackboard – it always worked.

A tragedy was uncovered while I was there. While ploughing his fields a local farmer took the machine much closer than usual to the deep drainage ditches which criss-cross the county and uncovered the wreckage of a Lancaster bomber, with the remains of the crew still inside. The aircraft was later identified as having been crewed by Polish airmen, and had been reported missing after a raid on Germany nearly twenty years earlier. Probably crippled by enemy aircraft or ground-fire, it had crashed into the soft ground by the drainage ditch and sunk out of sight in the swampy morass. As ours was the nearest RAF station, I was one of those who had the melancholy task of helping to carry one of the coffins, mine containing the remains of a young Pole who, had he survived the war, would have been about my age.

None of us had experience of carrying a coffin, and we found it to be very difficult. It was essential that it should not be allowed to fall from our shoulders, and the risk of this happening was reduced by each airman gripping the waistband at the back of the greatcoat worn by the man on the other side of the coffin, pulling him in as close as possible by keeping a tight hold, all of us pressing our heads against the wooden sides. Being servicemen, we instinctively walked in step with each other, which would have caused the coffin to sway from side to side, so we organised it that those on one side stepped off with their left foot, while the bearers on the other side did so with their right – problem solved. The sad remains of the crew were taken for burial service and interment in a cemetery in Newark, where there was, and no doubt still is, a Polish burial ground.

KLN was to bring me my next wife. Searching for music for the Network, I became a member of a tape club called Worldwide Tapetalk, where tapes on all topics were exchanged. Seeing the name Shelagh Bowyer in the lists, I contacted her, and over time our friendship grew. Eventually, she accepted my proposal, which I made from a phone box outside camp. Shelagh and her family had lived in Datchet, near Windsor, for generations; her father had been a Captain in Berkshire's regiment, but was drowned with many of his men while escorting a large number of prisoners of war to Canada, the liner *Arandora Star* being torpedoed in the Atlantic.

We were unable to get married until Shelagh's divorce was finalised, and so we were not eligible for a married quarter. Instead we rented a small house in Kirton Lindsey village. Shelagh had a beautiful voice and recorded some late-night programmes on the KLN Ferrograph, 'Dream Date with Shelagh', which were listened to with rapt attention by the audience of trainees. Shelagh already had a young family, and her daughter Mary has become a successful actress on television and in the West End. Mary and her husband Peter Waddington, another fine treader of the boards, gave me a scholarly-athletic step-grandson, Humphrey John. Mary's twin-brother Robert joined the RAF, then emigrated to Australia, where he succeeded in passing all the rigorous tests necessary to become captain of Boeing aircraft owned by Quantas Airline. Shelagh's other children included Richard, a television editor, and Sally, who raised a happy little family of her own.

It wasn't long before the authorities shook the dice once more and I was told to pack my kitbag again. Accordingly, on 18th May 1964 Shelagh and I piled into the VW Beetle and headed for Dover, boarded the *'Free Enterprise'* ferry, of later ill-repute, then pointed the car's bonnet towards our next assignation, Headquarters AAFCE (Allied Air Forces Central Europe), Camp Guynemer, Fontainebleau, in France. Once more we had to rent a small house,

20 Rue de Seine, in the quaint little village of Thomery sur Seine, the river itself being at the end of the road (definitely a *cul-de-sac*!). Shelagh's *divorce absolute* was granted, and naturally we wanted to get married as soon as possible. Apart from anything else, we would then become eligible for marriage and housing allowance (there were no married quarters there). We quickly approached the RAF Chaplain, who flatly refused to officiate on the grounds that we had both previously been divorced.

This was shattering news! We could have applied for extended leave in the UK but would have had to find somewhere to live and then stay there for the period of time necessary before marriage was legally possible. So, working on the basis that a captain of a ship was qualified to officiate at the marriage of his passengers (a wrong assumption, apparently), in desperation I wrote to the British Ambassador in Paris and asked him whether he could marry us. To our delight he replied saying that one of his staff was qualified, and he would be only too pleased for the wedding to take place there. And so, on 27th June 1964, we drove to the magnificently housed British Embassy at No. 39 Rue du Faubourg-Saint-Honore. There, a female member of staff was on hand to help my wife-to-be with make-up and so on after the journey, Richard turned up unexpectedly, and Shelagh and I were then joined in holy matrimony by another staff member, later receiving a most impressive marriage certificate, annotated as being issued in the 'District of the Consul-General of the British Embassy, Paris', and complete with Foreign Service consular stamps and a large imposing red seal.

We continued to live in Thomery. The village was a charming survivor of a bygone age, as was the nearby village of Moret sur Seine where washer-women still gathered on the river bank, scrubbing their laundry in its waters while exchanging local gossip. We had some electricity in our house, but the fridge was not powered, and we kept the contents cold with large blocks of ice which were delivered weekly by the ice-man, who put them into the large compartment in the machine while conversing with Shelagh, who spoke fluent French.

Life was never dull there. On one memorable occasion there was a cloudburst over the village, and a mini-tsunami rushed down our steep road towards the river a hundred or so yards away. En route, it poured onto our small patio and under the front door, flooding the house to a depth of at least two feet. Shelagh fled upstairs (I was at work in Fontainebleau) and shouted '*Ourage!*' from the bedroom window. A neighbour called for the fire brigade, and when, shortly afterwards, I returned home, it was to find my now dry but bedraggled kitchen full of French *pompiers*, resplendent in their shiny brass helmets, sitting around and chatting with Shelagh while drinking glass after glass of my plonk!

My drive to work led through the Forest of Fontainebleau, which meant I had to cope as best I could with the idiosyncrasies of French motorists, whose driving was frenetic, to say the least. It soon became obvious that the only cars without crumpled wings or dented bumpers were those still in the showrooms, and also that should the horn of a French driver's car cease to work he would be unable to continue driving and so would stop and have the vehicle towed to a garage.

It was about this time that Shelagh and I decided to give up smoking our usual twenty plus a day. This was less difficult when serving in the UK, but it was almost inevitable that when posted overseas alongside US forces the temptation to start again would become overwhelming, for, as mentioned earlier, a carton of two hundred Lucky Strikes cost only ten shillings (50p). But this time we managed to persevere and gave up altogether, although we weren't completely free of the pangs until a year later. Life was good, if only because, being on the Continent, most weekends we could just throw a few things in the 1960s rear-engined Fiat Multipla, for which we had traded the VW Beetle, and go exploring without having first to cross the Channel. The rear seats of the Multipla folded right down to become a flat metal floor, allowing plenty of room for camping gear.

But all good things come to an end, and on 26th December 1964 we left 20 Rue de Seine in our newly acquired, gorgeous VW Karmann Ghia coupe, as I was posted to become a member of Flight Safety (accident investigation), HQ Bomber Command, at High Wycombe, Bucks. After disembarkation leave we arrived on 21st January 1965 and eventually moved into married quarters there. The work, dealing as it did mostly with the analysis of aircraft incidents and crashes, was particularly engrossing in view of my technical background, and life improved considerably when, with effect from 1st March that year, I was promoted Flight Sergeant – three resounding cheers!

One of the big worries of a serviceman is where to live on leaving the Service. Savings rarely kept pace with house prices, and any property bought before retirement would have to be rented out with all the attendant risks. It so happened that at that time my mother and stepfather were living in a house overlooking Holy Loch, at Sandbank, near Dunoon in Scotland, and during one leave we visited them. A little distance away, near the shore line, was a small cottage, a 'Butt-and-Ben', just two rooms and a bathroom. It was for sale for £2000; I managed to get a loan from a very reluctant bank manager, and we bought it. A local estate agent rented it out on our behalf and kept a watchful eye on it during our absences, but whenever our leave coincided with it being unoccupied, we would stay there and pass many hours watching the American submarines, which were based in the Loch at that time, returning from their missions out in the Atlantic and elsewhere. After anchoring, the vessels would be surrounded by small craft bringing men and supplies from the buildings on shore, but it was much more fascinating to watch long white cylindrical objects, presumably the nuclear Polaris missiles, being hoisted vertically from the subs, seemingly an inch at a time, for inspection and servicing. We never thought to check whether the risk of a mishap was included in our household insurance policy – it would have been pointless, really; for who would fill in the claim? Eventually we sold the cottage for £4000 and put it towards buying another house later.

A mile or so from the RAF station at High Wycombe stood a lonely-looking derelict smock windmill, so called because the configuration of its wooden frame resembled that of an old-time peasant's smock. Lacey Green windmill had been built in the seventeenth century and was the oldest of its type left in the country. It had been used as a Home Guard post during the war. Now it was in dire need of restoration, and this was being undertaken by the Chiltern Society, so to 'get away from it all' I joined the friendly gang of volunteers working there at the weekends, taking photographs as the work progressed and, of course, frequently responding to the cry, 'Come and hold this while I hit it!'

By this time I had served twenty-eight years in the RAF, and finally I attained my ambition when on 1st July 1967 I was promoted to the rank of Warrant Officer. Handing in all my NCO clothing kit, I was issued with a new uniform and hat, both tailored of a superior material; the smart tunic with 'patch' pockets and bearing the badge of rank on each sleeve (colloquially known as the 'syrup tin', the badge resembled the sign on the lid of a well-known syrup manufacturer!). The new hat and beret were also adorned with Warrant Officer's badges. From then on I was to be addressed as 'Sir' by all those of lower ranks, flight sergeants, sergeants, corporals and airmen, and as 'Mister' by officers (oddly enough, thereby reverting to the title of a civilian). Holders of Warrant rank were, and doubtless still are, regarded as figures of much authority, having come up the hard way and so knowing the score, unlike officers, who, although superior in rank, understandably were not conversant with the other-rankers' way of life. A promotion invariably led to being posted to a station where a vacancy for that rank existed, and two days later, on 3rd July 1967, we packed up and departed in the Karmann Ghia to take up another staff post at HQ Signals Command, RAF Medmenham, Bucks.

That posting turned out to be fairly short, only ten months' duration – sometimes I wondered whether it was worthwhile unpacking – but I didn't complain, nor did Shelagh, when, 2nd May 1968, we stacked as much as we could into the coupe and left for one of our favourite destinations, HQ 2 TAF (Tactical Air Force) Munchen-Gladbach, West Germany – again.

Chapter Nine
MORE GERMANY –
AND SOME MOLINOLOGY

After driving halfway across Europe we arrived at HQ 2 TAF (Tactical Air Force) Munchen-Gladbach on 3rd May 1968. I was to take up a staff post in the Big House, and this time, when it was my turn for station duties, I would not be the orderly sergeant raising and lowering the RAF ensign; I would be standing facing the flagpole during those operations and saluting it – as the Orderly Officer.

We moved into a married quarter, and as the weeks went by I renewed my friendship with the Wittwers – I had my new wife to introduce to them and even more to talk about over many a glass of *bier*. We resumed our camping trips; I bought a new pair of essential green *lederhosen* ('what the well-dressed camper is wearing this year!'), and, to make more room for camping tackle, I sold the Karmann Ghia and replaced it with a VW Variant estate. We bought an innovative type of tent which could be attached to the rear rail of the luggage rack, and when opened out, with the tailgate raised into the open position, it formed a canvas extension to the car. Shelagh made some curtains for the car's side windows, and with the back seats flat – hey presto! – there was a warm and weatherproof bedroom plus a space in which to brew up.

We spent our weekends touring the Rhine and Moselle Valleys; Austria, Bavaria and Switzerland, visiting such places as

Oberammergau (our arrival fortuitously coinciding with the Passion Play which has been performed every ten years since 1634, except for the war years, as a thanksgiving for the ending of the Black Death); the fairy-tale Castle of Neuschwanstein, built on the orders of King Ludwig II of Bavaria; Lake Constanz, the fire-flies glowing in the undergrowth round the camp-platz; the source of the Danube at Donaueschwingen; and the ski-slopes of Garmisch Parten-kirchen. At many villages and towns we visited we made a point of buying the local *stock-schild*, a small tin shield, one and a half inches by one inch, each charmingly painted with a small scene of the particular place and the village's name. Supplied with each were two small pins with which to secure them to one's walking stick or hiking pole, and we followed suit, eventually adorning three of them with no fewer than eighty-six of the souvenirs, among them being those of Wurzburg, Berchtesgarten, Vaduz, Liechtenstein, Zell-am-Mosel, Innsbruck, Spa, and Rothenburg ob der Taube.

We discovered a park in which the paths were bordered by large stone toadstools, and by bending down and pressing one's ear to them, the music being played by the elves could be heard – enchanting! Another park had a tall tower with a notice at its foot stating that if one wished to see the maiden Rapunzel of fairy-tale fame lean from her high window and lower her auburn tresses, it was necessary to shout her name loudly. Being a typically reticent Englishman, I was reluctant to make an exhibition of myself. Eventually though, I yielded to Shelagh's persuasion and called out, whereupon Rapunzel appeared and the tresses came down, but not low enough to swarm up unfortunately. There were also theatre-like buildings where, instead of a film, play or an opera, one sat and watched vari-coloured jets of water rising and falling in time to music from rows of fountains along the edge of a stage .

We suffered one near-disaster when we visited the big joint-services shopping centre in the Canadian Zone of West Germany. We parked the Variant and went in, our casual browsing being rudely disturbed when, over the loudspeakers, we heard the announcer say 'The owner of AW857B – your car is on fire!' Frantically, we rushed out to find the service fire-fighters extinguishing the blaze; thankfully they had got there in time to limit the damage to the luggage area – in the Variant the engine was situated beneath the rear floor and the fire had apparently been caused by an electrical fault. The Canadians were more than helpful, for not only did they drive us home in one of their staff cars, but they also arranged for the Variant to be transported back to Munchen-Gladbach for repairs. Thankfully, the fire didn't start while we were on a camp platz, fast asleep.

The end of that overseas tour came all too soon; we loaded up the Variant, and left on 1st May for RAF Medmenham again. After disembarkation leave, 26th May found us in married quarters there once more, but my work not being particularly inspiring, after eighteen months or so I got itchy feet and volunteered for overseas again. Apparently there were two vacancies for one of my rank and trade, a post with NATO in Norway and another in Holland. I kept my fingers crossed; I never enjoyed the cold, and I also hoped to buy a new car, and buying one in Norway would entail bringing it all the way back by sea, whereas the Holland posting would be virtually on the doorstep. An added bonus, still recalling Lacey Green windmill with affection, was that the country would be chock-full of them. So cheers rang through the vast echoing halls – well, the lounge, anyway! – of our married quarter on reading the posting notice which read 'HEADQUARTERS, AFCENT (Air Forces Central Europe) BRUNSSUM, HOLLAND, NEEDS

YOU!' or words to that effect! Light-heartedly, we performed the ancient ritual of Marching Out, and on 28th December 1972 drove across the Continent in the long-suffering Variant to the Dutch town of Brunssum, in the east of the country, not far from the German border. There were no married quarters as such; instead we were allocated a house, no. 24 Roosevelt Straat, on a Dutch housing estate. Our neighbours were very friendly, as were all the people we met during our tour. The Dutch people had a soft spot for the RAF, since before retreating at the end of the Second World War, the Germans had deliberately flooded vast parts of Holland, and as soon as they had been driven out, scores of our Lancaster bombers had roared across the countryside at very low level and dropped food supplies to the starving families.

The Headquarters were situated in the buildings of what was originally an old coal mine, and I travelled to work daily by the transport apparently favoured by everybody else – a moped. Mine was the size – and weight – of a full-size motorbike; it was like straddling a fainting hippopotamus. And life in a tent resurfaced, for occasionally a NATO military exercise involving a mock invasion would be announced, and all personnel would retreat to somewhere in the countryside and there plot, plan, eat and sleep under canvas.

We bought a new white VW Beetle; the standard regulations stipulated that in order to avoid punitive purchase tax one had to own a car for a year overseas and not sell it until two years had elapsed after returning to the UK. Like just about everyone else we visited the magnificent bulb fields at Keukenhof and, as was the custom in those days, drove back with the bonnet festooned with the 'slinger', a long 'rope' of intertwined tulips, the ends secured to the side mirrors. We later bought a caravan, the like of which we had never seen before or since. It was a second-hand Belgian model called a 'Wa-Wa' and was just big enough for two people. It was ingeniously designed to reduce drag to an absolute minimum when being towed; similar in shape to an ordinary caravan but sliced horizontally, the two halves were hinged together at the front; the upper half was the slightly wider of the two and was lowered for towing, overlapping the lower half to some extent and thereby giving the van a much lower profile; when parked it was easily raised and bolted into the 'normal' position, so we could stand upright inside it. It sounds crazy, but it worked.

As always Shelagh had brought her tape-recorder from England with her, and as we toured the country she took up a new hobby, recording the sounds of the carillons in the towns we passed through. Dutch bells play tunes, not peals, and if we approached a town at five or so minutes to the hour, she would tell me to stop and let her out so that she could hit the switches and catch the music. And while she was on the look-out for bell-towers, I was watching out for windmills. Millers on the Continent were working millers, not the part-timers one sometimes encounters on this side of the Channel, who operate solely to sell little bags of organic flour and the like. During our weekends we toured Holland and the nearer parts of France and Belgium, stopping, recording carillons, photographing mills and chatting over tea with the millers' families. On our travels I logged the location and condition of more than a hundred mills, a record which I later presented to the Windmill Section of the Society for the Preservation of Ancient Buildings in London for their archives.

The study of windmills is known as 'Molinology', from the Latin *molaris* for grinding (the word molars for the teeth with which we grind our food comes from the same root). Windmills were part of the very fabric of many Dutch communities. After a death in the village, the funeral cortege would wend its way to the cemetery, and, as it passed along the lanes, each miller would rotate the cap of his mill so that the sails faced the sombre procession as it moved along. During World War II millers passed vital messages for the underground movement by the way they positioned their sails when not actually grinding the grain. The saying 'he's a man of mettle' (metal) originates from the way of life of millers. The two large stones which grind the grain need to have the grooves between which the grain passes frequently re-cut, 'sharpened' as it were, and this was done by men who visited mill after mill throughout the district. A miller would identify a new man by asking to see the backs of his hands; if he saw little specks of steel embedded under the skin near the man's knuckles, specks which had broken off the edges of the mill bills (the chisels) while they were re-cutting the grooves, he would be satisfied that the man was a genuine 'man of mettle' and would employ him. Another saying, 'taking the wind out of one's sails' originates from the intentions of someone to build a mill upwind from another's, thereby depriving the latter of his source of power and therefore his livelihood. I quoted those sayings when giving talks on the subject to NATO audiences, and answered questions such as 'why do all windmills have two doorways?' I also explained that wind and water mills are unique in that they create power without changing in any way the motive power that they utilise: burning coal changes it in to cinders; nuclear fuel leaves a dangerous residue; wood leaves ashes, but the wind and water turn the sails or waterwheel and pass on, completely unpolluted; no exhaust, no smoke, no chemical change.

Brunssum was situated not far from the German border, and the nearest village, Waldfeucht, had a working corn-grinding windmill. We spent many happy hours with the miller, operating the machinery, even using the mill bill. And it so happened that early in 1974 I was contacted by a staff member of the *RAF News*, our 'firm's' newspaper, who wanted to include an article in the paper designed to show that young servicemen and women didn't spend all their off-duty time imbibing *bier*, *schnapps* or *genever* in the local taverns and that, on the contrary, they occasionally visited places of interest. The journalist had heard of my interest in windmills and my contact with the Waldfeucht miller, and asked if I would mind taking a few service people there for a photograph with which to illustrate his article. I had no objections, and so we all went out there, posed with the windmill in the background, and in due course the article appeared. Having by then served over thirty years in the RAF, I had long since given up reading the *News*, but because I was featured in that particular edition, of course, I bought a copy.

I read through the rest of the contents and happened to notice a small paragraph mentioning that vacancies would shortly be occurring for Yeoman Warders at the Tower of London. This was food for thought indeed. A burning question, one that haunts every serviceman, was what to do on leaving the Service. I was fifty-two years old and would have to retire in three years time. I would, to all practical intents and purposes, be unemployable, except perhaps as a shelf-loader in a supermarket or a car-park attendant. Shelagh and I discussed the 'Tower' advert. What would it be like to leave the RAF, the junior Service, and become a member of the oldest uniformed body of men in the world still carrying out the duties for which they were originally formed – guarding the Tower of London and all those who lived within its walls? What would it involve – having to learn history? Showing tourists around? Parading in yet another uniform? What were the qualifications? And where would we live? Well, we could at least enquire, so we sent for the particulars.

I was informed that to qualify I had to have attained the rank of Warrant Officer or Sergeant Major (thereby being capable of dealing with hundreds of civilians) – box ticked. I would need to be one hundred percent physically fit (standing out in the open in all weathers every day) – another box ticked. I had to possess a clean crime sheet (the Crown Jewels should not prove a temptation) – well, yes, box ticked! And finally, I had to be recommended by my Commanding Officer (would he really be that glad to get rid of me?). If accepted, we would be allocated living accommodation in 'Her Majesty's Royal Palace and Fortress, the Tower of London' – what an address! What would it be like to live in the oldest continually inhabited castle in the world, to walk where Henry VIII strode; where Sir Walter Raleigh was imprisoned; where the Little Princes played; where Anne Boleyn was beheaded? Having met the requirements, I submitted an application and was informed that I would also have to be interviewed, together with my wife, by the Resident Governor of the Tower, Major General WDM Raeburn, CB, DSO, MBE, MA… so if I cared to call in the next time I was on UK leave?

Preferring to settle the matter one way or the other without undue delay, I immediately put in for leave, notified the Tower, and within a week or so, via rail and ferry, eventually entered the Byward Gate of that historic edifice, and was utterly overwhelmed by my surroundings and the sheer mass of humanity, all shapes and sizes, seemingly from every country of the world, which seethed around us. Yards away a Yeoman Warder was giving a guided tour, expressing himself loudly to a hundred or more tourists. Shelagh turned to me and asked 'Do you think you'll be able to do that?'

and I recall just shaking my head in total bewilderment and exclaiming, 'I don't know!' In fact, after thirty-five years' service I couldn't even envisage what civvy street would be like.

To a career serviceman, civilians seem to belong to an alien civilisation. They have a different way of life, a totally different culture. They live in neighbouring houses in the same town as each other for decade after decade; they don't march or take orders, or have to lay their kit out, or risk court-martial. They are not taught how to shoot or bayonet people, nor are they suddenly told to pack and board a ship bound for heaven knows where – or told when to get their hair cut! Such acclimatisation has to be faced by every serviceman on leaving the services, but if I accepted this opportunity, I would not get slowly accustomed to it by living in a quiet street in some small town, I would be thrown among thousands of civilians every day – two and a half million a year!

We were escorted to the Queen's House on Tower Green, where, in the richly panelled room in which Guy Fawkes had been harshly interrogated, we sat facing General Raeburn and discussed my RAF service and our hopes and ambitions, questions obviously designed to assess my competence for such a role. Apparently, we made the required impression, for the Resident Governor said he would recommend my suitability to his superior, the Constable of the Tower, but he added that there was a long waiting list and, rather than raise our hopes unduly, we should put the idea at the back of our minds, because it may never come about; a case of many are called but few are chosen. So we returned to Holland and the old coal mine.

However, some little time later I received a letter enquiring whether I was still prepared to apply for my retirement from the RAF and became a Yeoman Warder a few weeks hence. I replied immediately, accepting the invitation, and we started to make preliminary preparations. Then disaster struck! One morning I woke to feel a sharp pain in my side, a sensation that seemed to me could be only one thing – appendicitis. Good grief, I remember thinking – pneumonia in the Atlantic, typhus in East Africa, poliomyelitis in the UK, and now appendicitis in Holland – whatever next, the Black Death? Shelagh got the car out and we drove across the border to the nearest RAF Hospital, where the MO questioned me. When I told him my diagnosis, he replied – and I quote – 'Don't be silly, Mr Abbott, you're much too old to have appendicitis!' Within the hour I was in surgery, later to leave not only minus one appendix and facing an indeterminate period of convalescence, but also bereft of our dream of the Tower. Disconsolately, I wrote informing the authorities there, and they accepted my withdrawal.

Some months went by and then out of the blue came another letter from the Tower – an increase in the number of yeoman warders had created a vacancy – would I be available in the very near future? I certainly would! Accepting by return of post, I applied to my superiors to be released from my post there and return to the UK in order to retire from the RAF. Initially, difficulties arose. NATO was understandably reluctant to let me go, entailing as it would, the need to request the Ministry of Defence for a replacement, and had I been wishing to leave in order to take up an ordinary type of job, my application could have been rejected. But on being told that I had been invited to become a Yeoman Warder in Her Majesty's Tower of London, no further objections were made; indeed, everyone was only too helpful. I soon completed all the necessary departure paperwork and, excited by the prospect of a new and challenging career, booked our passage on the Channel ferry, sold 'Wa-Wa', replaced it with a small trailer,

131

loaded it and the car up to the gunwales with household effects, and on 15th November 1974 I left Brunssum and headed to a very unusual home!

In the North African Campaign, 1942.

Blackburn Skua Two-Seater Dive-Bomber.

'My' Spitfire – Hoping nobody presses the start button! 1944.

Practice makes perfect – Suez, 1953.

Camp Defences, Suez Canal Campaign, 1953.

Checkpoint, Fayid Shopping Centre, Suez, 1953.

Going Native in Iraq, 1954.

Bow Fishing in River Euphrates, Iraq, 1955.

Chapter Ten
LOCKED UP IN THE TOWER

Landing in Dover, we drove north into London; it had been a long tiring journey from Brunssum, and I had to get accustomed to driving on the left again; there was no GPS in those days, and I didn't know my way through the suburbs. Luckily, on approaching the city in heavy traffic, our small trailer bouncing along behind the Beetle, I saw Tower Bridge in the distance and beyond it the Tower. Aiming in that direction, I eventually crossed the Bridge, turned left, and found myself at the top of Tower Hill, and there, leading off to the left, was the road leading straight down to the Tower gates. My heart sank as I saw the 'No Entry' sign. Straight on led to I knew not where – Westminster, Fulham, perhaps even Bristol! Throwing caution to the winds, in defiance of the sign, I turned left and slowly drove down the hill – only to brake as a large member of the Metropolitan Police stepped out and held up his hand. At the prospect of my new career ending in tatters in court, all I could do was to wind the window down and babble 'I'm going to be a Yeoman Warder there, and I don't know the way in!' The officer smiled and waved me through!

Driving along the Wharf by the river, we entered the Tower complex via the East Drawbridge near to the Bridge and drove along between the inner and outer walls until we stopped outside our new home, No. 25 The Casemates, next door to John Holmes, also ex-RAF, and his wife Rita, who had arrived and moved in a week earlier. These were two of the many apartments set within the thickness of the outer wall which encircles the castle, and were originally the Tower rooms which, in troublous times, accommodated the gun crews and ammunition for the cannons mounted on the battlements above. Some of the many small towers, constructed at intervals along the battlements, are also apartments for Yeoman Warders and their families. These were built as small guardrooms, having a door each side leading out on to the battlements, so that, should there be an attack at any one point, the defenders could run round along the top of the wall and through them to the hotspot, instead of having to go down the steps, along at ground level, then climb up again. During times of threat, soldiers would continually man the battlements, and among the facilities provided for them were, of course, toilets. These closets, now long gone, extended out over the moat, one featuring in the ancient records against the date 7th March 1733, when 'A Poor Soldier on his Post on the North Lyne [the battlements facing the City], the box and house of easment fell doun into the Ditch with the poor fellow in it, which so bruised him that he never Spoke, and dyed in two hours after.'

Nos. 25 and 26 were of an odd design, one family living in the rooms each side of a central, communal stairway. Of three stories, each residence had a 'loft extension' which was the bathroom. The accommodation was unfurnished, so on arrival Shelagh and I slept in our ex-camping sleeping bags until we could purchase the necessary furniture – which was quite a change from finding everything one required when Marching In to a married quarter.

A quick visit to RAF Uxbridge was then necessary in order to be 'demobbed', terminating my thirty-five years service – so it was farewell to the Royal Air Force. Already fading were the memories of the Gladiators and the Spitfires, the Hurricanes and Dakotas, the instructional blackboards and staff posts, office desks and statistical graphs, barrack rooms and married quarters, drill parades and kit inspections, Marchings In and Marchings Out – life was going to be very different. Now I would be joining my thirty-five colleagues, mostly ex-Army men, with a flavouring of RAF. Some of them had been at the Tower since the 1950s and 1960s, among them Bob Harton, the Yeoman Gaoler, ex of The Queen's Regiment, George Armstrong of the Grenadier Guards, John Howson of the King's Own Yorkshire Light Infantry, Don Bunker of the King's Own Hussars, Jack Studham of the Durham Light Infantry, Cedric Ramshall of the Royal Artillery, and not forgetting John Wilmington of the Queen's Own Hussars who, in addition to normal duties, also cared for the eight Tower ravens, the Queen's Ravens, each with their individual names and quirky characters, who hopped at will around the lawns.

The bonds between us were strong – most of us were veterans of one campaign or another, we had the same services background, our families lived along the same street – well, the same battlements! – and we got on well together. The Tower officers, the Resident Governor General Raeburn, his Deputy Colonel Hindmarsh, the Master of the Armouries Mr Norman, and of course our padre, the Revd Llewellyn, were all approachable and friendly – altogether, a great team. Their wives joined in our social events and helped create a quite unique community spirit within the castle's walls, and it quickly became apparent to me that the Tower was, in reality, a village set in the heart of one of the most modern cities in the world, with the Yeoman Warders and their families its residents. We have a Lord of the Manor in the Resident Governor, who lives in the Queen's House, the ancient timbered building erected in 1530 as a residence for Anne Boleyn, who occupied it only as a prisoner before being beheaded on Tower Green – our village green. The postman and milkman make their daily rounds, and we have our own doctor and chaplain, the latter baptising and later officiating at the marriages of our children in the village church – the Royal Chapel of St Peter ad Vincula. A village inn is of course essential. Once there existed three, the King's Head, the Golden Chain and the Cold Harbour taverns, but now we have our own club, which provides the liquid sustenance so necessary after spending a long hot day smiling into tourists' camera lenses. Prior to World War II the Tower had its own police station and fire brigade, even its own school for the residents' children. During the war warders had their own allotments in the moat, where they grew vegetables to eke out the meagre rations. Also in the moat there still remain little gravestones marking the burial places of our pet dogs and cats, with rather more important ones near the Middle Drawbridge marking the graves of deceased Tower Ravens. And all patriotic villages have a flagpole; the one atop the White Tower flies the largest Union Flag of any public building in the country, measuring 12 ft (3.6m) by 21ft (6.4m). In winter, because of the strong winds, a smaller flag is flown.

On Guy Fawkes nights, because he and his confederates had resided in the Tower, albeit unwillingly, we and our families would congregate in the moat, partying on the cakes our wives had made for the occasion. And at Christmas time the Resident Governor and his wife would invite us all to the Queen's House, where we could explore the Bell Tower – prison of Queen Elizabeth I, Sir Thomas More and others – and the bedroom once occupied by Queen Anne Boleyn. To live in such a close community, sharing the same traditions, is like being one of a large family, and whenever I return to the Tower I am greeted as if I were a relative just dropping in.

Shortly after my arrival, my neighbour John Holmes showed me how to don the blue undress uniform with which I had been issued. Buttoned down one side and across the shoulder, the high-collared tunic has the advantage of having no lapels, useful when clearing the Tower Wharf of druggies or winos at closing time, as it deprives them of the hand-hold essential to grasp while they attempted to head-butt their captor! A disadvantage was that in summer it was very hot to wear while standing on duty out in the open. In the heatwave of 1976 it became customary on returning home after a long day to turn the tunic inside-out, hang it on the line, and let it drip!

An issue police whistle had to be attached by its chain to one of the shoulder buttons, the whistle parked inside the top of the tunic for use if help was required – nowadays of course the inevitable and invaluable walkie-talkie is also issued. The tunic has very deep pockets in which to keep hankies and so on; I also kept a small bottle of smelling salts in mine, with which to revive fainting ladies who, having just flown in from foreign parts with a crowded itinerary to see the sights and so foregoing breakfast, tended to keel over during a long wait in the ticket and Jewel House queues. I recall one such young lady recoiling hysterically when I produced it and attempted to hold it under her nose. Obviously, she did not have such restoratives in her country, and she must have thought I was trying to drug her preparatory to putting her on the Tower's Rack!

On 12th December I was sworn in as a Yeoman Warder by the Resident Governor in the Queen's House, and my name entered against the number 37 in the Tower's records. In 1985 my good friend and fellow Yeoman Warder, Brian Harrison, researched fascinating details about those previously recorded against that particular number, dating as far as back 1664 (prior to that date, continuity in numbers was not maintained) and expertly scribed my 'family tree'. Incidentally, the origin of the nickname 'Beefeater', which is usually ascribed to us, has been erroneously attributed to the word '*bouffetier*', one who tastes the food to ensure its non-toxic quality, but it appears no such word in the French language exists; a more likely derivation is that, as members of the royal bodyguard, they were encouraged to keep their strength up as much as possible and so were allowed to eat as much beef as they wished from the king's table, whereas the ordinary servant of the court had to wait until the end of the meal and consume whatever food had been left on the plates.

As might be expected, my first year was a busy one. I had to visit Hobson's, the court tailors, in Tooley Street across the river, to be measured for my State Dress, the splendid red and gold medieval uniform reputedly designed by Henry VIII's court painter Hans Holbein. In those days commoners were forbidden by law to wear any clothing of that particular shade of red, the dye reportedly being only obtainable from the East, and that in but small quantities; consequently, it was restricted to the livery worn by all royal attendants, bodyguards, horse-drawn coach drivers and outriders, swan-uppers, barge-crews and the like. They still wear uniforms of that colour, of course, as do present-day huntsmen, their Tudor-age predecessors having to apply to the sovereign for permission to enjoy a sport which was otherwise the sole prerogative of the Crown.

The tunic, hand sewn with gold thread and tailored for the wearer, is a very heavy garment, the material and its lining being thick, and one definitely needs the assistance of one's wife in donning it. Like the blue undress uniform, it is buttoned down one side, and the collar clips beneath the chin and under the ruff which cushions one's beard should one be hirsutely endowed. I had allowed mine to grow, partially to enhance the 'Tudor' image, but also to have five minutes extra in bed! The first few days of growing one was a scratchy and unsightly experience, and because beards were forbidden in the RAF and also, except for a very few, in the Army, one never knew whether a 'respectable' one would be forthcoming – but my efforts were rewarded.

The legs of the breeches are secured by bands beneath the knee, rosettes called Knee-bows, consisting of short-folded ribbons of red, white and blue silk sewn on to a leather patch, being attached thereon, and similar Foot-bows adorning the insteps of one's shoes. I also had to be measured for my Tudor Bonnet, the high-crowned black velvet hat encircled with the royal ribbons. In order to estimate the size of headband required, the tailor positioned around my head a device more reminiscent of the Spanish Inquisition, called a conformateur, consisting of a wide metal ring with screws around its circumference, these being 'gently' tightened until just touching the scalp.

Red stockings (nowadays tights) are part of the uniform, and as I considered that garters were overly restrictive, and also, because the cameras would inevitably be clicking non-stop, wrinkled stockings were a definite no-no, my wife Shelagh went to Selfridges to buy the obvious alternative, a suspender belt. On being asked the required size, she deliberately paused, then, not lacking a wicked sense of humour, answered 'I'm not sure – it's for my husband!' The assistant raised an eyebrow but refrained from commenting.

The ruff itself is an important part of the ensemble. It was added to the uniform during the reign of Henry VIII's daughter Elizabeth;

she wore one and so it became high fashion, her courtiers and members of her bodyguard having to follow suit. It is made of bleached Irish linen and is difficult if not impossible to wash, launder or iron, so when soiled, is replaced by a new one. Horse-shoe shaped, it is held apart before donning the tunic, then slipped around one's neck and tightened at the back by means of the long tapes threaded through its hem, these being crossed to keep it in place, brought round and tied at the front of the wearer.

The sword belt, complete with weapon, buckles around the waist, and is even worn when attending Easter and Christmas church services. The Tower's Royal Chapel of St Peter ad Vincula is one of the few places of worship in which men are allowed to carry weapons, the reason being that in medieval times kings or queens at prayer were vulnerable to assassins and so their bodyguard had to remain fully armed. On a lighter note, care has to be taken when sitting down in the Chapel's pew-chairs lest one's sword impales a colleague in the row behind! The final accessory is the eight-foot-long partizan (pike). In times of war it was designed to be held at about forty-five degrees pointing towards the attacker, its nether end firmly pressed into the ground. The speedily approaching enemy knight would then be kebabbed by the blade, his skewered torso sliding down the blade, and the two smaller blades curving outwards each side preventing it from progressing further down the shaft. The current-coloured silk strands around the shaft were originally rags on which the warder would wipe his bloodstained hands. It is not an easy uniform to wear, but once donned, one feels as resplendent as a ten-foot high multi-coloured playing card!

Nor was that all. Still hardly believing that I had had the good fortune – nay, honour – to become a Yeoman Warder, on 29th

January 1975 I was told to attend St James' Palace, where I was sworn in as a Member of the Queen's Body Guard of the Yeomen of the Guard Extraordinary. The Yeomen of the Guard are all ex-service civilians who serve part-time and are called forward whenever required for specific occasions such as the Maundy Money Ceremony. Our title of 'Extraordinary' signifies that we are 'extra' members; we reinforce them when necessary and 'hold the line' when the Queen is inspecting them, usually at Buckingham Palace

Our historical reputation as traditional guardians of the Royal Palace, the Tower of London, endows us with a certain mystique in the eyes of the public; they are never quite sure of what powers we possess, and this conception is advantageous to us in controlling the considerable numbers of visitors. However, to cope with those few who visit the Tower with evil intent, we were all sworn in soon after arrival by two Justices of the Peace as Special Constables of the Metropolitan Police and issued with Warrant Cards. William the Conqueror was to blame, of course, for having the Tower built so near Tower Hill Underground Station, thereby allowing every villain in the City to get to his unsuspecting victims with ease! Seriously, the Tower was and is a happy hunting ground for pickpockets. Groups of tourists, intent on listening to their guide, are vulnerable; one thief extracts a wallet or purse, passes it to his accomplice outside the group, and both disperse. While taking a guided tour, I once warned the men present to safeguard their wallets – whereupon each man felt for his back pocket, revealing its location to any watching baddie. It was always heartbreaking, when checking at closing time that no one was still in the toilets, to find empty wallets, purses, and handbags, their contents, money, credit cards, airline tickets, driving licences, private papers, everything, stolen.

As well as the multi-swearings in and the everyday duties (some of which have changed since my sojourn in the Tower in the 1970s and 1980s) I, like other 'new boys', had to learn the basic history of the Tower before giving guided tours. The tours are known as 'Specials', a term originating in early Victorian times when the warders just stood around, and a guided tour had to be specially ordered in advance. It is usually a once-weekly duty and consists of three tours on the day. The history was contained in a little yellow book with which I had been issued, and so all available off-duty time was spent studying it, either at home or more often walking round the moat in the evenings, coached by a helpful colleague, his contribution consisting mainly of saying exasperatedly 'Not 1453 - 1553!' or 'Of course you can remember what happened to Henry VIII's wives – divorced, beheaded, died, divorced, beheaded, survived!' Only half convinced I was ready for the worst day in a Yeoman Warder's life, when he has to be tested by taking the Resident Governor on a guided tour and demonstrate his competence, I took a deep breath and informed the Chief Warder.

Just as executions and similar ordeals take place early in the morning – and no, I didn't eat a hearty breakfast! – my initiation on 31st January 1975 was similarly timed. The nerve-racking event took place before the public had been admitted, but workmen and office workers were entering the Tower, and I had to face General Raeburn and address him as if I were addressing a large tour group – very loudly, clearly, historically accurately, avoiding slang, swear words, colloquialisms and dialectic phrases. Despite the invaluable techniques I had learned as an instructor, I was not looking forward to it.

For those readers who have not visited the Tower, I should explain that a guided tour lasts about an hour and involves conducting one's tour group, stopping at five designated locations and describing the historic significance of the immediate surroundings, and so I, the Chief Warder and the General, moved from one to the other until we finally completed the tour. There was a long pause, then the General said 'That was very good, Mr. Abbott!' – the verbal baptism was over!

Having passed the test, the usual procedure was to personalise one's talk, to embroider it and make it more informal, in order to teach the visitors our history in a humorous manner. For instance, I would point out the window of a particular room, explaining that it was in there that Guy Faulkes was severely interrogated, 'or, as we say nowadays, he was helping the police with their enquiries!' To stand on a stone block and look down at the sea of faces, each person hanging on one's every word, imbues one with a sense of power. As any good orator knows, a crowd can be moulded to respond to his words. For instance, on Tower Green, where the queens were beheaded, I would inform the group that Henry VIII's motto was 'Tails I win' then pause to have the group chant 'Heads you lose!' accompanied by loud laughter! Similarly, my comment 'That was the trouble with Henry VIII – always chopping and changing!' never failed to bring about a hilarious reaction. But it wasn't all that easy. It's one thing to give a talk in a hall or lecture room, but it's quite another thing addressing a group out in the open at the Tower, trying to make oneself heard over the noise of the crowds of tourists walking past, the workmen hammering nearby, a helicopter hovering overhead and the sound of the inevitable police sirens on Tower Hill.

Of the 878 guided tours I conducted, it seemed that some of the listeners were more impressed by my oratorical style than others. On one occasion a letter was received by the Resident Governor from the USA referring to me by name and asking whether I could be allowed to visit the States, there to spend a few weeks giving talks to universities across Alaska. As this would have necessitated a lengthy absence from duty, it had to be declined, as was another, even more laudatory, invitation in June 1976, written by another American, Mr James Autry, Vice-Chairman of the Dallas Chapter of the 'Young President's Organisation'. Having been on one of my tours, he referred in glowing terms to my presentation, adding 'his manner was impeccable and his bearing was a true credit to your Nation and The Queen'. He explained that the purpose of his Organisation, which had 3000 members in fifty foreign countries, was to make better presidents through exchange of education and ideas, and that each month its Dallas Chapter had a guest speaker talk to them about government, art, medicine, science and so on, one recent speaker having been Astronaut Tom Stafford, Commander of the Apollo-Soyuz space ship. In the coming year (1977), he wrote, they had planned to include three members of the President's Cabinet, the President of General Motors, Dr Lee Clark-Head of Cancer Research, Mrs Lyndon B. Johnson, and Dr Von Hapsburg, the former Crown Prince of Austria. His letter concluded 'I was wondering if it could be arranged for Mr Abbott and his wife to come to Dallas at our expense to address our Group. As you and I both know, we need to be inspired to keep this world free and I think Mr Abbott, as your messenger, could be a valuable asset.' At the thought that I was considered worthy of joining such an august assembly in helping to choose the next American President, I could hardly get my Tudor Bonnet on! Unfortunately, for a variety of reasons, it was not possible for me to accept the invitation.

As custodians of the Tower, a tradition stretching back over many centuries, our duties consist of manning various points about the Tower around the clock. During the daytime most are within the complex, warders being given a different post each day to afford us some variety, with a few posts outside on the Wharf. One was at the East Gate by Tower Bridge, when it was not unusual, on opening the Gate at 6.30am, to see large rats scurrying around the area. These voracious-looking rodents lived in the vast customs warehouses where now stands the Tower Hotel and expensive apartment blocks overlooking the river.

All the entrances are manned by Yeoman Warders of course, one being the Byward Tower, the outer tower where the byword or password had to be given – incidentally it contains the oldest continually manned guardroom in the world, the Middle Drawbridge and East Drawbridge being the others. The Byward Tower, the main entrance, is manned through the night by the Yeoman Warder on watch duty. The Watchman also plays a vital part in the Ceremony of the Keys, which has taken place every night for at least the last 600 years and is the oldest military ceremony in the world. Shortly before 10.00pm, the Chief Warder or his deputy proceeds to the Byward Tower and there takes possession of the Tower's Keys and the ancient candle lamp. He then returns as far as the Bloody Tower archway, where awaits the Tower Guard, a non-commissioned officer and four soldiers of the particular Regiment currently on ceremonial duties at this and other palaces. He hands the lantern to one of the soldiers, and they then escort him back to the Byward Tower, where the Watchman, clad in the traditional red watch coat, has already closed the heavy doors in the archway. The soldier with the lantern holds it up to illuminate the lock, which the Chief Warder then secures. As he is doing so, the two ranks of soldiers turn inward and present arms, because, of course, the Keys are the Queen's Keys. Having locked the doors, the Chief Warder resumes his place between the ranks of soldiers, and the party march back towards the Bloody Tower archway, where stands a sentry on guard. On hearing the approach of footsteps, he levels his rifle and bayonet and challenges in a loud voice, 'Halt! Who comes there?' The Chief Warder replies, 'The Keys!', the sentry then shouts, 'Whose Keys?', to which the Chief Warder replies, 'Queen Elizabeth's Keys!' The sentry exclaims, 'Pass, Queen Elizabeth's Keys, and all's well!' Standing there in the shadows, it requires little imagination to envisage the same ceremony being enacted repeatedly over the past centuries, the Chief Warder or Porter, as he was once known, standing in exactly the same spot, shouting in the same stentorian voice 'King George's Keys!', 'King William's Keys!', 'King Henry's Keys!'

Upon hearing the sentry's reply the Keys party march through the Bloody Tower archway to where, on the big steps leading up to the Broadwalk, is drawn the Tower Guard, the Officer of the Guard standing in front of them, his sword held in salute. The Keys party halt, the Chief Warder takes two steps forward, doffs his Tudor Bonnet, shouts, 'God preserve Queen Elizabeth!' and all the soldiers shout 'Amen!' The bugler then sounds the Last Post coincidental with the old clock on the Waterloo Block chiming the hour of ten. The Keys are then taken into safe custody until the morning, and the soldiers resume their duty of patrolling the Tower through the night hours, challenging, if necessary, anyone they might encounter for the password. This, authorised on behalf of Her Majesty, is revealed to but a few authorities and is a different word every day. As the ceremony has been performed over such a period, there can't be many left, so they'll probably have to start all over again! Incidentally the word 'doff', used when the Chief Warder raises his Tudor Bonnet, is a combination of the words 'do' and 'off'. Similarly, when we put a hat or garment on, we 'do – on' it – we don it.

In defiance of the air-raids during World War II, the Ceremony of the Keys was still conducted each night, the only difference being that those participating wore steel helmets. During my service the regulations decreed that residents could not leave the Tower after midnight, and if they had not returned before 2.00am, they would have to sleep alongside the junkies and druggies on the benches on Tower Hill until the doors of the Byward Gate swung open at 6.30am.

To be present at the Ceremony of the Keys, enacted as it is in the very heart of a vibrant and modern city, is to experience an emotional moment, especially during the playing of the Last Post, the call which traditionally reminds all servicemen of their fallen comrades. And it is my opinion that the most historic *airspace* in the country, even more than that surrounding the coronation chair or within Westminster Hall, is the airspace within the Bloody Tower archway. For literally hundreds of years that was the only entrance to the inner ward of the Tower. These were the towers in which the high-ranking prisoners were incarcerated, the torture chambers in which they suffered, the Green on which they met their end. That very airspace was traversed by the kings and their families who lived in the Tower, the captive queens awaiting execution, royal captives such as Sir Thomas More, Sir Walter Raleigh and Guy Fawkes – a veritable host of those who had fashioned our past. And to pause beneath its portcullis at night is to experience an atmosphere almost tangible; one can almost hear Anne Boleyn pleading that she 'should not be put in a dungeon', Princess Elizabeth declaring that she 'never thought to have come in here as a prisoner', the two Little Princes crying in the room immediately above one's head. You may have read history; there you can feel it!

However, the material world sees that particular one, and indeed all the other archways, as merely passages through which the tourists swarm, most of them heading for the nearest Yeoman Warder to photograph, so one smiles until one's teeth go dry. I always found it satisfying to provide pleasure for tourists who, after all, had travelled from far and wide to visit the Tower, by acceding to their requests for photographs standing next to me as indeed did my colleagues. Appealing moments would sometimes occur, as when I'd see, some distance away, a couple of children looking up at their parents, obviously asking them for a photograph with me; I would stretch out my arms, palms facing outwards, and they would run towards me delightedly, take hold of my hands, Dad would give me a thank you look, and we'd all smile into the family camera!

Occasionally, emergencies could occur involving small children who had got lost among the milling herds of tourists. My personal strategy was to induce the crying child to sit on the chair in the nearest 'warder's box' – a large sentry box – and attempt to calm him (it was usually a boy – little girls seem to stay close to Mum). Because our visitors hailed from every country across the globe, soothing words would be useless, so, ignoring the crowd which had gathered around eager to see how I handled the situation, I would slowly produce a wrapped sweet from my tunic pocket and equally slowly start to remove the sweet-paper but deliberately twist the ends of the wrapping paper the wrong way, i.e. tightening it even further, while frowning at my lack of success. The effect was almost magical; the child's laments would gradually cease as he watched almost hypnotised by this peculiarly dressed person who, although obviously some sort of an adult, was unable to unwrap a toffee! I would try again, then shake my head, finally give up, and hand it to the child who, of course, all tears by now forgotten, would know exactly what to do! It was usually about this time that the mother, in an overwrought state of anxiety, would burst through the spectators and take over, expressing her relief by shaking the child and chiding him for straying – panic over!

On another occasion a small boy, looking through the big iron gates at the entrance, slipped his head between the railings, and couldn't withdraw it again. His yells and the appeals for help from his frantic mother brought me to the spot. What to do? Cut through the bars with a hacksaw? Part them sufficiently with a car jack? Send for the Fire Brigade? And then it came to me, from where I know not. He couldn't withdraw his head because of his ears so, amputation being out of the question, I went to the other side of the gate, lifted his body off the ground, instructed his mother to hold it just above horizontal, then gently moved his head down, his chin on his chest, and eased him backwards so that he exited with his ears pressed flat against the sides of his head, the way he'd gone in. For that I got a round of applause!

Disabled tourists are often brought to the Tower, and as ex-military ourselves we pay special and sympathetic attention to injured servicemen, some of whom are paraplegics or who had lost all their limbs in battle. Similarly, whenever I met blind children or adults, I would take their hands and trace the royal cypher on the breast of my tunic with their finger-tips.

Some tourists craftily take photographs for commercial reasons.

Seeking to include me in a subsequent advertisement for some product in their own country, a group of Oriental gentlemen once asked me to look up into the sky and point but I didn't fall for that.

Many questions featured ghosts, and, eventually, after telling tourists so many times that we had so many ghosts that they even walked through each *other*, they inspired me to start researching any such experiences described in Victorian and Edwardian books about the Tower with a view to writing a book on the subject, an ambition which I realised a few years later.

The different languages are a problem, but we all have smatterings of foreign lingo picked up during our tours overseas – in 1979, on the occasion of the State Visit of the President of the Republic of Kenya, I greeted him in Swahili, much to his surprise and delight! So we learn to smile in Spanish, shrug our shoulders in French and point in Urdu! Sporting a beard, I found I attracted Japanese and Chinese tourists in particular, with whom to be photographed, no doubt because their menfolk tend not to be so hirsute.

Being on duty anywhere in the Tower, one is called upon to answer questions such as whether Anne Boleyn was beheaded on Tower Bridge, or whether those are the real Crown Jewels (no, madame, they're just well-sucked wine gums!). Some tourists ask more unusual questions: one American said that he knew the Crown Jewels were genuine, but were they where he saw them, or were they in an underground chamber and was he looking at their hologram! Thinking rapidly, I replied that on the grounds of security I'd rather not answer that – it was a thought-provoking question, though. Questions were often posed about the security of the Jewel House, and I would remind them of the owner of a Rolls Royce who queried the power of its engine and received the makers' one-word reply – 'Sufficient!'

Among the thousands of visitors to the Tower each day were occasionally one or two who were more interesting or interested in our history than usual, and it was my custom to put a bit of icing on their holiday cake by inviting them to our apartment in the evening, partaking in a glass or two of wine, and taking them on the Ceremony of the Keys. One such person was a young American, Joe Rodota,who, a year or so later, via a friend of his in this country, sent me a watercolour portrait he had painted of me, using the inevitable photographs, as a 'thank you' for our hospitality. Other invited guests were the attractive young American members of a Barbershop Quartet Competition, who were visiting England and the Tower as part of their prize. Wearing their winners' crowns, the young ladies harmonised in our lounge, the melodies no doubt coming as a shock to its thirteenth-century walls.

Not all tourists were 'ordinary' members of the public; anyone who is anyone visiting London, foreign royalty, celebrities, film stars, is invariably brought to the Tower and handed over to a Yeoman Warder for a personal guided tour. In June 1977 I conducted 'Chip' Carter, son of the then president of the USA, and Chip's girlfriend Caron around (the security 'heavies' guarding them were somewhat miffed at having to leave their guns at the gate).

Another celebrity visitor proved to be astronaut David Scott, a member of the crews of Gemini 8, Apollo 9 and 15, and after showing him around I invited him to bring his wife to the Tower and visit us, an invitation he accepted. Shelagh was looking forward to meeting our guests, and, on the evening of 11th March 1981, he and Lurton sat and chatted in our apartment before we all strolled around the grounds. When all the tourists have gone and twilight descends, the Tower becomes what it really is under the veneer of modern civilization – an ancient stone time-machine, full of historic memories.

As we walked along, the moon hung low over the White Tower, and it was difficult to believe that I was actually in the company of one of the very few men who had walked on that heavenly body! But I really couldn't let this American 'colonist' get away with all the glory – I pointed out to him that had it not been for the Tower of London, he wouldn't have even reached the Moon, because the seventeenth-century charts made by the Astronomer Royal, John Flamsteed, who studied the heavens from the north-east turret of the White Tower, were the origins from which the ones used at Cape Canaveral eventually evolved. David hesitated for a moment then conceded the point, admitting that one of the geographical features on the Moon was the Flamsteed Crater!

We also discussed the ghosts – what else, in the gathering gloom – and we both agreed that nowadays, in this world of computers, micro-chips, electronic marvels and space travel, when everything can be, has to be, discovered and rationalised, brought into the open and de-mystified, let us have something that can't be explained. We remained friends, and, on his return to the States, he sent me his thanks and a picture of himself 'up there'.

Another unusual tourist was a gentleman about my age who in 1977 explained that this was the second time he had been to the Tower – the first time was as a German prisoner of war! He related that he had been a crew member of a U-boat sunk in 1940 by the Royal Navy, and upon being captured he and his colleagues had been told that they would be sent to the Tower. Aware of its grim reputation, they resigned themselves to the fact that, as enemies, they were being sent there to be executed, but were overwhelmed to find they were treated kindly and well fed for some time, before eventually being transferred to a prisoner of war camp. He added that, despite that, he still recalled the feeling of utter dread on hearing their destination after capture.

One year a Tall Ships Regatta took place in the Pool of London, their officers and crew visiting, among other attractions, the Tower, and I was detailed to give a guided tour to the doctor of the sailing ship *Danmark* moored off Tower Pier. As was my wont, I also invited him to our residence that evening and took him on the 'Keys'; in return, some days later, he gave me a guided tour of the *Danmark*. On noticing some of the crew scrubbing the decks with long brooms and lots of sea-water, I commented on their efforts to make the vessel clean and smart-looking, only to be informed by my host that that was not the purpose – soaking the planks like that caused them to swell, thereby making the upper decks water-tight in rough seas; one never stops learning! The ship was due to sail on the early morning tide at day-break so Shelagh and I got up early and mounted the battlements which overlooked the river, and sure enough the *Danmark*, all its sails spread in picturesque splendour, sailed slowly past – and there in the half-light of dawn, we saw the Doctor and members of the crew lined up along the rails, returning our waves of *bon voyage* – quite a romantic moment.

Some of our personal visitors expressed surprise that parties and festive events were held by the Yeoman Warders and their families in their casemates or the moat, virtually in the shadow of buildings in which prisoners had been incarcerated for years, some even being tortured and executed; my reply was always that people live in close proximity to present-day prisons such as Wandsworth and Pentonville, which house 'lifers' and where not so long ago hangings took place, yet they still celebrate birthdays and the like!

As in any major tourist attraction, emergencies occurred within the Tower and had to be dealt with quickly and efficiently. While I was there the IRA were active, no fewer than forty bomb attacks occurring in the City during 1974 and 1975, and we were an obvious target. When a 'Red Alert' (the highest security warning) was in force, I felt I was back in a troopship, at any time half expecting a explosion which would result in scores of severely injured tourists. A bomb had actually been detonated in the basement of the White Tower on 17th July 1974, just three months before my arrival. There are no windows in that chamber; had there been, they would have shattered and much of the blast would have harmlessly escaped; as it was, the full force was felt by those within, one woman being killed, others, many of them children, suffering broken limbs and other injuries. The obvious precautions were in force during the 1970s; tourists' back-packs and handbags were searched as a matter of routine, but such measures could not have prevented, for instance, parts of a bomb being smuggled in then assembled, the timer set and the completed device placed where it could inflict the most casualties. Nor was that all; anyone outside the Tower could, and indeed did, phone in and say they'd planted a bomb there, then ring off. Hoax or not, no chances could be taken, and we had to clear every tower and herd the hundreds of tourists out into the open on the Broadwalk. Dealing with such numbers, many not understanding English, proved a problem; avoiding a rapidly spreading panic being essential, I used to tell frantic tourists not to worry until they saw me running – then to try to pass me!

It was during those dangerous times that I received a suspicious package through the post. Small and rather heavy, the writing was somewhat indistinct and it bore no return address. In view of newspaper reports regarding letters and parcels being delivered to government agencies, which, on being opened, injured the recipients, I suggested to Shelagh that rather than opening it, I would throw it in the bin. She rightly demurred, saying that, if I did it could explode in the council tip and possibly harm the workmen. There was only one thing to do, so, carrying it carefully and very gingerly across Tower Bridge, I walked into the Tower Bridge Police Station and, placing it on the Sergeant's desk, told him who I was, where I lived, and added my suspicions. He backed away slightly, then explained that they had no facilities there, but he would arrange for it to be taken to Bow Street headquarters where, after being X-rayed and subjected to explosive-sensing equipment, it would be opened up by robotic devices under remote control by members of the bomb squad.

Ten days later I received a phone call from him, inviting me to come to the station 'where I would find something of interest to me'. Intrigued, I wasted no time in crossing the Bridge again and entered his office. There on the desk, amid the wrappings, was a letter and an oblong tobacco tin; he removed the lid to reveal a Victorian print block, the small blocks of wood with lead letters, numbers or designs attached to them which were used in the printing of books – and the design on the one in front of me was that of a Yeoman Warder, arms outstretched in greeting! The mystery was solved! Some years earlier we had bought a house in Witherslack in the Lake District from my mother, who was moving to Kendal, and we had rented it to a young couple, one of whose friends collected such bibliographical memorabilia, and on seeing the 'beefeater', my tenants decided to send it to their landlord! It is now my lucky charm, my 'Diddyman', and appears somewhere or other in all the books I have written since then.

Two important events took place in 1975. One was the

installation of a new Constable of the Tower. His is an ex-officio post, although it is one of great tradition and importance, the Constable being one of the few officers who can approach the Sovereign directly, rather than having to go through a government department, for he is the Constable of Her Majesty's Royal Palace and Fortress the Tower of London. The Ceremony takes place on Tower Green. On that occasion Field Marshal Sir Geoffrey Baker was installed, and we Yeoman Warders, being in State Dress, together with Guards of Honour from the Royal Regiment of Artillery and the Honourable Artillery Company, plus detachments from the Parachute Regiment and others, were part of an impressive occasion indeed.

The other event was that of the Ceremony of Beating the Bounds. In early centuries, where questions of grazing rights, crop-planting and such like were concerned, it was essential for villagers to know where their village ended and the next one began; accordingly in order that the location of the village bounds could be passed on to future generations, a method of acquainting the youngsters of the village was adopted; they were taken to the boundary posts and made aware of the sites by striking them (the youngsters, not the posts!).

At the Tower it used to be celebrated annually, with Richard II decreeing in 1381 that 'The Constable shall upon every Ascension Daie goe in procession worshipfully about the Tower, having with him the Lieutenant and Warders and all the freemen and inhabitants within, in their best arraye.' Now it is celebrated at three-yearly intervals, and on 8th May 1975 we Warders in State Dress, accompanied by the residents of the Tower, our families and children, took part in a short church service conducted by the Tower's padre Revd Llewellyn then formed a procession, willow wands being given to the children. We next proceeded round the Liberty of the Tower – the traffic along Tower Hill being halted – the boundary marks rather than the youngsters being struck, the Chief Warder exhorting them by shouting, 'Whack it, boys, whack it!', which they did with gusto, using their willow wands. After that we continued our perambulation around the Tower, re-entering it by the East Gate near the Bridge, and concluded the ceremony with a hearty rendition of the National anthem.

I mentioned earlier that I had privately been sworn in as a Yeoman Warder by the Resident Governor in the Queen's House, but while researching our records I came across an account of previous Swearing-in Ceremonies actually taking place in the open on Tower Green, all the other warders being present. Intrigued, I investigated further, to discover that it had last been enacted seventeen years earlier but had, for whatever reason, been allowed to lapse. Generally, when any tradition is discontinued for such a length of time, it is almost impossible to have it reinstated, but, on approaching General Raeburn on the subject, he agreed that it should be revived.

The first one to be so sworn in was Jack Chaffer, on 17th February 1976, the ceremony taking place on Tower Green after public hours. All the Yeoman Warders 'in Hollow Square' faced a table at which the Resident Governor in full uniform, together with other Tower officers, was seated. Mr Chaffer, wearing civilian clothes, stood within the hollow square also facing the table and repeated the Swearing-in Oath, line by line, after the Resident Governor. After that we all resorted to our Club set within the outer wall of the Tower, where we welcomed our new colleague in accordance with the following ancient practice.

In centuries long gone the post of Yeoman Warder was eagerly sought after, despite it having to be purchased for the enormous sum of 250 guineas (a guinea being £1.1 shilling) in the same way as army officers in the past bought their commissions. The post carried many perquisites such as living in a royal palace, being excused jury service and such usually compulsory parish jobs as street sweeper, constable and the like. Having become a Yeoman Warder, the practice when wishing to retire was to sell the post to a willing applicant, and thus recoup the initial purchase price. However, should one die in harness, as it were, the Lieutenant of the Tower would take over, sell the post and retain the fee for himself! So we drank to Jack's health with the obvious toast 'May you never die a Yeoman Warder!'

Fortuitously some time earlier, I had been tidying an old store room near the Chief Warder's office and had discovered a large pewter punch bowl. Taking it home, Shelagh cleaned it, and its age became apparent, for inscribed round the sides were the words 'God Preserve King George and the Royal Family'. The bowl then must have been made between 1714 and 1727, during the reign of George I. It could not have been a later George, since there was no number after the name, and he could not have known whether there would be any more George's. Queen Victoria didn't sign herself Victoria I, for the same reason. Once cleaned, the ancient artefact then became the Swearing-in Bowl containing the libation with which to drink the health of a new Yeoman Warder and welcome his family to our little community.

Surrounded as I was by historic and interesting buildings, and possessing a questioning mind, I found myself noticing local edifices and asking 'Why?' Why were some of our towers round and others square? What was that small round building immediately outside the Tower's main gates? What prevented the two towers of the

Bridge falling inwards and squashing the frail-looking walkway connecting them? What was vaguely familiar about the traffic bollards lining the road leading down to Billingsgate Market (then on the riverside on Tower Street)? And what was the purpose of the sixteenth-century iron rings set in the outer wall of the battlements above our apartment?

It would be most unfair to leave readers in suspense, so – square towers, like houses, were obviously easier to build, but when, in the thirteenth century, cannon became the major weapon, enemy cannon balls fired at the corners of the towers quickly brought about defeat by the collapse of such fortifications, so they were eventually superseded by round ones, their shape diverting much of the impact.

The small round building which stands at the front of the Tower bearing the inscription 'London Hydraulic Power Company' is virtually unnoticed by the hordes of tourists passing through the gates. Actually, it was the entrance to the Tower Subway, the precursor of the London Tube. Built, or rather dug, in 1869, it bored through the clay to Bermondsey on the opposite river bank. Originally, passengers would travel in cable-hauled trams, but later the trams were removed and people were allowed to walk across, although it was reportedly an unnerving experience, the noises from the river craft passing immediately overhead sounding uncomfortably close! The Subway was closed in 1896 when Tower Bridge was opened, and, as I observed when I had the opportunity to peer inside, it is now a passageway for water mains and other conduits crossing beneath the river. I admit I chickened-out and refrained from climbing down the steel ladder which seemed to lead into the very bowels of the earth.

The towers of the Bridge are held upright by their 'chains', actually long curved girders attached to each one, their ends eventually vanishing into deep apertures in the ground on each side of the river. One day I happened to be passing 'our' end of the bridge when workmen were inspecting the security of the anchored extremities there, and on looking down any doubts I may have had about the Bridge's security were definitely dispelled.

The traffic bollards? Standing vertically, they might have looked like that, but actually they were originally cannon captured during the Napoleonic Wars, and, when Billingsgate was a thriving fish market, the buyers would load their horse-drawn carts very early in the morning and set off back up the hill to deliver their purchases to hotels and restaurants in the City. But the hill is steep, and so the driver would give his steed a short respite by stopping the cart and allowing it to slide slightly backwards until the tailboard was brought to a halt by one of the cannon/bollards.

Finally, the iron rings on the battlements. During unrest in the City in medieval times, many cannon were positioned on the outer battlements facing the city, but the walkway is narrow, and, when fired, the cannons' recoil would have propelled the heavy weapons backwards to crash into the roadway below, so, to prevent this, short chains were attached to the cannons' undercarriages and to the rings set in the crenellated parapet.

In 1976 Shelagh and I moved into a smaller apartment, No. 16 The Casemates. Opposite to us on the inner wall was the Martin Tower, which was the Jewel House when Colonel Blood sought to solve his cashflow problems – and failed. It was also once the prison of Gunpowder Plotter Ambrose Rookwood, who was later hanged, drawn and quartered in Westminster in 1605. In earlier times its unwilling occupant was Henry Percy, Earl of Northumberland, whose ghost was reputed to stride along the adjoining battlements in full armour; one wonders whether it (he?) centuries later looked down over the parapet when spies of both world wars were executed by firing squad in the rifle range which stood below.

The outer wall of our apartment was six feet thick, pierced only by an arrow-slit through which we could look across the moat towards Tower Hill Underground Station; it also proved to be a cool depository for my beer. Some Sundays, when I was not on duty, we would hop on a bus to Petticoat Lane, one of our major purchases there being a black kitten which we christened Phredd (he was never very good at spelling!). He enjoyed life in the Casemates but always steered clear of the Tower ravens whenever those birds of ill-repute ventured into 'his' area! Not for nothing is the name of a gathering of them an 'Unkindness of Ravens', their beaks being capable of dissecting an unwary pigeon in a matter of seconds. As stated earlier, the Yeoman Warder who was also Raven master at the time was my good friend John Wilmington, and, when he was on leave, one of his colleagues would stand in for him; Shelagh and I spent many a hot evening chasing the ornery critters across the lawns into their individual cages; they would flutter away, flapping their clipped wings, until they decided it was their bedtime; they are the true Kings of the Castle. Replacement birds are obtained from the high fells of Scotland, the Lake District and similarly wild regions. The tradition regarding the ravens, namely that should they leave the Tower, the sovereign would lose his or her throne, is believed to have originated from a story in Celtic mythology, in which Bran the Blessed, a god of the underworld, engaged in battle and, on being mortally wounded, directed that his head be cut off and buried in the White Mount i.e. Tower Hill, facing France; as long as it remained buried, England would never be invaded. The significance of the saga is that the name 'Bran' is

Celtic for raven.

Later that year I developed tinnitus, a constant hissing in the ears (not coming from the audiences in my guided tours!) This was confirmed by the specialists at Guy's Hospital, who also told me that there was neither treatment nor cure. The ailment was attributed my RAF service, including as it did the constant testing and running of aircraft engines after servicing them. In those days ear protectors were unknown, but a claim to the RAF resulted in a small pension. However, compared to others much less fortunate, I consider myself lucky that I sustained nothing worse during the war and subsequent years.

Quite a lot seemed to happen in 1977. As I was still a member of the Society for the Preservation of Ancient Buildings, I received an invitation to be guest of honour at their banquet held in the Banqueting House in Whitehall, the truly magnificent building which in the past had been used for the St George's Day dinner for the Knights of the Garter, the 'touching for King's Evil' – the sovereign touching the sufferer to 'cure' scrofula – and the celebrations of Charles II's restoration to the throne. However, during the banquet I found myself occasionally looking up towards the rows of windows, through one of which the doomed Charles I passed on his way out on to the balcony, where the scaffold and the axe-wielding executioner awaited.

An invitation also came Shelagh's way from the producer of BBC's 'Woman's Hour' to broadcast the woman's angle on living within the confines of the Tower. Problems did exist, for instance, coming back with the shopping and walking straight in past the long queues; it was futile to say 'I live here!' to the protesters, because of course nobody actually *lived* there! And where d'you dry the washing? Where it's always been dried, on the battlements, except that in the old days it included doublets, not singlets!

Shelagh, fascinated by the Tower's history, sought to further her research by visiting the British Library but was disappointed by being informed that she would need a pass and, they being restricted in number, none were available; however, should she leave her address, she would be notified as and when. Accordingly, she told them – the Tower of London – whereupon one was immediately forthcoming!

An intriguing event took place in the moat when, early one morning, lorries started to arrive at the front gates and their drivers, Belgian farmers, then proceeded to lay out a dazzling display of begonias in the design of the royal coats of arms of their – and our – sovereign. When, after many hours, it had been completed, word came that protocol had not been observed as strictly as it should have been, because the Belgian one was on the left – which, strictly speaking, should have been occupied by the British one – so the farmers re-arranged the display accordingly! It remained for three days and proved to be quite a spectacle to Londoners and tourists alike, until the blooms withered away.

Shelagh also had a nasty shock that year, for one of the tourists told me that postcards portraying me in State Dress were on sale in all the souvenir shops along Oxford Street, Regent Street and elsewhere, and everywhere she went shopping, there was hubby looking at her. Evidently, some commercial company had sent a professional photographer to the Tower with orders to get a picture of one of us, then churned out thousands of postcards – alas I received no royalties; we are public property!

While I was at the Tower, the rafters of the thirteenth century Bloody Tower were being replaced, the old ones being thrown in the skip, so I seized the opportunity to obtain a chunk of one of them; the carpenter kindly fashioning it into the shape of an execution block and carved the appropriate cut-outs each side as on the actual block. I adapted it into a time-piece, hollowing it out and installing a clock mechanism, with face and hands. Looking at it now, I sometimes wish that it could speak and thereby end the age-old controversy as to whether the two Little Princes in the room beneath it were murdered on Richard III's instructions or not. Actually, his guilt was apparent at the time, for in the same month as he was crowned, he bestowed honours on two of his closest friends; one of them, John, Lord Howard, became Duke of Norfolk, and his other friend Lord William Berkeley was made Earl of Nottingham. But the younger Prince was not only Duke of York but also held both the Norfolk and Nottingham titles – so how did Richard III know they were by then vacant and available?

The White Tower itself contained a truly magnificent collection of suits of armour and medieval weaponry, and one of the wardens who supervised that museum agreed that I might accompany him on his nightly patrol. I joined him near midnight, and we walked through the hall, up the spiral stairs and past the many large show cases filled with life-size figures clad in complete suits of armour. Only the dim security lights illuminated the room and I must admit that 'spooky' wasn't the word for it; I could have sworn that unseen eyes were watching me through the slits in the visors of their helmets as I walked past, and that, had I turned suddenly, I would have seen one of them move!

In July I was detailed to take part in the Royal Tournament in Earls Court Exhibition Hall. Until recently regrettably cancelled, the tournament was the highlight of the military year, a show in which mock battles and epic events were performed, a superb recruiting advertisement for the armed forces. The two daily performances ended with the Ceremony of the Keys, and I first played the role of Watchman, marching behind the Chief Warder and escorted by four guardsmen across the vast arena to the artificial Tower backdrop at its far end. The Queen Mother attended the evening performance, and I had been 'promoted' to play the part of the Chief Warder, one that I performed with much trepidation. As the time for our entrance grew near, we, the Keys party, waited in the wings and listened to the display taking part, cavalry charging at speed round the arena before thundering off to cheers from the hundreds of spectators. To provide a suitable surface for the equine events, the floor of the hall had been covered with inches of sand, and the horses' hooves had left hollows in it, cavities in which a certain 'Chief Warder', blinded by the searchlights directed on him as he led the Keys party out and advanced towards the far end, would surely trip and fall headlong, losing his Keys and all shreds of dignity in front of the royal guest! Fortunately, I didn't, but nevertheless, after having to march 'Eyes Front' and dazzled by the searchlights, I breathed a sigh of relief when finally I had to doff my Tudor Bonnet and rattle the rafters with my 'God Preserve Queen Elizabeth!'

The year 1978 was crowned, in more ways than one, by being the year in which we celebrated the 900th anniversary of the building of the White Tower in 1078, and so on Thursday, 23rd November we kept all the public out and invited our two special guests, Her Majesty the Queen and His Royal Highness the Duke of Edinburgh. The royal party arrived at 3.00pm, trumpeters atop the White Tower playing a fanfare. Her Majesty was greeted by the Constable and the Resident Governor, the latter presenting her with the Gold

Keys of her Palace and Fortress. Proceeding to Tower Green, she received a Royal Salute from the 2nd Battalion Coldstream Guards and a further Salute from the Body of Yeoman Warders. She then inspected us, walking along our ranks, and this was followed by our giving her three rousing cheers, and marching past the dais. Her Majesty and his Royal Highness signed the visitors book and then formal photographs of our guests and the Yeoman Warders were taken.

It was then time to relax in the marquee erected near the Green, the royal couple taking tea with us, circulating and chatting with us and our families. The Duke paused in front of Shelagh and myself to enquire what it was like living in the Tower, and asked the inevitable question 'Yes, but what about the ghosts?' Shelagh explained that I was researching the subject and intended to write a book about them. It was published shortly afterwards, the book reviewer of the *Daily Express* adding that 'it would keep the Beefeater in beef for the rest of his life'. It did too and it is still on sale in the Tower's souvenir shops! Being a Member of the Queen's Body Guard, I sent signed copies of that and my subsequent books about the Tower to members of the royal family, Her Majesty The Queen, of course, and the Duke of Edinburgh, Prince Charles and Diana, Princess of Wales, Prince William and the Duke of York, among others. Appreciative acknowledgements were always received but, as is the custom, signed on their behalf by their personal secretaries.

During the royal visit members of the media were much in evidence, one inspired reporter demanding that rather than the usual tourist-greeting smiles, three colleagues and myself should adopt grim visages more befitting castle custodians. We did so, the result subsequently being featured on the front of the *Sunday Telegraph* magazine and its German equivalent. A photographer friend of ours, Charles Torrington, seized the opportunity and photographed me in State Dress; enlarging the result, transferring it on to canvas and mounting it, he included it in an exhibition of his work in London. The impressive portrait now graces my lounge. Some learned person once said, 'Clothing maketh the man', and of course had I been in civvies he wouldn't have wasted an inch of film on me.

On another day, while passing the Lanthorn Tower, I paused to watch some diggers who were excavating near to where the old Roman Wall once traversed the castle's grounds. About six feet down they uncovered a pair of human knee-caps, so, putting down their trowels, they carefully brushed the soil away, and, finally uncovered a complete skeleton. He lay on his side, a gaping hole in his skull being visible, and his knees were drawn up as if he had been lowered gently into a grave that was too short for him. I hastened to get my camera, then slithered down into the mud and photographed him – unusually for the Tower, he didn't smile for me! The archaeologists took the remains away and dated them to about AD70; he'd been lying there, unknown and undiscovered, for over two thousand years, maybe millions of visitors having passed over his bones.

It is hardly surprising that, with the Tower's history, such buried artefacts are constantly coming to light, but when workmen, removing some turf on Tower Green in order to check domestic conduits, uncovered what appeared to be an extensive layer of brickwork, the digging was suspended and the Tower's archaeologist Geoff Parnell took over. More turf was removed until eventually a large area of the brickwork was exposed. I, on duty on the Green that day, looked on as some of the bricks were loosened and removed – and Geoff and I found ourselves looking down into an underground chamber! Widening the hole, he dropped six feet or so down into it, and I, determined to see what was in there, followed. The large chamber had a wide-arched roof and an earthen floor; it was disappointingly empty, and although it might have been some sort of cellar or dungeon, it was concluded that it was more likely to have been a 'soak-away' for drainage of waste water from the nearby Tudor buildings. It was later sealed up again, the turf replaced, and now tourists stroll across it, unaware of what lies beneath their feet.

Not quite so ancient was the disused store-room I inspected about that time. It was situated in the outer wall of the moat beneath the Tower Bridge approach road, and it had a grim history of its own. It was the temporary morgue used during both World Wars in which the corpses of some of the enemy spies who had been shot by firing squad in the rifle range, which was once situated, as mentioned earlier, opposite our apartment, were placed pending their removal to various cemeteries.

Another macabre depository for human remains which I inspected exists only yards away, within the base of the north tower of the Bridge. It is known as 'Deadman's Hole', and its use dates back to the nineteenth century, when the Yeoman Warder going on duty to open the East Gate at 6.30am had the task of checking the water's edge for the corpses of those who had committed suicide by drowning during the night – regrettably the living conditions of the poor of the East End were such that this was not infrequent. He then had the job of hauling the cadavers ashore using a long handled triple hook and depositing them in the 'Deadman's Hole' to await collection by the parish undertaker.

Members of the Body were often invited to attend functions at various places and I was Guest of Honour at a big parade held at

Chichester on 12th August 1979. I don't recall what was being celebrated, but I do remember standing in a vehicle resembling the Popemobile, an open topped Land Rover, and holding on to the rail with one hand and waving with the other as the procession drove through the streets lined with cheering spectators.

On another occasion the Tower was asked whether two Yeoman Warders were available to fly up to Newcastle, there to escort the Lord Mayor at the official opening of their new shopping centre. The invitation was put to those who would be on a day off, and my colleague Joe David and I accepted. On the day, wearing our blue undress uniforms and carrying our partizans, we attracted much attention from members of the public at the railway station to Gatwick Airport. Nor were the air hostesses less taken aback; pointing out that weapons were not allowed in the passenger compartment, they insisted the pikes be stored in the luggage hold. At Newcastle we were treated royally, being met at the airport and taken to our hotel. The ceremony passed off successfully, His Worship being gratified by having such a semi-regal escort, and we flew back to London the next day.

Other pleasant perks came our way. Warders were sometimes invited to nearby luxury hotels, there to regale the diners with tales of the Tower while they were waiting for the next course, namely the Baron of Beef. This dish was usually brought in to the dining room suspended from a pole and borne on the shoulders of two of the cooks, who would then carve and serve it up. Afterwards we would dine in a side room and return home, our appetites also satisfactorily replenished.

Ghosts came into our lives again, when, in May 1979, Shelagh woke up to see a tall man dressed in dark clothing standing by the bed, the figure vanishing as she sat up. We asked the Revd Llewellyn what we should do, and, as he had also advised other warders and their families over similar visitations, he suggested that we kept an open Bible by the bed. This we did, with great success, and no further supernatural visitors were received.

My researches on that particular subject still ongoing, I was invited to give a talk to the renowned Ghost Club, and when, in the following year, I had completed a manuscript of my proposed book, I approached Field Marshal Sir Geoffrey Baker GCB CMG CBE MC, the Constable of the Tower, asking him whether he would write the Foreword as an endorsement. To my delight he wrote back, telling me to write it and he'd sign it! The manuscript thus completed, all I needed was a publisher, and of course it had to be William Heinemann Ltd., their logo being a windmill. So the mighty presses started thundering and brought forth *Ghosts of the Tower of London* – "In the 1970s firm footsteps were frequently heard ascending a rear stairway in the Queen's House. So convincing were these sounds that eventually two residents decided to investigate. On hearing the measured tread, one resident immediately went to the foot of the stairs, his companion going to the top via an upper corridor. Slowly one man ascended, the other man descended – to meet no-one but the other!" Shelagh penned some appropriately spooky verses for that book and my next one; as a tribute to her many qualities, some are included in the Appendix.

Its publication received much publicity, and I was invited to go on the airwaves by most of the London radio stations and be interviewed. An unusual coincidence occurred: on leaving one studio, I was running late for a similar interview at another so I hailed a taxi, on hearing my desired destination, the cabbie, recognising the building from which I had just emerged, asked me whether I was a broadcaster; on admitting it, he replied that he had just been listening to my last interview on his cab radio! Interestingly, colleagues and workmen at the Tower subsequently came to me and said they were glad I'd written that, because now they could relate the paranormal happenings they had experienced two, three or four years ago but hadn't liked to tell anyone for fear of being laughed at!

One was a fellow Yeoman Warder living in the Casemates who described how, in the early 1980s, he and his wife became aware of a figure which came out of a room, passed across the corridor, and disappeared into one of the arrow-slits which pierced the opposite wall. It moved quickly, never visible for more than a couple of seconds, and appeared quite frequently to them, and they referred familiarly to it as the 'Flitter'. Guests staying in other rooms complained of a feeling that they were not alone and of hearing deep, measured breathing, and this sensation had also been experienced in other apartments in the Casemates, sometimes accompanied by other, more unpleasant emanations. In one, the occupants became aware of a strong dank smell around ten o'clock each night for over a fortnight, a smell reminiscent of mouldering clothes. There was also a feeling of intense evil where the smell was strongest. In that particular apartment the three-year-old son of the family was once found sitting at the end of the bed, whimpering and tense, and, as described to me by his mother, 'looking at something through his closed eyelids'.

Children seem to be very susceptible to supernatural visitations. In the terrace of houses once the Tower's hospital, the family in one of the flats told me that although their young son frequently played in one corner of the lounge and once or twice a month he would run out of it and stay a few feet away, staring into the corner and crying. No amount of cajoling would induce him to return to his usual spot, even when his father went there and tried to coax him. And a visiting 1920s resident of the Tower related how Eileen, the teenage daughter of a Yeoman Warder then living in the Broad Arrow Tower situated on the inner encircling wall, felt far from alone when mounting the spiral stairs up to her bedroom. On one occasion the 'presence' walked around the spiral ahead of her, abruptly stopping when she stopped, and her bedroom felt suddenly cold and damp. A search revealed nothing but empty rooms and locked doors.

This extra awareness seemed to be possessed not only by children but also by animals. In 1979 the poodle owned by a colleague of mine, who lived a little further along the Casemates, would growl and bark while looking up at Northumberland's Walk. And from poodles to labradors; two of which lived in one of the houses on Tower Green overlooking the execution site of the doomed Tudor queens. Their owners, my good friends Yeoman Warder Dave and 'Mo' Cope, were awakened at one thirty in the morning by a gentle knocking on their bedroom door. The sound grew louder and more insistent, but on opening the door, no-one was there. Although everything was checked for the possible source of the noise, radiators, loose window catches, etc., the knocking continued until 4.00am, the two dogs meanwhile barking so wildly that eventually they had to be shut in the kitchen.

I quickly came to realise that part of the shock caused by a supernatural experience is the sheer unexpectedness of it although one's training has been to prepare one not to be caught unawares. Even Yeoman Warders and Army sentries are initially taken aback, but because of their service background quickly recover and react with their usual efficiency. For instance, in the 1970s it was reported that a sentry suddenly became aware of a crouching figure watching him from behind the locked glass doors of the Waterloo Block. The silhouette was unmistakable, being outlined by a bright light behind the figure, and even as the sentry stared, the shape moved away. The soldier acted promptly, summoning assistance and, together with other members of the guard, searched the locked building from top to bottom, but nothing untoward was found. It should be remembered that all this occurred during the IRA era, when all residents and soldiers were on particularly high alert at all times; moreover, under those circumstances anyone foolish enough to try to hoax the sentries ran the risk of being shot.

The Tower's ghosts seem to be everywhere! In January 1982 one of my colleagues, who had been on duty as Watchman in the Byward Tower, told me what had happened at about 4.30am. He related how he had been sitting opposite the huge stone fireplace – which now holds just an ordinary gas fire – with the electric lights on, when he became aware of a buzzing sound, like that of a fly. He then found himself looking at a roaring fire of logs or coals. In front of the fire two men were standing, side by side. He said both men had beards, and that they both had 'spindly' legs, as if they were in State Dress, wearing breeches and stockings. They seemed to be talking to each other, then stopped, one seeming to lean forward and look at HIM! Next minute, my friend said, they and the roaring fire suddenly disappeared, leaving the Watchman dumbstruck and hardly believing what he had just witnessed. That poses a fascinating question – who thought who was a ghost?

Some years after I had left the Tower, I was contacted by an Officer of the Guard in 2002 who told me of an occurrence involving one of his sentries while on post facing the Wakefield

Tower, near Traitors' Gate. In the middle of the previous night, he suddenly saw the figure of a man wearing a hat and a long black coat mounting the steps leading up from the base of that tower. On reaching ground level the 'man' turned left and passed under an arch leading into the Inner Ward. The sentry, aware that all the Wakefield doors were locked, and that rationally there could not have been anyone at the foot of those stairs anyway, immediately called out the guard and a thorough search was carried out, with the almost inevitable negative results. The officer passed his phone over to the sentry and on talking the somewhat shaken young man through his experience, I had no doubt whatsoever that he had seen what he had said he had seen, inexplicable or not.

Even Shelagh and I experienced a peculiar phenomenon, one so ordinary and common-place as to cause no unease at all – at first. We just began to smell hot, freshly baked bread, yet no-one was baking bread or cakes anywhere in the vicinity. A similar 'visitation', one that seemed natural initially but turned out to be inexplicable, was experienced by a Yeoman Warder who lived on an upper floor of the Waterloo Block. He told me that he was just entering a corridor when he heard a voice say 'Oh, sorry!' He turned to see a man also approaching the swing doors six paces away. One door being propped open, the man passed through and turned the corner. My colleague, now curious, followed – to find no one in sight, all other doors locked and securely barred. He told me that the 'man', far from being clad in 'ghostly' Tudor dress, wore an ordinary suit and a 'wartime type' brown trilby hat. The Waterloo Block is relatively modern and did in fact house Joseph Jacobs, a German spy awaiting execution by firing squad in the Tower in 1941.

But in case it should be thought that only the Yeoman Warders, their families and soldiers are susceptible to such occurrences, I was informed by two workmen that when they unlocked the heavy wooden door of the Salt Tower one morning they heard the sound of footsteps on the floor above, footsteps which slowly paced back and forth. Eventually, the sound ceased, and it was a very reluctant couple of workmen who ventured up the spiral stairs to the chamber in which severely tortured Jesuit priests had once been incarcerated, only to find nothing to account for the mysterious sounds.

The Salt Tower also featured in yet another eerie event a year later. While I was on duty a few yards away, I was approached by a young workman who told me that, having finished the job he was doing in the upper chamber, he closed the door after him and started downstairs. Halfway down the unlit spiral he suddenly heard the sound of stamping feet in the room he had just vacated. Puzzled, and thinking that someone, somehow, had got in, he retraced his steps, only to find the room empty, the light still on (the switch being at ground level). It was then that the understandable reaction set in, and pausing not, he fled down the stairs and out! Calming him down, I, somewhat hesitantly, I must admit, accompanied him back inside, and we conducted a thorough search. But the sound could not be duplicated by making the floorboards creak or windows slam, and, when I positioned the young man halfway down the stairs, only my stamping feet could reproduce the exact sounds he had heard.

Perhaps the most inexplicable and blood-chilling visitation during my time there occurred in the Royal Chapel of St Peter ad Vincula, the last resting place of the three beheaded queens and those executed on Tower Hill. The Chapel's organist told me that late one evening he had been practising in the darkened chapel, the only illumination coming from the small organ light immediately above the music rack. While playing, he suddenly heard the heavy entrance door open and close, and, assuming it to be a patrolling Yeoman Warder, he turned round and looked over the organ screen. No-one was there, but, as the last echoes died away, he looked up – to see a face, glowing eerily, about fourteen feet from the floor, against a supporting pillar near the chapel door. For seemingly minutes, he said, he stared unbelievingly at the apparition as it floated there, then saw it fade away. Badly shaken, he admitted that although he had frequently practised his music late at night, in future he'd make sure that all the chapel lights were switched on.

So far I had lots of reports involving shapes, dim figures, outlines, dark suits and trilby hats, but nothing prepared me for the detail contained in a letter I received from a customs officer, whose office was in the Customs House just west of the Tower. He was a member of a rummage crew: officers who search for any contraband hidden in secret lockers and behind panelling aboard yachts arriving in St Katherine's Docks to the east of the Tower, and because of his job he possessed an uncanny eye for detail and a photographic memory. Having read my *Ghosts of the Tower of London,* he wrote to me describing what he had seen earlier that year while en route to work via Tower Wharf. In order to preserve spontaneity I quote the account in his own words:

"Though I have passed by the rear of the Tower hundreds of times, this was the only time I felt or saw anything. It was 7.30am on 11 March 1980, a slightly misty morning. As I was approaching Traitors' Gate, I noticed a blue light which was flickering and therefore drew my attention. On looking down I was amazed to see a group of people in what appeared to be Tudor dress. There were about eight or nine of them. Leading the procession was a very big man dressed in a leather apron, closely followed by two men carrying pikes or something like that, then two more men very well dressed. They wore red velvet with gold thread or brocade, and one had a small ruff, also a lace collar under the ruff. One seemed to be red-headed and had a small beard, the other dark, no hat, and a small beard; his costume came up to his neck, no ruff, long puffed sleeves and several rings on his fingers. One man had a long gold chain.

Behind them were two women in their early twenties, both very richly clothed. One seemed to be dressed in grey material, silk and brocaded, with a low neckline. Both women had a small tiara, which appeared to have rows of pearls on the crown of their heads. The other woman's dress was of a brownish colour. Both had necklets of pearls, double loops, also a golden chain and pendant of some sort, long sleeves but without frills. The hair of one of them was sort of auburn, the other brown. Both dresses were studded with pearls, diamonds, etc. and gold thread or something like that. The woman in brown was holding a box against her chest with both hands. It was quite a small box, more of a casket than a box. The woman in grey was clasping a prayer book with a cross on it. Following them were two more men carrying pikes. They were dressed the same as the other pikemen, with black hats and capes or cloaks. The figures seemed to be gliding along as in a boat, and the blue light was above them seemed to move with the figures, growing fainter all the time they were in view.

The impression only lasted about a minute or two, then there was some movement along the wharf and they all vanished like **a** puff of smoke. I cannot say whether what I saw was real or not, but I can assure you I don't want to see it again for it left me feeling greatly puzzled and feeling a great deal of sadness, also very cold. I have had many sleepless nights since then, it is a welcome to have happened in daylight and not at night, which could have had a disastrous effect. However at no time did I feel any menacing or evil feeling towards me, only, as I have already said, a feeling of overwhelming sadness and coldness. As well as being an observer, I felt that someone or something was also observing me, to what purpose one cannot tell. In my case there was no fear but a knowledge that I was privileged to see it. I can only say once more that I hope never to see anything like it anymore."

The Wharf also featured in a letter forwarded to me by the Tower from a Mr Arthur D. John of Redlands, California, dated 7 April 1995, in which he explained that his daughter Shannon, together with her school group, had been visiting London and took many photos, including the one he enclosed. It was of Traitors' Gate, but an apparently gloved hand appeared at one side of the photograph, having a Tudor-style ruff at the wrist. His daughter had stated that there was no-one else in the vicinity and she was not aware of the hand until the roll of film was developed after her return to the USA, and so he was interested to know of any similar occurrences.

At first I admit I was sceptical, wondering whether this was a hoax to fool the Tower authorities, but then I realised that, if that was the case, the photo would have been publicised in the American press and not sent to the Tower. I wrote to Mr John and as well as thanking him, asked him whether he would forward the negative for without that any investigation would be impossible. He responded by sending the entire roll of film which contained the one with the 'ghost hand'. As this was such a fascinating subject I contacted an acquaintance, a journalist on the *Daily Telegraph*. He asked me to send it by rail from where I was living in Kendal and he would have a courier waiting at the London end who would take it to Kodak headquarters (it being Kodak film) for analysis.

After some time I received a report from them stating that they had subjected the negative to a wide range of technical investigations and confirmed that the picture was not a double-exposure and the hand was there at the time of exposure – it had not been inserted later by computer-graphics or any other means. They obviously could not suggest that it was of any supernatural origin, but drew attention to the bluish halo around the hand, reminiscent of the electro-florescent glow said to show natural emissions from human bodies (it is believed by some that such colours outlining people are indicative of their moods, orange for happiness, darker colours for depression). I forwarded a copy of their findings to Mr John and, tongue in cheek, reproached Shannon for not standing further back – had she done so, the whole of the owner of the hand would have been in shot! This made me think – if one walked round the Tower continually operating a camera, what would develop? In the photograph, the hand appears to be resting on the railings, but this cannot be so since they were only put in place during the nineteenth century to prevent tourists from falling into the water. The macabre history of Traitors' Gate, the entrance through which the ill-fated Katherine Howard, her entourage and escort passed, along with the ghost hand and the customs officer's experience, must surely have some significant connection.

Many families live in the Tower for a considerable number of years yet encounter nothing untoward. Others take such happenings in their stride, accepting them as inevitable manifestations of the Tower's bloody history. I believe that, when all is said and done, the Tower's ghosts don't really care whether you believe in them or not!

As the existence and traditions of the Tower's Yeoman Warders are so well known, it was hardly surprising that in May 1980 we received a visit from the Incorporated Ancient Order of the Beefeaters of America. I presented the President with a signed copy of *Ghosts* and then, standing at his side, we and the seventy or so members posed for the inevitable formal photograph. The book also attracted the attention of yet another American, Hollywood star Jack Palance. His company was considering making a film about the supernatural, and on 18th August 1981 he visited the Tower and perched with me atop the Bloody Tower's flat roof while we discussed the paranormal.

Yeoman Warders occasionally perform royal escort duties, and on 18th May 1980 three colleagues and I accompanied His Royal Highness the Prince of Wales at the Royal Performance of *Star Parade 1940-80* at the Drury Lane Theatre. During the interval we all withdrew from the royal box to an inner room for a brief respite from the audience's gaze. Once away from the cameras, the media and the public, members of the royal family relax and chat, and it was on that occasion that the Prince complimented me, saying 'What a magnificent beard!' I must say I felt rather honoured to have my beard praised by a future King of England! Actually, I suspect that he was somewhat envious, since he had to shave off the one he grew while serving in the Navy.

Yet another royal encounter occurred on 3rd June 1982, when my colleagues and I reported for duty at Buckingham Palace where a garden party was to take place. I had been detailed to flank the Terrace Steps leading to the lawns, down which the Queen would later walk but, before the event commenced, large numbers of the invited public were milling around the grounds in utter confusion. On seeing an aged Rover 90 saloon appearing some distance away, I 'pulled rank', ordering the throng to move out of the way, then pointed my hand at the driver of the oncoming car and gave him a peremptory flick of my fingers, beckoning him to come through. As the car drew level, who should the passenger be but Her Majesty! She nodded and gave an understanding smile. Caught completely off-guard, I didn't even have time to salute as the car moved on – how was I to know that that particular vehicle was her favourite transport between the stables and palace! Luckily, it was not considered a case of *lese-majesty*, so I escaped a court-martial – or even having to return to the Tower under escort as a prisoner!

Contrary to the much-held belief that no-one could have possibly escaped from such a well-guarded and formidable fortress as the Tower, I discovered reports of a few who did escape, and, because little on that subject had been published, I started researching with a possible book in mind. Living in the Tower was a considerable help, for it meant that I could visit the room in which an escaper had been incarcerated, absorb the atmosphere of his confines, look from the arrow-slits through which he must have peered, walk the very route to freedom he must have taken, then return to my apartment and write his chapter, an advantage that an 'outside' author could never have.

While researching, I heard about one who had escaped then been recaptured and imprisoned in a town in the south of the country. It so happened that, while marshalling the long and slow-moving Jewel House queue one day and chatting to the tourists, one of them mentioned that she lived in the same county, so I explained my project and asked her whether she'd mind unearthing any information about my escaper with which I could embellish my account. She agreed, and little did I know the beneficial effect it would have on her until, some weeks later, I received a letter which contained much detail she had discovered for me in the libraries and elsewhere. In her letter she added that, at the time we had met, she was taking a break from her personal and domestic problems to visit London in the hope of alleviating the extreme depression from which she was suffering. On returning home and immersing herself in the search I had asked her to undertake, her feelings of despondency were completely dispelled, and her thanks for inadvertently being instrumental in her recovery were rewarding indeed.

Great Escapes from the Tower of London was published in 1982 and included the story of an abortive escape by a woman prisoner who, alas, was subsequently re-captured. In a letter among the State Papers of Lord Lisle, dated 28th March 1534, it was stated that 'Wolf and his wife Alice Tankerville will be hanged in chains at low water mark upon the Thames on Tuesday.' Executions such as this took place at Execution Dock at Wapping. After being hanged on the gallows erected on the shore, the corpses were chained to a stake at the low-water mark and left drifting there for three high tides as a horrific warning to those on board the hundreds of ships entering and leaving the Port of London.

While compiling that book, I came across references to Americans who had been held as prisoners in the Tower (and hadn't escaped!). This surprised me, as I'm sure it would any of the vast numbers of American tourists who visit us. After more intensive research I reaped a rich harvest, not only discovering exactly who had been incarcerated and why, but also providing the answer for a query I had long wondered about, namely who was the 'Downing' in Downing Street?

George Downing was the nephew of American Governor John Winthrop and had the distinction of being the second man to graduate from the renowned Harvard University. Downing came to England in 1645 and became a high-ranking officer in Cromwell's army, a dedicated Roundhead and Member of Parliament for Edinburgh and later Carlisle. In 1654 he married into a titled family and three years later was appointed British Ambassador in Holland, although he never concealed his thorough dislike for the Dutch. When Charles II was restored to the Throne in 1660, Downing wasted no time in changing sides; he swore allegiance to the King and blamed his former socialism on his earlier life in America. Samuel Pepys described him as 'an ungrateful villain with no good conscience', and this was borne out when Downing betrayed his former Roundhead colleagues to the King, one of whom was his ex-commanding officer in the Commonwealth Army, Colonel Oakey, knowing full well that they would be gruesomely executed. For his servile conduct he was knighted in 1663.

However, eight years later Charles II, needing to antagonise the Dutch for political reasons, sent Sir George to Holland again, knowing that his presence would exacerbate the situation. Sir George, feeling threatened by the public demonstrations against him, deserted his post and returned to England. On 7th February 1672, he was imprisoned in the Tower. At the end of March he was released to continue his political career in a more minor role. Many of his contemporaries considered him to be avaricious and treacherous, and in New England, any man who betrayed his trust was described as 'an arrant George Downing'. One wonders, however, whether it was because of his skills in the political field, rather than his disloyal hypocrisy that the street which contains the Prime Minister's residence was named after him!

My list of unwilling American guests of the Tower would not be complete without including a wealthy vice-president of South Carolina named Henry Laurens, who, in 1780, sought to enlist the Dutch to come to the aid of his countrymen in the American War of Independence against Great Britain. Captured at sea during his journey, he was brought to England, and, on arrival at the Tower suffered the indignity of being greeted by the Yeoman Warders on duty who derisively whistled 'Yankee Doodle Dandy'! In those days it was customary to billet a prisoner in a warder's house or tower, there to be guarded, fed and generally looked after by the warder and his family. Laurens was placed in the custody of Yeoman Warder James Futterill. Board and lodgings in the Tower, even for prisoners, were never free, and Laurens had to pay his warder a guinea a week for purchasing and cooking his food, although he refused a bill for £97.10.0, the cost of guarding him.

During the next fifteen months he was subjected to repeated questioning by members of the Government but remained loyal to the American cause throughout. I discovered that he suffered severely from gout and was nursed by Mrs Futterill and her daughter, with whom he became great friends, and, in fact, he left a legacy to his 'nurses'. He had nothing but contempt for Colonel John Gore, the Deputy Lieutenant of the Tower. He was released, on crutches, on New Year's Eve 1781 and later interceded with the authorities on behalf of American prisoners of war – captured seamen held in ordinary gaols – visiting them and contributing £200 towards extra food and provisions. In April 1782 he was exchanged for a British officer captured by the American colonists and returned to America via Holland. Once home, he dined out for years on his experiences as a prisoner of the 'enemy' and liked to be called 'Tower' Laurens.

Prisoners were very lucky not to end their days on Tyburn gallows, at the junction of what is now Edgeware Road and Oxford Street/Bayswater Road, adjacent to Marble Arch, where, set in the stones of a small traffic island there, is a symbolic plaque bearing the words 'Here stood Tyburn Tree, Removed 1759'. Curious readers should beware inspecting this for themselves – such is the density of the traffic thereabouts, yet another tombstone would be inscribed 'Died at Tyburn'!

I was given permission to bring some visiting friends to the nearby Tyburn Convent, where they keep relics of the 105 Carthusians, Benedictines, Jesuits and others who met their ends on the Tyburn Gallows between 1535 and 1681. The nuns received us graciously, and, on hearing that I was a Yeoman Warder of the Tower, suggested that I probably knew more about those whose remains they revere than they did! The humble and devoted nuns who guard those martyrs' memories so jealously possess qualities at which we can only marvel, lacking them ourselves.

Earlier in this chapter I recounted my visit to St James' Palace to be sworn in as a Member of the Queen's Body Guard of the Yeomen of the Guard Extraordinary, but it wasn't until much later that I realised we had no document that recorded I had done so. My application to the Resident Governor, Major General Mills, that a document should be introduced, was approved, and a suitably worded certificate, designed by the Queen's Scribe Donald Jackson, has since been presented to each warder on qualifying [see

Appendix] – a testimonial to be treasured by the subject, his family and his successors.

During the summer of 1982 Shelagh and I went on leave to Cumbria in order to visit my mother who lived in Kendal. We stayed in Grange-over-Sands, fifteen miles away, and while idly looking in the window of an estate agent there, we noticed an attractive eighteenth-century house for sale, overlooking Morecambe Bay. Curious, we visited it and immediately fell in love.

We still owned Bownas Cottage in nearby Witherslack, which we'd bought from my mother, and by chance it was valued at the same price as this one. But we were reluctant to buy only to leave it empty for much of the year, and to let it would risk it being ruined by uncaring tenants. I was rapidly approaching the age at which I could apply, not for retirement, for being a Yeoman Warder is a life appointment, but to be transferred from the Yeoman Warders' Active List to the Supernumerary List and thereby leave the Tower. We came to a momentous decision and arranged the sale of the Witherslack house and the purchase of Gowan Lea then returned to the Tower and submitted the application to leave. It was a sad but exciting moment when, in October 1982, the gates of the Tower closed behind us and yet another new life lay ahead.

Outside our home beneath the
Tower Battlements.

'What about the ghosts?'
asked the Duke.

A guaranteed cure for sluggish adrenaline.

The Body of Yeoman Warders
with HM The Queen and HRH.

Kendal Mace Bearer, 1983.

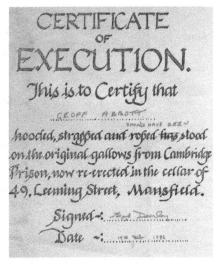

CERTIFICATE
OF
EXECUTION.

This is to Certify that

GEOFF ABBOTT

SHOULD HAVE BEEN

hooded, strapped and roped has stood
on the original gallows from Cambridge
Prison, now re-erected in the cellar of
49, Leeming Street, Mansfield.

Signed ~:

Date ~:

Dernley Hanging Certificate.

THE WHITE HOUSE

WASHINGTON

May 22, 1987

Dear Bud and Shelagh:

Thank you for your thoughtful message and for
the copy of your delightful book. Your words
of encouragement and gesture of friendship are
truly appreciated.

I look forward to reading about the illustrious
history of the Yeoman Warders of the Tower of
London who, as you point out, "represent the
glories and traditions of England."

You have my heartfelt thanks and best wishes.

Sincerely,

Ronald Reagan

Yeoman Warder and Mrs. G. Abbott
Gowan Lea
Cart Lane
Grange Over Sands
Cumbria LA11 7AB
England

A letter from the President.

HADLEY-APENNINE, AUG 2, 1971

To BUD AND SUE ABBOTT WITH WARM PERSONAL REGARDS
AND MANY THANKS FOR THE HOSPITALITY, AND FOR SHARING
THE HERITAGE ON WHICH RECENT JOURNEYS BY THE
"COLONIES" HAVE BEEN LAUNCHED!

Dave Scott
GEMINI VIII
APOLLO IX, XV
MARCH 11, 1981

Astronaut David Scott's Thank You Letter.

On the occasion of the visit of

Her Majesty the Queen
and
His Royal Highness Prince Philip, Duke of Edinburgh

on
Thursday, 23 November 1978
The Constable of Her Majesty's Tower of London
Field Marshal Sir Geoffrey Baker GCB. CMG. CBE. MC
invites

Mr and Mrs G Abbott

to a Reception in the Tower

Please bring this
invitation with you

EiR

The Lord Chamberlain
is commanded by Her Majesty to invite

M. G. Abbott

to a Parade followed by a Reception
in the Garden of Buckingham Palace
to celebrate The Queen's Golden Jubilee
on Friday, 5th July 2002

Uniform (with decorations),
Morning Dress or Lounge Suit

10.15-11.15 a.m.   Guests to be seated
11.30 a.m.   Inspection
12.00 p.m.   Detachments march off

You are hereby invited...

Here's one I executed earlier!

14th August, 2001

Dear Mr. Abbott,

The Queen has asked me to thank you for your letter of 10th August with which you sent a copy of your latest book entitled "Crowning Disasters". Her Majesty much appreciated your thoughtfulness in sending this gift to her.

Yours sincerely,

MRS. DEBORAH BEAN
Chief Correspondence Officer

Geoffrey Abbott, Esq.

Royal Thank You Letter

Chapter Eleven
AUTHOR, HELICOPTER PILOT
AND TV STAR

We arrived at Gowan Lea, our new 'real' home, and proceeded to carry out extremely un-service-like modifications, such as putting shelves up and painting the walls in the colours *we* wanted. The house overlooked Morecambe Bay, whose shores were home to countless sea birds: gulls, oyster catchers and the like. Grange-over-Sands is a small but welcoming town, with lots of local societies, and when the news was flashed around the secretary circuit that there was a 'Beefeater' in town, I was inundated with invitations to give talks on the Tower. Within the first eight years I presented no fewer than 200 slide-illustrated talks across the Lake District, so the ego-trip certainly didn't end with the Tower.

In the following year I noticed an advertisement in the *Westmorland Gazette* for a mace-bearer to the mayor of Kendal, so, not averse to getting back in uniform again and intent as ever to maintain traditions of whatever variety, I applied and was accepted. Mace-bearers, or sergeants at mace, were originally the Sovereign's Bodyguard, and, because the mayors of cities and towns were his or her representatives, they too had to have a bodyguard. While closely escorting a mayor, their duty was to ensure that no-one intervened between them and their charge. Over the centuries the club-like maces evolved into symbols of the city or town, the 'handle' ends lavishly decorated with the town's arms, crests and mottos. Mace 'handles' became enlarged or replaced with larger 'handles', and eventually the decorated end of the erstwhile weapon grew bigger and heavier than the 'hitting' end until they were almost impossible to carry. The obvious solution was to carry it the other way round. So every existing mace, including the impressive one made of gold on the table in the House of Commons, is in reality being carried upside down!

Kendal has two maces, one very slightly heavier than the other, and being the newcomer I had to carry that one. My uniform, unlike that of a town crier or Yeoman Warder, was a smart suit with a peaked cap made of Kendal Green material, worn with medals. Parades took place three times a year and consisted of the two mace bearers following our leader, the sword bearer, who was in turn followed by the Mayor, the bewigged Town Clerk, and members of the Council. Unlike similar parades in the RAF or at the Tower, the procession from the Town Hall to the Parish Church and back was little more than a gentle amble accompanied by a great deal of talking in the ranks, and I had to restrain myself from suggesting that I gave them a bit of drill in the evenings!

In due course, as my colleagues retired from their duties, I progressed up through the chain of office, as it were, first carrying the lighter mace, and ultimately becoming Sword Bearer. The Kendal Sword, dating from the reign of Charles II, is three feet eleven and a half inches in length, and I had to be very careful not to kebab the Mayor when turning round. The post of Sword Bearer was different from that of the Mace Bearer in that the Sword Bearer was not a bodyguard but was the symbol of the Sovereign's authority. It is for this reason that the figure surmounting the Old Bailey Central Criminal Court holds a balance in one hand and in the other, not an axe or a noose, but a sword.

I performed the civic duties for more than twenty years, savouring the cheering crowds lining Kendal's streets, the members of the congregation rising to their feet as we led the Mayoral Party into the Church, and the glass of port in the Mayor's Parlour afterwards. Kendal Castle is believed to have been the birthplace of Catherine Parr, the last wife of Henry VIII. Once, while visiting a London shop specialising in old prints, I came across one of Queen Catherine and purchased it. Since, to my surprise, no picture of her existed in the Town Hall, I presented it to the Council, and it now adorns a wall in the Parlour. I retired as Sword Bearer in 2005 and was presented, at my last parade, with a superbly engraved cut-glass decanter by the members of the Council. In my acceptance speech I thanked them – and pointed out that I had escorted more than twenty mayors and had never lost one of them!

In view of the success of the couple of books I had published while at the Tower, I continued to write. The most-asked questions posed at the Tower were about torture and executions. I suspected that the public relished reading about those particular gory subjects, and I eventually had four publishers and was completing one book a year. My aim was always to have the reader comment 'Well, I never knew that!'

In 1985 I wrote *Beefeaters of the Tower of London* – "the night before Simon, Lord Lovat, was beheaded, he and his Yeoman Warder rehearsed the execution using a bed pillow as the block to make sure that the old man's neck would not be too thick for the block's groove". While researching for material, I came across a volume written in 1885 by an author named Thomas Preston containing details of Yeoman Warders and was surprised and delighted to discover something I never dreamed existed: a Coat of

Arms of the Yeoman Warders (he called it 'Trophy of Arms'), the design including the White Tower, the Crown, a Tudor Rose and two partizans. I included it in my book, and my colleagues decided to adopt it, having had it verified and accepted by the College of Heralds. We now sport it, not only on our sweaters and blazers, but also engraved in our glassware.

My *Tortures of the Tower of London* was published in the following year – "The Jesuit priest John Gerard said, 'We went to the torture chamber in a kind of solemn procession, the guards walking ahead with lighted candles. The chamber was underground and dark, particularly near the entrance. It was a vast shadowy place and every device and instrument of human torture was there. They pointed out some of them to me and said I should have to taste them. Then they asked me again if I would confess. 'I cannot,' I said."

About that time I received an invitation to be Toastmaster at a St George's Day Dinner, 23rd April 1986, at Hoghton Tower, near Preston in Lancashire. The banquet took place in the magnificent hall of the building, and I found myself seated next to the England football celebrity Sir Tom Finney. History relates that when King James I visited Hoghton Tower in August 1617, the main course included a large piece of roast beef, and His Majesty was so impressed by the sumptuous meal laid out on the still existent seventeen-foot long table that, tradition has it, he touched the side of beef with his sword and exclaimed 'I name thee Sir Loin!'. It is highly likely that I was the first member of the Sovereign's Bodyguard to have officially crossed the threshold of that impressive hall since that king and his bodyguard entered, nearly four hundred years earlier! At the appropriate moment in the proceedings, all the guests were called upon 'to be upstanding' and drink to the Loyal

Charge. Accordingly, I loudly announced, 'God for Elizabeth, England and Saint George!' to which all present responded in good voice with the same words and quaffed their wine in salutation.

In the previous chapter I mentioned a young American named Joe Rodota who had sent me a watercolour he had painted of me, and in May 1987 we received an unexpected letter from him. In it he thanked us again for the evening spent in our Tower Casemate and went on to say, 'I am currently working in the White House for President Reagan, as the Deputy Director of Public Affairs, and should you ever visit the USA while I am there, I would be only too happy to give you a private tour of the building.' We replied, thanking him, and I also enclosed a copy of my book *The Beefeaters of the Tower of London* and included an extra one for his boss, writing on the title-page 'To the President and his wife, with best wishes from Bud (my nickname) and Shelagh Abbott', together with one of my souvenir-shop postcards.

Shortly afterwards I received another letter from Joe in which he thanked me for the book, adding, 'As for the President's book and postcard, I sent it along to him and I expect you will be hearing from him and Mrs Reagan shortly.' Sure enough it wasn't long before a much-impressed postman delivered a large envelope bearing the imposing words *"FROM THE WHITE HOUSE, WASHINGTON"*. The letter started with 'Dear Bud and Shelagh', and, after thanking me for the gift, was signed by the President himself. The fact that one of the two most powerful men in the world at that time could take time off from concerning himself with the Cold War and the nuclear threat and actually sign the letter said a lot about his outgoing personality.

Shelagh and I usually did our main shopping in Kendal, and on one particular day, while driving there along the A590 through the countryside, I noticed a heron standing motionless only a matter of yards from the roadside. On our way back a few hours later, we saw that the bird was still there, so I pulled off the road and went to investigate. I noticed that one of its feet seemed injured, so I approached it cautiously – herons have very sharp and pointed beaks. It allowed me to get near and didn't move as I slowly put one arm round its body, keeping my head turned away in case it suddenly attacked my eyes. There was a bungalow a little distance away, so hoping, in those pre-mobile days, to be able to phone the RSPB, the three of us went to the front door and Shelagh knocked. The door was opened by a woman who, on hearing Shelagh's explanation and seeing my burden, exclaimed 'Don't bring that in here – wait outside!' Apparently, the reason for her protest was that her lounge walls were lined with shelves bearing china and glass ornaments, and she was worried that the heron might escape.

So I sat on the bench clutching the large bird to my side and feeling for all the world like the late-lamented celebrated comedian Rod Hull and Emu – although MY bird was not a dummy arm! The heron – we'd already christened him 'Harry' – stayed motionless in my grasp, his eyes alert and bright, as Shelagh brought me a cup of tea and informed me that the RSPB was on its way. About twenty minutes later a van drew up and one of their inspectors got out. He examined the bird and told us that it was very emaciated – I could feel its ribs almost protruding through its skin – and due to its crippled leg, probably caused by it having been trapped in a wire fence recently, it hadn't fed for some considerable time. He further pointed out that only a very sick bird would have allowed me to approach it in the way I had. Putting it gently into the large cage in the back of the van, he explained that it would be nursed and given plenty of fish to build up its health but warned us not to raise our hopes too high. Alas, a week later he phoned to say that Harry the heron was too far gone to recover and had died shortly after the rescue.

Just as archaeologists digging in the Tower's grounds come across unexpected artefacts, I too continued to dig into the Tower's shadowy past and came across unexpected historical facts, which inspired me to write *Mysteries of the Tower of London* in 1988: "In September 1664 a man named Edmund Halley, a salter who owned several houses and an inn called the Dog Tavern in Billingsgate, became a Yeoman Warder. He had married Ann Robinson, and while living at Haggerston, she gave birth to a child on 8 November 1656, whom they also christened Edmund. Surprisingly he grew up to be bright and intelligent, so much so that he was educated at Queen's College, Oxford, and qualified as a mathematician, with a strong preference for astrology. After graduating he developed his studies of the heavens, and surprised his learned colleagues by forecasting a total solar eclipse in 1715, and six years later, in 1721, he became Astronomer Royal. However all his previous discoveries were themselves eclipsed by his predictions regarding a certain astronomical event, one so remarkably accurate that the celestial body itself which passed the Earth at regular intervals was forthwith known as 'Halley's Comet'! But disaster struck the family when his father, Yeoman Warder Halley, left the house on 5th March 1683, and was never seen again until, on 12th April, his lifeless body was found in a field near Stroud in Kent. At the inquest the jury brought in a verdict of murder, but his possible assailant was never discovered. His corpse was buried in the cemetery of the church in

Barking, Essex. So how did he meet his death? Was he ambushed by a highwayman or footpad? Slain during a fight with a cutpurse? We will never know – it is a mystery." My publisher did not hesitate to get the book into the bookshops, especially those within the Tower's precincts, there to satisfy the curiosity of those tourists agog to read about the Tower's mysterious happenings.

Nor was that all, for I had long been collecting Victorian and Edwardian picture postcards of the Tower, and, having amassed a few hundred, I had a selection of them published later as *The Tower of London As It Was.* Subsequently, rather than put the no-longer-needed cards away in a drawer, I offered them to London's Guildhall Museum; they were gratefully accepted, and as the *Abbott Collection* they were made available, not only to those researching the many changes which had taken place to some of the Tower's buildings and those in the surrounding area but to others more interested in the costumes and dress accessories of long-gone visitors.

Late in that year I had a sudden fit of nostalgia and visited RAF Cosford, one of the training stations I had attended nearly fifty years earlier. I presented the Commanding Officer with a copy of one of my books and a charming WRAF Officer conducted me round the camp. I was shocked and horrified to find that the parade ground was being used as a car park. That was always God's Own Acre in my day – simply to set foot on the very edge of any parade ground was to receive seven days jankers! It was my own fault – I'd forgotten the motto again – never go back!

Two years later I had a book *Lords of the Scaffold* published, which was based on the lives and experiences of many executioners – "In the 1850s there was an Irish hang*woman*, and so fearsome was her reputation that parents threatened their children by saying that if they didn't behave they'd send for the dreaded Lady Betty!"

Some little time after that I received a letter from a Lancastrian model-maker, David Atkinson, congratulating me on the preciseness of the dimensions of scaffolds which I had included in the book, details which he had found invaluable. A warm friendship with him and his wife Jil (herself a skilled artist and no mean dress designer) developed, and they were very supportive when in 1993 Shelagh died of multiple ailments. Later, happening to discover that they'd never seen the sights of London, by way of repaying them for their sympathetic help, I organised an interesting tour of the City. It included such mundane events as riding in a London cab, crossing over the Thames on Tower Bridge, sailing on the Thames by river-boat, and walking under the Thames via the tunnel at Greenwich. Much less humdrum was watching a sitting in the House of Commons from the public gallery, and the highlight undoubtedly was an overnight stay in the Tower of London, a certificate signed by the Resident Governor to that effect subsequently being framed and displayed in their lounge. They certainly deserved it.

The title of my next book was one I came up with myself and seemed appropriate for a history of torture instruments. *Rack, Rope and Red-hot Pincers* was published in 1993: "The French assassin Francis Ravaillac was punished by having his right hand burned, then torn with red-hot pincers; this was followed by having scalding oil and molten lead poured into his wounds, after which he was torn asunder by four horses and his remains burned to ashes."

Many of my books included references to executioners and I, through the good offices of David Atkinson, was able to meet one. He was Syd Dernley, who had been assistant to the late, great Albert

208

Pierrepoint, and had taken part in more than twenty hangings. In 1994 I visited him at his house in Mansfield, Nottinghamshire, and took the opportunity to resolve something that had puzzled me for ages. Most accounts of hangings mention that the knot was positioned under the victim's left ear but never explained why. I just had to find out. At first I thought that it was because a particularly vulnerable artery was located there but on checking with my doctor – who, knowing me, was not overly surprised by the macabre question – was assured that both sides of the neck were anatomically identical. I then wondered whether there was an esoteric reason; was it because the word 'left' has a related adjective of 'sinister' and so was more applicable to a hanging?

Alas, the reason was nothing so bizarre. On the scaffold the rope hangs down from a hook, and, in order to save time when the victim is positioned on the drop trapdoors, the rope is coiled up so that the noose hangs at head level, being held there by a thread which snaps on the victim's descent. After hooding him or her the hangman takes the noose, holds it level between both hands and drops it over the victim's head – and as most hangmen are right-handed, that is the hand in which he grips the noose's knot, and so it ends up under the victim's left ear. After Syd had explained all that, I turned to chat to his wife Joyce – only to feel a noose dropped around *my* neck by my host! Fortunately, he took it off again, but it was, I must admit, a somewhat unique sensation. As proof of my 'execution', he presented me with the appropriate certificate.

During the next few years I visited many antique collectors' fairs and bought ancient handcuffs, leg-irons, a ball and chain (later presented to Lancaster Castle as exhibits) and even swapped some copies of my books for a genuine execution axe. I also acquired a small guidebook, the covers of which 'are made from the wood of the old gallows tree of Doune Castle' in Scotland. I wondered what tales it could relate.

On the stall of one dealer at an antique fair in Wetherby, Yorkshire, I saw an antique I could simply not ignore. It was a bronze death mask which I purchased for £50. In times past, following the death or execution of many famous or infamous figures, a wax mask would be made of the face, from which a mould would be formed and a number of bronze replicas produced. Mine is finely detailed, every wrinkle visible, and I sometimes find myself looking at the closed eyelids and wondering what my reaction would be if they suddenly opened and I found myself staring straight into his eyes. I have made every attempt to discover his identity – sending photographs of him to the National Portrait Gallery, Edinburgh University and even to Scotland Yard's Black Museum, but all to no avail.

Long ago I had written the memoirs of my troopship days and the various units on which I had served, and I presented copies of the memoirs to the RAF Museum, Museum of London, the Imperial War Museum, Guildhall Museum, the Fleet Air Arm and Greenwich Naval Museums, the Parachute Regiment archives and the US Airborne Museum, among others, for the benefit of their researchers, since my own books had involved so much research themselves. One evening in 1994 I received a phone call from a David Scott, a photographer who lived in Scotland. He introduced himself by saying that he had read all my books, which commended him to me immediately! He invited me to accompany him on a visit to the 'drop room' in Barlinnie Gaol, Glasgow, which was about to be demolished and replaced by an ordinary cell so many years after the abolition of the death penalty. He had arranged to photograph it before its move to the Royal Scottish Museum. I had always been meticulous in adding as much detail as I could in my books, and the opportunity to confirm the accuracy or otherwise of my descriptions of the drop room was definitely not to be ignored. So, on the day we had arranged, I drove north, taking a roadmap and street map of Glasgow. It was my first visit to a prison, and it was strange to find my request for directions met with such wary looks from the locals! Eventually, I found the large group of buildings and parked the car in the forecourt, then entered the front office block. I found myself facing a reception desk; to my right was a large area crowded with women and children, evidently waiting to spend time with their incarcerated spouses and fathers. At the desk I was greeted by David Scott, together with a senior prison officer assigned to show us around, and Frank McCue, a gentleman about my age who had served there as a prison warder for many years and had twice spent the night in Barlinnie's condemned cell guarding prisoners due to die on the following morning.

We passed through the front offices to the prison itself, which was made up of five Victorian blocks, one of which we entered. Inside it resembled a cathedral, long and narrow, with high windows at its far end. There were cells all along each side, above and below a railed walkway, over which prisoners leant and greeted us with no-doubt highly descriptive but thankfully inaudible remarks. Warders were very much in evidence, and we mounted the iron steps leading to the upper floor and entered the end cell on the left-hand side. This was the condemned cell, and Frank and I sat on the bed while I signed the copy of one of my books he'd brought. The cell was as I had expected – cold with stone walls and minimal furnishings; the thick steel door incorporated a peephole, the steel surrounding it tapering away so that, on looking in, the warder's view was not restricted in any way. Shortly afterwards, Frank led me round the walkway to the cell in the corresponding position on the opposite side of the block which was the execution chamber itself. It differed from all the other cells in that it had two entrances: one a standard-sized doorway through which the sheriff, chaplain, chief warder and other officials entered; the other was three times wider to permit the condemned person and the warders walking one on each side of him or her to pass. The chamber was large, and my attention was immediately attracted to the 'drop' in the centre of the room. A large opening, it was covered by the two wooden trapdoors, and overhead a thick wooden beam spanned the cell. In the far right-hand corner, a steel ladder led up to the loft above the beam; below the ladder was an aperture through which the executioner and his assistant would descend into the 'pit' in order to cut the hanged person down after the specified hour had elapsed. Frank demonstrated the method of preparing for a hanging by chalking a letter 'T' across the gap between the trapdoors so that the upright of the letter was bisected by the gap. He invited me to stand on the drop with one foot each side of the T's upright stroke and my toes just touching the crossbar of the letter. This was to ensure that I would fall vertically and not strike my head on either side of the opening when the drop lever was pulled. Above my head three hooks projected from the beam; the short chain to which the noose rope would be attached was suspended from the centre hook, and ropes from the outer two would be gripped by the warders standing on planks straddling the pit so that they didn't accompany the doomed person downwards. The trapdoors themselves were, of necessity, very heavy, and, in order to prevent them bouncing back when released and striking the rapidly descending victim, retaining catches were set in the walls of the pit. The visit proved invaluable, allowing me to confirm at first hand that the descriptions I had included in my books were accurate.

The execution chamber was converted into a normal cell the following year and Frank kindly sent me a small piece of the stone wall as a grim souvenir of my visit and of bygone executions. This I have had mounted on a base of polished wood.

Later that year my *Book of Execution,* containing a very large number of different methods of judicial extermination, was published. As a change from concentrating on writing about English executioners, I followed it up in 1995 by writing *Family of Death,* the biography of the celebrated Sanson family, six generations of whom bestrode the scaffold, the most notable being Charles-Henri, Monsieur de Paris, who despatched so many aristocrats, both men and women, during the French Revolution: "The King's favourite, Mme Du Barry, was so faint that my [Charles-Henri's] son Henri had to support her. She kept speaking to me, begging for mercy. I was more moved than anyone, for this unfortunate woman reminded me of my younger days, of the time that I knew her... When she saw the guillotine she became overwrought and struggled with my assistants and tried to bite them. She was very strong, and three minutes elapsed before they could carry her up on to the platform. She was frightful to look at, and to the very last moment she struggled."

It was while researching the French Revolution that I noticed an incident in which Charlotte Corday, assassin of the Revolutionary leader Marat, was decapitated by the guillotine, and when one of the executioner's assistants picked up her head and slapped one cheek – the other cheek also blushed. How could this be possible? Could the nerves still be alive? Could she still react to the outrage? I then recalled the oft-recounted story regarding Anne Boleyn's execution by the sword on Tower Green, which stated that when her head was held high 'her eyes and her lips went on moving'. So could consciousness continue after beheading? Was it feasible? After all, nowadays hearts, livers, kidneys and other organs remain 'alive' long enough to be transported long distances and transplanted into a critically ill recipient, and the brain is just another organ...

My curiosity aroused, I continued to research other out-of-print books and accounts of experiments carried out by various learned people. One avowed that there is sufficient oxygen stored in the brain for consciousness to remain for seven seconds or more. In 1795 a Dr Seguret, a professor of anatomy, had actually obtained: "...two freshly severed heads, exposed them to bright sunlight, and opened their eyelids, whereupon 'the eyelids closed of their own accord, with an alertness that was both abrupt and startling – the entire face then assumed an expression of intense suffering. One had its tongue protruding, and a student pricked it with the point of a lancet, whereupon it withdrew into its mouth and its features grimaced as if in pain". An anatomist, Dr Sommering, reported cases in which a head had grimaced when he inserted a finger into its spinal canal, and he had also heard severed heads grinding their teeth. The most dramatic account came from Dr Beurieux, who, having placed a severed head on a bench, saw the face relax, the eyelids half close. He called the victim's name, and slowly the eyes opened and the pupils focused on him: "...not with a dull, blank look, but alert and concentrated; then after several seconds the eyelids closed again. Once more I called out, and once more the lids opened and those undeniably living eyes fixed on mine, only to close again, the eyes taking on the glazed look of the dead." So could Queen Marie Antoinette have seen the wicker basket coming up to meet her as her severed head fell? Could Anne Boleyn have looked into the eyes of those around the Tower scaffold as the French headsman held her head high? We will never know – and volunteers are definitely in short supply!

A machine similar to the guillotine and its English forerunner, the Halifax Gibbet, was the 'Scottish Maiden'. This death-dealing machine was believed to have been introduced into Scotland by James Douglas, Earl of Morton and Regent of Scotland, who, while returning home from a visit to the English court, passed through Halifax and noticed its gibbet, maybe on a market day, when it could well have been in use. Evidently impressed, he had a similar one constructed, it being known as the Scottish Madin or Maydin, a name perhaps derived from the Celtic mod-dun, the place where justice was administered.

With a view to including the Maiden in some future book I eventually featured it in *Who's Who of British Beheadings*, published in 2001 – I studied drawings of the device, then was delighted to discover that the original machine was on display in Edinburgh Museum of Antiquities, so in 1996 I travelled north across the border again and, with the friendly assistance of the staff, made copious notes of the Maiden's construction. It consisted of two ten-foot long oak uprights connected by a cross-bar at the top and mounted twelve inches apart on a wooden base, supported in an upright position by bracing beams at the rear. The axe blade was an iron plate faced with steel, thirteen inches in length and ten and a half inches in breadth, its upper side weighted with a seventy-five-pound block of lead, which travelled in the copper-lined grooves cut in the inner surfaces of the uprights. It was retained at the top by a peg attached to a long cord, which, when pulled by means of a lever, allowed the blade to hurtle downwards to where the victim's neck rested on a wooden bar. To ensure that the blade passed completely through the victim's neck, the bar had a wide groove cut in its upper surface, filled with lead to resist the impact of the falling blade, and, to prevent the victim from withdrawing his or her head, an iron bar, hinged to one upright, was lowered and secured to the other upright before the cord was pulled.

In many cases it <u>was</u> 'her' head: poisoners Isabell and Ann Erskine paying the price in 1614, Janet Embrie for incest in 1643 and minister's wife Margaret Thomson for adultery three years later. Ironically, James Douglas himself, found guilty of complicity in the murder of the Scottish Queen's husband Lord Darnley, was taken under strong escort to the Grassmarket where the Maiden awaited, suffering beneath the rapidly descending blade in 1581. The Halifax Gibbet operated in the same way except that there was no executioner – instead the rope which released the blade was stretched out and grasped by as many of the spectators surrounding the scaffold as possible, and if they considered the victim was guilty, they all pulled the rope.

I was later invited to take part in a series of history programmes broadcast by Scottish radio, the recordings started as I stepped off the train in Edinburgh. The producer had booked a hotel room for me, and on arriving there I was informed that the only one available was the Honeymoon Suite, which sadly had no bride in it awaiting me. The next day was occupied with more interviews, the last taking place while having a wee dram in the public house situated in the Grassmarket, mine host presenting me with a tie, its crest being, appropriately enough, a gallows, complete with a suspended victim.

In 1995 Charles came into my life. I had been in London to discuss a project with one of my publishers, but, unable to keep away from the stalls of antique markets that might just have the odd pair of old handcuffs or a porcelain figurine of a Beefeater for sale, I visited a favourite stamping ground of mine, Portobello Road, where I saw Charles for the first time. He was standing on the cobbles outside an antique shop with tourists gathered around him posing for photographs. He was a fibre-glass life-sized model of a Yeoman Warder, and although his paint was somewhat faded, nevertheless he was in good trim, and more importantly he had a 'Victorian'-type face akin to those seen on ships' figureheads which gave him an air of authenticity. I went in and asked the owner how much he was asking for Charles, telling him that I was his flesh-and-blood equivalent. Arriving back in Kendal, I made up my mind to give Charles a good home. I phoned the shopkeeper, who agreed that as I was a bona fide Yeoman Warder he would reduce the price to a very reasonable level – the deal was struck.

The next problem was how to transport him to Cumbria. Various removal firms stated their willingness, but pointed out that he would be collected from the antique shop, then taken to a depot and subsequently loaded and off-loaded into different lorries along with other goods destined for delivery to this area, and so they could not guarantee 'his' safe handling. There was only one thing for it – I would have to collect Charles myself. (I had already christened him after Charles-Henri Sanson, the leading character in my *Family of Death*, since my fibre-glass friend had been paid for out of that book's advance royalties.)

At that time I had a Honda CRX, a small two-seater hatchback coupe, and on sitting in the passenger seat and lying back as stiffly-straight as I could, I realised that 'Charles', not being hinged at the hips, simply would not fit in the car – but he would if I removed the passenger seat altogether. Accordingly, I did so, and informed the shop owner of my intention, then motored down there. On arrival he asked whether he should swathe Charles in bubble-wrap: 'Certainly not!' I exclaimed, 'How undignified!' So, opening the car's hatchback, we gently slid him in. The 250-mile journey home was hilarious. Every time I had to slow down for traffic jams or roadworks, other motorists would manoeuvre alongside and point out my instantly recognisable companion, apparently in a state of rigor-mortis, to their open-mouthed passengers! Now with his paintwork smartened-up, his royal cypher burnished, he stands proudly in the corner of my lounge; visitors are initially startled, then delighted to see him, and he blends in perfectly with his appropriate surroundings – the axe, the block, a severed plastic head, and the instruments of medieval persuasion.

During the same year I happened to read of the illness affecting King Hussein I of the Hashemite Kingdom of Jordan, so having served in that country, I wrote a letter of condolence and posted it to the Jordanian Embassy in London. I later received a gracious reply, but unfortunately His Majesty died not long afterwards.

Until recently the Tower Wharf was part of the route of the London Marathon, and the Yeoman Warders on duty assisted in keeping it clear for the runners by controlling the throngs of spectators. For this they were each given one of the same medals as were awarded to the race marshals and competitors. In 1998 I heard from my good friend and ex-colleague Brian Harrison that he had come across the medal he had been given for doing this in 1986; he said that he noticed that the figure engraved on it was the one of me on the postcard that went on sale in the souvenir shops all those years ago. He sent it to me, although he stipulated that I should return it as it was part of his Tower memorabilia. As soon as I saw it, I could only agree that it was me in State Dress! It seems likely that the company manufacturing the 1986 medal had been asked to find a Beefeater for that year's design and mine was the most accessible image available. I sent the medal back to Brian and then contacted the Marathon organisers. They were fascinated by the story and said they would include it in their magazine, and would also check to see whether any medals of that year were still around. Three weeks later I had a letter stating that one, complete with its 1986 ribbon, had been found and was enclosed. Wow – even the winner of an Olympic gold medal doesn't have his or her image engraved on it!

Most peoples' lives are governed by voices, some more unforgettable than others. Mine ranged through 'Deliver the leg of lamb to Mrs Jones at No. 18', spoken by the butcher; 'Get fell in on parade!', by the RAF Sergeant; 'You are now a Yeoman Warder!', by the Resident Governor of the Tower of London; and now 'Lights, camera – action!' by television producers, because the eventual wide circulation of the books launched me on a TV career which was to span the coming years. My debut came about in January 1999, when I received a letter from MPH Entertainment, a television company based in California, in which the producer Adam Hyman said that Rob Goubeaux, the writer/co-producer, had been quite intrigued by the accounts in my books of ghosts and escapes from the Tower (I had been told that some of my books were in the Library of Congress, Washington DC), and asked whether I would take part as a consultant in television interviews with the film director in a London hotel. At the prospect of such excellent publicity for my books, I accepted the invitation with alacrity – after having looked into millions of cameras at the Tower, looking into a single television camera would hold no terrors for me!

So I travelled down to London and located the West End hotel in which an overnight room had been booked for me. The extensive interviewing went very well, by all accounts, and subsequently I appeared in the programme *The Bloody Tower of London* on the History Channel and Channel Five.

MPH Entertainment contacted me again in September; could they send a crew across to Kendal? No problem, and it was almost comical to see the expressions on the faces of the presenter and crew of two (camera and sound) as they entered my lounge and saw the execution axe, ancient handcuffs, leg-irons, and ball-and-chain! We got to work quickly, having no fewer than three programmes to record that day: *The Tower of London, Dr Guillotine and his Execution Machine,* and *The Bodysnatchers*. I, duly miked up, perched on the corner of the table, the presenter, a charming young lady, to my left, the camera and sound men kneeling on the floor facing us. The cameraman made sure I kept in shot by watching a small monitor screen which duplicated the camera's viewpoint, and having started to learn the technique, my first question to the presenter was 'Where d'you want me to look – at you or the camera?' It does vary, as readers watching the TV will no doubt realise. I was told to reply to the presenter's question but look into the lens all the time, and we went to work, had a lunch break, then pressed on.

While we were filming about the bodysnatchers (the sub-human jackals who dug up freshly buried corpses and sold them to surgeons, desperate to obtain specimens with which to teach the rudiments of surgery to their students), the subject of 'articulators' came up. I explained to the camera that these were men who, on finding that the exhumed body was too putrefied to sell to the surgeons, would steal just the bones and rebuild them into useable skeleton specimens. I explained that the articulators would probably sit at a long table and wire the bones together in their correct order, no doubt chanting that well-known song, 'The ankle bone's connected to the leg bone, the leg bones connected to the hip bone!' I wasn't sure whether the Americans would consider that too flippant, but on viewing the entire programme later on the History Channel, I was delighted to see that it hadn't finished up on the cutting room floor. After six hours on camera we were all totally exhausted, but we'd got everything we wanted in the can, so all present were pleased with the results.

I spent quite a lot of 1999 in front of a TV camera. A letter was forwarded to me from the Tower from Jamie Simpson, the BBC producer of the series *Meet the Ancestors* who wished to get in touch with, 'Yeoman Warder Abbott, author of *Rack, Rope and Red-hot Pincers,* as we wish to speak with someone with a good knowledge of execution. This is in regards to a half-burnt skeleton discovered by an archaeologist while digging in an Anglo-Saxon cemetery in Cambridgeshire.'

Upon my phoning him, he mentioned the half-burnt skeleton again, whereupon I suggested, not altogether facetiously, that it could have been the remains of a witch, but that rain may have interrupted the procedure while she was being burnt at the stake. We agreed on a time and date, and on 28th October 1999 he, the presenter Julian Richards and Sarah, the continuity girl, visited my home; Julian and I sat facing each other across the table, Jamie Simpson did the filming and Sarah did the continuity, as the questions and answers flowed. The victim could have been a witch but might also have been a heretic; they were burned to death either to prepare them for the nether regions they would surely encounter because of their 'wrong' religion, or to burn the 'wrong' religion from their souls. Another possibility was that the woman, if indeed the remains were those of a female, could have been executed in that fashion, having committed 'Petit', or 'Low Treason' (as opposed to High Treason, conspiring or assassinating the King, which carried the penalty of being hanged, drawn and quartered), by planning or actually killing her husband, the 'king' of the family. Such women did not suffer the appalling death of disembowelling and dismemberment, it being considered too indelicate to expose a woman's body for such a butcherly purpose, so they were burned to death instead. The interview was all done and dusted within an hour and a half, the programme appeared on BBC 2 the following year.

There's a stage in everyone's life when they reach the conclusion that they've already experienced every sort of excitement going: that there's nothing fantastic left, they'd 'done it all'. I'd been in World War II and the Suez Canal Campaign, lived in the Tower, written books, carried the town's sword, been on TV – what else? Now, at the age of seventy-seven, life should consist of more than Kendal Mintcake and Sticky Toffee Pudding – I wanted to inject something more stimulating in my complacent existence, a new challenge altogether. Deciding exactly what was difficult. I'd always enjoyed getting airborne; although having flown in heavy bombers, two-seater fighters and dive-bombers, conventional light aircraft didn't have much appeal for me. I wanted something different from just flying in one direction – forwards – so how about learning to fly something that could also fly backwards and sideways, and even remain more or less stationary in the air as well – a helicopter!

Large helicopters, such as those operated by Air Sea Rescue and police forces are, of necessity, mainly computer-controlled – should they need to hover or fly at a given speed on a certain compass heading, the appropriate button is pressed – but where's the challenge in that? A manually controlled type was obviously the answer, so in August 1999 I took myself to Heli 2000, a helicopter-training school based on Blackpool Airport, and explained my intentions. The instructor, Captain Mike Cull, started by saying that of course I would first need to learn all about the theory of aero-dynamics, the function of control surfaces and suchlike, but when I pointed out that I had served thirty-five years in the Royal Air Force and had been an aero-engine fitter on Spitfires, Hurricanes and many other aircraft, he said, 'Oh well, let's go!' and led me out on to the airfield, to where one of their fleet of two-seater Robinson R22 helicopters was parked.

The R22 is a hands-on manual machine. Being small, with a large rotor, its controls are so hyper-sensitive that if you should hiccup while you're over Blackpool you'll probably find yourself looking down at Leeds or even Hull. The relatively powerful air-cooled engine is situated almost in the small of your back, so despite the radio headset, the noise is deafening and the vibration is akin to being trapped inside a coffee-grinder. The concentration required to make it do what you want it to do is intense – it's like trying to control a soap bubble that has overdosed on crack cocaine and that's the challenge. It's also essential that at all times during instruction both occupants should be aware of just who is in charge of the temperamental beast, and this is made clear by the use of the phrase, 'You have control', the recipient replying 'I have control'. I occasionally found myself uttering the first phrase in a voice rising to a high-pitched crescendo when the helicopter tried to find out how many times it could spin round under its rotor before I could remember what I'd read on page 17 in the instruction manual; it was at those moments that I found myself wondering why I hadn't taken up embroidery or square-dancing as a hobby instead!

To those of my readers not conversant with just how a helicopter flies, I offer the following analogy: imagine you are holding a large golf umbrella, to the handle of which is attached a powerful but small vacuum cleaner, pointing upwards. You switch the cleaner on and as you open the umbrella slowly, figuratively speaking, you rise from the ground, stopping at a given height by ceasing to open the umbrella any further. Then, by pointing the umbrella slowly forward, sideways or backwards, you would find it 'blowing' you in the direction selected. Now replace the idea of opening of the umbrella with the rotor blades twisting to dig deeper into the air, and substitute an engine for the cleaner, add a rudder bar to help you turn, and there you have it. Mind you, it's a lot more tricky than that; the pull of gravity, the varying strength and direction of the wind, and the sheer cussedness of the machine itself, all need to be controlled by ultra-sensitive co-ordination of hands and feet, so flying manually, and more importantly, hovering is no easy task – to quote Mike, 'If you can't learn to hover, don't waste your money!'

The various manoeuvres – turning, climbing, descending – are partially achieved by the use of the 'collective', the lever at one's side, in co-ordination with the 'cyclic', the control column (it is not called the joystick; the only joy is the sadistic pleasure felt by the helicopter itself when, on noticing that you're momentarily distracted, it promptly goes into a steep left-hand turn without any warning!) Having gone through the necessarily complex start-up checks – there's no scramble take-offs in an R22 – started the engine and got the rotor swishing round overhead, the aircraft gently rocking from side to side, a gentle lift-off then takes place; a quick check of the instruments is followed by raising the collective lever slightly, causing the helicopter's skids to leave the ground, then easing the cyclic forward – whereupon the grass flashes past beneath one's feet as the helicopter hurtles across the airfield. No matter how often I've flown, the sensation is incredible – who needs Ecstasy tablets?

Possibly the worst thing that can happen at any time is total engine failure; there's no hard shoulder to pull on to, just the hard ground coming up rapidly to meet you, so the first lesson concerns the action to take immediately, and that is to push the collective lever down, thereby turning the rotor blades 'flat' so as to stop climbing, then hopefully to descend like a sycamore leaf and try to glide it down; but as a helicopter has the gliding capability of a house-brick, and wearing a parachute is a physical impossibility…! Needless to say, it's essential at all times to expect the unexpected and react correctly and instantly; flying one is a guaranteed cure for sluggish adrenaline and not for the squeamish; one wrong move can prove disastrous, Mike Cull once reminding me, 'The R22 is small – but it bites!'

On one unforgettable occasion in the early days, the instructor told me to go on out and start up the helicopter while he rang Air Traffic to tell them of our intentions. I had never done that before without him being present, but the Abbott pride was at stake, so off I went. I climbed in clutching my check-list, and commenced carrying out the pre-start sequence – check this, switch that, unlock the other – my actions going slower and slower, my anxious glances towards the hangar getting more and more frequent and desperate. Would I have to turn the engine starter key before he arrived?!

Eventually, I reached the point of no-return. I paused; had I done everything on the list, or would the machine suddenly lift off, roll on to its side, topple on to its nose? Still clasping the list in a clammy hand, I double-checked each item again, then took a deep breath and turned the key! The engine behind me clattered deafeningly into life, and the rotor started its lazy rotation, the R22 swaying rhythmically – and at that moment the instructor emerged from the hangar and nodded approvingly as he climbed in – panic over!

About that time, dog-lover Jil Atkinson wanted to attend the International Dog Show in Brussels, so, David having to remain to look after the many animals they boarded in their kennels, I accompanied her to Brussels, flying, for the first time in over fifty years, from Manchester Airport – my old stamping ground, 'Ringway' – though fortunately the pilot didn't decant us over the Tatton Park drop zone. While serving in Germany, I had often driven through Brussels, but to walk through its cobbled streets and historic square at night was unforgettable, and the show itself certainly took some licking, in more ways than one.

David and Jil, also looking for new challenges, particularly those which involved historic costumes, expressed a wish to become, of all things, a Pearly King and Queen – well, why not? Accordingly, I, being one of the traditional characters of the London scene, a 'Beefeater', contacted some members of London's well-known families of Pearlies, and to cut a long story short, in 2001 David and Jil, both clad from head to foot in the splendidly pearl-button-adorned costumes which she had created, were crowned by the Londoners as the Pearly King and Queen of Lancashire, the only Pearlies existent outside the capital! I had obtained permission from Kendal Council to wear my Sword Bearer's uniform and, carrying a sword obtained by David, led the long procession through cheering crowds along the streets of Barrowford. Long may Pearly King David and Pearly Queen Jil reign!

The year of 2001 saw me in front of the cameras again. World of Wonder's producer Mark Rossiter invited me to participate as consultant in *The History of Torture and Punishment*, the two programmes being broadcast on Channel Five in November of that year. Then producer Anna Keel, of another UK TV company, Uden Associates, contacted me, and we filmed *Secrets of the Guillotine*, again for Channel Five, the following December.

I even found time to write another book, *Crowning Disasters*, about things that went wrong at coronations, and there were certainly many in the days before the all-seeing eyes of the television cameras were installed in Westminster Abbey – "Queen Victoria was a very small lady, and had to have a coronation ring made especially for her, so the jewellers manufactured one to fit her fourth finger, the little finger, in accordance with the instructions received from the College of Heralds. The latter authority however was ignorant of the fact that in the pre-Reformation Service books the thumb was counted as the first finger, and when, during the coronation ceremony, the Archbishop attempted to put the newly made ring on the Queen's THIRD, wedding finger, she demurred. He insisted however, so she had to remove her other rings first and allow him to force the already tight ring on to the larger finger. This caused her considerable pain throughout the lengthy proceedings, and indeed the ring could only be removed later in Buckingham Palace after she had immersed her hand in ice-cold water for some time."

That was followed, yes, by yet another TV approach, this time by the Triage Entertainment Inc. of Sherman Oaks, California, their researcher Sharon Griffin writing to say that they were producing a two-hour special on the history of punishment, adding: '...considering your expertise on this subject we would be honoured to have someone of your stature to be a part of our show, and wonder whether you would consider being involved.' When my blushes had faded, I accepted and, filming in my lounge, we spent three and a half hours getting *Punishment* just right for their History Channel and Channel Five, the programme appearing in June 2002.

In February of that year I was again in front of Uden Associates' cameras, this time, appropriately enough, being filmed in the crypt of St Bartholomew's the Great in London's Smithfield. The subject was Queen Mary Tudor, and soon after that I was on location in Deal Castle, Kent, not as a consultant, but for the first time playing the part of yer aktual executioner, wearing an axeman's costume of leather jerkin, mask, etc, provided by the wardrobe people – very enjoyable! This was in *What the Tudors did for Us,* Adam Hart-Davis being my victim, and the producer Page Shepherd subsequently writing to thank me for the use of my torture props and congratulating me as being 'a terrifying executioner'. I don't really know whether that's a compliment or not! I must add that there were no scripts or auto-cues in any of those programmes, everything being 'off the cuff', so all that activity kept me mentally on my toes. I had hoped that by appearing in all these television productions I would be offered roles in other types of programmes (as the dashing hero?), but it was not to be; I had been type-cast as an executioner, producers saying unkindly that I looked better in a mask, although too old to play Batman!

Many authors spend their lives in a state of uncertainty, wondering whether they'll be able to find a willing publisher and, having found one, whether the book the book will die within the first year? So it was much to my surprise and delight to be informed by Headline in 2002 that the Japanese rights to my book *Execution* had been sold to Harashobo Publishers of Tokyo – the text was translated into Japanese, of course, but at least the pictures were in English!

By now, having been dubbed the 'Flying Beefeater' on Heli 2000's website www.heli2000.co.uk, my airborne capabilities were improving considerably; clad in a bomber jacket, jeans and wearing a peaked cap, I was occupying the right-hand seat of the chopper and feeling capable and confident at the controls (incidentally, the cap is adorned with a cloth badge commemorating the exploit of Apollo 15 and bears the names of its crew, Worden, Irwin and my friend David Scott, although I don't aspire to attain *their* record altitude in the R22!) In the same way as one finds oneself suddenly – and almost miraculously – able to balance perfectly on a bike, I had found myself enjoying flying the helicopter without laboriously thinking what each hand and foot should be doing; it was almost a dream-like sensation, being able to relax, as if I were actually part of the machine, and I realised that I was responding almost automatically to any unexpected hiccup – well, most of them, anyway!

I find little fun in flying high, where all sensation of speed is lost, so I stay thirty feet or less above the ground over the airfield practice area – that's really exhilarating. Over inhabited areas, of course, a height of a few hundred feet is mandatory, and even that poses a challenge when coming in to land, by having to continue keeping a wary eye open for other aircraft in the circuit and others taxi-ing on the ground, while deciding when to start descending, at the right approach angle, and at what speed: too high and fast entails over-shooting, pulling out and going round again, too short an approach means levelling out and creeping ignominiously over the airfield boundary, almost hearing Air Traffic Control tut-tutting!

Among my favourite manoeuvres are flying 'figure eights'; staying about twenty feet above the ground, I fly the aircraft like an aerial motorbike, aiming it at speed towards a turning point where I then bank round almost vertically, taking care not to slide-slip and join the scenery, and bring the nose round until I'm facing in the opposite direction, crossing my previous track to another point where I bank round again in the opposite direction, in a figure eight pattern – cool, man, cool! A 'Quick Stop' is equally mind-blowing. As its name suggests, it calls for a fast approach, then ease the cyclic stick back so that the nose comes up and the helicopter stalls, momentarily poised at an angle approaching the vertical. Stopping in the air like that is defying the laws of gravity, and the thing will fall away to one side or the other and has to be corrected even faster than immediately, or else. It is then allowed to bank under control on to an even keel again. On one occasion, while flying with my good friend Graham Cash, he introduced me to a somewhat mind-blowing variation; I was aware of his allowing the aircraft to stop in mid-air, then suddenly realised I was looking straight ahead – at the ground! He then of course pulled out and levelled off, whereupon I naturally had to try the manoeuvre for myself – fantastic! Henceforth, he's known as 'nose-dive' Graham!

Flying sideways, like a crab, is achieved by easing the cyclic mere millimetres to one side or the other, the aircraft then floating as bidden (usually!). The manoeuvre is easy when the wind is blowing in the desired direction but deucedly tricky when trying to propel it against the wind. Every movement of the controls requires only finger – or toe – pressure, and not much of that either, and this is never more essential than when flying backwards. Following a hover into wind, easing the cyclic fractionally rearwards results in the aircraft dipping its tail almost imperceptibly as it moves slowly 'in reverse', it then being necessary not to lose height. It would of course be dead easy if there was no such thing as gravity; if there was no breeze at all, or if there was, it was blowing in exactly the same direction and speed ALL the time; that the tail didn't have ambitions to get ahead of the nose; and also if the R22 hadn't got a mind of its own and didn't want to play this silly game anyway! And a very wary eye has also to be kept on the look-out for other aircraft, for R22s are not fitted with rear-view mirrors – nor do they go beep-beep when travelling backwards, nor, being small and mostly glass, do they paint (appear) on the radar screens of the airliners taking off for foreign parts..

To date I have flown four different types of manual helicopters, R22, R44, Bell 206 and a Schweizer 300Cbi. All of them have their own particular characteristics, but the four seater models, being slightly larger and therefore heavier, are more docile and rather more predictable, so less exhilarating to fly. I must admit that the sound of rotor-slap is music to my ears, even sweeter than the once delectable bubbling murmur of a Spitfire's Merlin engine. And for introducing a new and exciting chapter to my life, I am indebted to my instructors and fellow pilots over the past twelve years, Mike Cull, Bill Scarrett DFC, Simon Fletcher, Graham Cash, Dominic Hickson, Andy Campbell and Terry Butterfield for all their expertise and patience; may they always 'have control'.

In flights across Blackpool I occasionally find myself looking down at one of the most outstanding and memorable buildings of the town – no, not its Tower or the Big Wheel of the Pleasure Gardens – but Little Marton Windmill, its sails and white superstructure clearly outlined against the background of greenery.

It is cared for and supported by a group of dedicated enthusiasts led by Shirley Matthews and deputy Ann Allen, and, my interest in molinology being undiminished, I too am one of the 'Friends of Little Marton Windmill'.

As a more-or-less follow-up to *Crowning Disasters*, I wrote *Regalia, Robbers and Royal Corpses*, mainly featuring the origin of crown jewels and the state of the royal remains immured in the vaults of Westminster Abbey: "when the corpulent Queen Anne died in August 1714, courtiers were reported to have commented that due to her size, her coffin was almost square!" – how cruel.

But on the 5th July 2002 I was privileged once again to find myself in the presence of The Queen – and it was a day like none other, for it also included the most exhilarating road journey of my life. It all took place when I attended the 'Parade for the Golden Jubilee of Her Majesty', at which she inspected members of the Body of Yeoman Warders, the Military Knights of Windsor, Her Majesty's Body Guard of the Honourable Corps of Gentlemen at Arms, The Queen's Body Guard of the Yeomen of the Guard, The Queen's Body Guard for Scotland (i.e. The Company of Archers), and the In-pensioners of the Royal Hospital, Chelsea, on the lawns of Buckingham Palace.

I sometimes visit London to discuss book details with publishers or to take part in television programmes, and I occasionally stay in the Tower with my great friends, Yeoman Warder Alan Fiddes and his hospitable wife (and superb cook!), Eve. On arrival I usually make my way to the Royal Chapel of St Peter ad Vincula (currently under the aegis of the genial and caring Canon Roger Hall and his wife Barbara). My visit to the Chapel is not, as you might imagine, to thank the Deity for my safe journey but for the reassurance I gain on inspecting a wooden tablet therein, on which is inscribed the names of deceased Yeoman Warders, on seeing that my name is not among them!

On that particular occasion, however, I went down on the previous day to do some big-city shopping and also to visit my favourite print shop in Cecil Court, off Charing Cross Road. There, to my surprise, I found one portraying the Company of Archers participating in an archery shoot in the early 1920s, so I purchased it and, on meeting their Captain on the following day, presented it to him for their archives.

But it was on the following day that it all happened. We, the Yeoman Warders, assembled outside the Tower's gates and boarded a coach, bound for Buckingham Palace. We set off with two motorcycle police outriders escorting us, blue lights flashing, sirens sounding. Because on no account should Her Majesty be kept waiting, the necessary traffic arrangements had been made, and unbelievably we went through every traffic light controlled junction, whether the lights were at red or not, from the Tower in the east to the Palace in the west without stopping, nothing, but nothing slowing us down! I had seen police cars and ambulances travelling like that (and even they slow down somewhat at traffic lights) and even watched films of Russian dictators being driven in that fashion, but I never believed it would happen to any vehicle in which I was a passenger; it was like the Red Sea parting as we approached. At the sight of our police escort and the speed of our progress, people on the pavements stopped and stared in wonderment, obviously assuming we were some kind of royalty, so a few of us gave them the slow regal hand wave – great fun!

We arrived at the Palace, the coach parking in the forecourt, and we strolled through the archway out on to the lawns. Together with other past members of the Body, I took my seat on the stands which had been erected and occupied the time by reminiscing about old times with other erstwhile colleagues, until eventually the uniformed phalanxes took up their positions in a wide arc, and The Queen made her way round the parade and inspected them. Marquees had been positioned nearby, and afterwards, while the Pipes and Drums of the Royal Scots, the Band of the Irish Guards, and the Pipes and Drums of the Highlanders (Seaforth, Gordons and Camerons) took turns in providing a musical background, the Palace staff served us with drinks and delicacies, and Her Majesty circulated, having a few words to speak to each of us. It was a great and unforgettable day out.

In August 2002, as a result of the American editions of my books, I received a letter via one of my publishers from those responsible for the publication of the *Encyclopedia Britannica,* the editors inviting me: '…to participate in our project of reviewing every article in our 40 million word data-base, by revising and updating our articles on torture, beheading, drawing and quartering, exile and banishment, flogging, the guillotine, hanging, lynching and scalping. We would also like you to write new articles regarding the rack, the wheel, and caning. We would also like you to review a variety of articles relating to torture in the *Encyclopedia Britannica's* 11th edition (1911) – blinding, boiling to death, branding, ducking and cucking stools, fetters and handcuffs, tarring and feathering, and treadmill… updating and rewriting them if considered worthwhile', the letter ending, 'I hope very much that you will be able to work with us.'

I must admit I considered it a privilege that, from all the other authors, and indeed specialists on such subjects, I should have been the one to be approached, and of course I accepted the invitation. It was somewhat of a daunting task, because although I had most of the information they required, and obtained further material from Amnesty International HQ, I had to revise my writing style. I write the way I talk – indeed my colleagues at the Tower say that when they read my books it is as if I'm addressing tourists on guided tours. But the format required for text books calls for the information to be worded in a much more formal style, and it was not until after much re-wording and re-phrasing that by the deadline of 31st December I finally submitted the work to the publisher. Thankfully, they expressed their complete satisfaction and sent the promised fee, my name being included among the contributors to that epic publication.

A book I'd written earlier finally hit the bookshop shelves, one also based on things that went wrong, but this time on the gallows. With the title *The Executioner Always Chops Twice*, it was subsequently published in paperback as *Execution Blunders* – "At a hanging of two criminals in 1723 the hangman was drunk and, believing there were three for execution, attempted to put one of the ropes round the neck of the parson who was there to give spiritual solace to the condemned men, and it was with much difficulty that he was prevented from doing so!"

These TV invitations were coming so thick and fast that I thought I'd remedy a deficiency in my collection of macabre props. I had leg-irons, handcuffs, etc. and the execution axe – but no block! Eggs with no bacon? Sausages and no mash? Something had to be done. I knew all the necessary dimensions of an execution block, of course, and owned many illustrations, so turning to the Yellow Pages, I contacted Mr. Kevin Quine, an expert cabinet maker in Seatle, north Cumbria, and, having explained my unusual request – there can't have been many such gruesome artefacts manufactured over the past few centuries – he agreed to make one. I drove up there, and he pointed out the piece of timber destined to be hewn to the required shape. On asking him what sort of wood it was, he replied that it was hemlock. Although he was unaware of it, the eerie coincidence struck me immediately, and I explained that hemlock was also the name of a plant which, in ancient Greece, was used as the means of execution for Athenian philosopher Socrates, who, having been found guilty of being 'an evil doer and curious person, searching for things under the earth and above the heaven, and making the worse appear the better cause, and teaching all this to others', was sentenced to death and in 399BC died after drinking the poison. What type of wood, therefore could be more fitting for an execution block? Accordingly, one was made at a very reasonable price and held in readiness in the lounge, next to its soul mate: the axe.

The gruesome twosome weren't required in the BBC programme *The Tower of London*, in which my contribution was to say a few words about the ghosts, nor were they when, on 24th October 2002, I was consultant in *The Executioners*, directed by John Keeling of DGP TV of Soho, that not appearing on Channel Five until some two years later.

During the ensuing lull I decided to write a book featuring women who had been executed, and in line with my decisions regarding lurid titles, *'Women on the Scaffold'* seemed a little tame, but eventually I came up with a much better one, *Lipstick on the Noose*: "what to wear on the scaffold? For the guillotine, an off-the-shoulder blouses, short-sleeved dresses for lethal injection, upswept hairstyle for the axe, no metallic bangles or sequins for the electric chair, and there was no point in using perfume in the gas chamber" – the publisher giving it their full approval and the public their patronage.

Having been a motorist for many, many years, I had always driven fast but carefully, but my record of never having been stopped by the police was shattered one evening in 2003 when driving in Kendal. I became aware of headlights immediately behind me, and so on slowing and turning right I made sure I gave the correct signals. The headlights followed me, and I realised they were those of a police car; I stopped and was approached by the driver, a female police officer, who said that when I braked the brake lights came on, but one of them went out when I signalled the right turn. I thanked her and said that I wasn't aware of it, it being impossible to press the foot brake and check the brake lights at the same time, but that I would of course have the fault rectified forthwith.

She then asked me how much I had had to drink that night. I admitted that while dining with friends I had drunk two glasses of wine, whereupon she produced a breathalyser and invited me to blow into it. Apprehensively, I did so, worried that because I rarely drank anything too intoxicating, two glasses of wine might show I'd drunk to excess. As I continued to blow, I mentally visualised the banner headlines in the next edition of the *Westmorland Gazette* – 'Kendal Sword Bearer gets the Chop!' Similarly horrific thoughts assailed me; would I have to return to the Tower – as a Prisoner? I had been sworn in as a Special of the Metropolitan Police – how would the Commissioner react? And because I was still a Member of the Sovereign's Body Guard – what would the Palace say? The situation was fraught, the moment dire – but then I barely refrained from embracing the delicate and shapely Arm of the Law when she said, albeit sounding somewhat thwarted, that the result was negative – I was reprieved! Actually, she was quite correct in the action she took; any motorist stopped for 'a moving traffic violation', even a tail-light out, can be breathalysed.

More TV filming, this time on 23rd July 2003 for Tiger TV, the location being in the shower room of a leisure centre somewhere in London, the instrument used not an axe but a quantity of water. The programme was called *Pubammo*, designed to provide and illustrate questions or 'ammunition' for pub quizzes, and my role was to inflict the 'Chinese water torture' on the 'recalcitrant' victim. The producer had recruited a young man who submitted to being strapped down on a bench, his head firmly and rigidly held in position by a makeshift wooden vice. A contraption had been constructed above his head which incorporated a tap and a water tank, and I had verbally to exhort him to confess while slowly adjusting the tap so that a drop of water fell on to his forehead every few seconds. As many minutes passed, I must say he endured it very well indeed; by falling on the exact same spot every time, the drops must have had a most unpleasant effect – but that's showbiz! I felt the urge to write again, and having seen so many guidebooks to the Tower, written by 'outsiders' and fairly innocuous in nature, I decided to write a more bloodthirsty version (what else?), its chapters, moreover, being arranged in the order in which visitors toured the Tower. This, *A Beefeater's Grisly Guide to the Tower of London,* published in 2003, proved very popular in the Tower's bookshops and elsewhere: "The last man to be executed in the Tower was a German spy Joseph Jakobs who, on 14th August 1941, was escorted to the rifle range near the Martin Tower. There, having broken his ankle when landing by parachute, he was strapped into a chair and blindfolded; a circle of linen was pinned over his heart as the target and at 7.12am precisely a fusillade of shots from the firing squad of eight Scots Guardsmen rang out, and the condemned man slumped in the chair, fatally wounded."

At last the opportunity to use my new execution block came along in that year when I was approached by the BBC and invited to enact the decapitation of Tony Robinson in the series *The Worst Jobs in History*. The proposed date was, appropriately enough, 5th November, and the location was in my adopted home-town, on Kendal Castle Hill. Tony and the crew assembled at my house and then we drove up to where the ruins of the castle provided a superb backdrop. 'Lights, camera, action' was followed by the filming of the inevitable banter between victim and executioner, as I demonstrated how he should use the axe on a water melon, with hilarious, albeit very messy results. A joint of meat was then placed on the block, and at the thought of hacking at something more like a human neck than just a piece of fruit, Tony, axe in hand, looked at it, hesitated, then said soberly, 'It isn't funny anymore, is it?' I agreed – of course it wasn't. Later, more melons hit the dust in fragments. Afterwards, I delivered my opinion of his performance; his wrist action wasn't too bad, his swing adequate, but it lacked accuracy to the extent that the block needed minimal repairs.

I also learned something about executions on that occasion; something of which I'd never been aware. I had always been contemptuous of the medieval executioners, in particular the notorious Jack Ketch, for frequently needing more than one stroke to sever his victim's head, but it was not until, suitably garbed and masked, I 'beheaded' Tony, and realised that on swinging the axe high above my head in order to gain the necessary momentum on the down stroke, the vision-restricting mask prevented me from seeing not merely the back of his neck, but anything of him at all. We live and learn – my belated apologies, Mr. Ketch!

Later that year, I had a phone call from Outline TV in London inviting me to take part in a programme which was being planned, one of a series entitled *Bloody Britain*, and asking me whether I knew of a good location. I told them they could forget the Tower, it being very expensive and, due to the multitude of tourists, filming would be very restricted. But recalling the sinister dungeons and the scarcity of visitors to Deal Castle, I recommended that as an excellent location. And so it was that I found myself down in Kent. I arrived at night and somehow found the hotel where accommodation had been reserved for me. Coming down for breakfast the next morning, I sat down at a table in the dining room, looked out of the window, and was amazed to see water splashing on the other side of the road. I asked the waiter whether there had been some flooding during the night, and received an answer that made me feel approximately two feet tall 'That, sir,' he said, in a butler-like manner, 'is the English Channel!'

The sound and cameramen arrived, together with my 'victim-to-be', Rory McGrath, a comedian with whom I thoroughly enjoyed working. Some of the filming took part in the dungeon, the full-size model of the rack provided by the company proving most functional – as were the thumbscrews, Rory discovering it the hard way! We then adjourned outdoors, where my 'victim' was slowly hanged, drawn and quartered. I found it difficult to keep a straight face and look like a death-dealing executioner while having to extract his bowels – a string of sausages – from his innards, followed by a piece of liver and a sheep's heart! Again we worked without a script, the cross-talk being totally spontaneous.

For another episode of the same series, the producer needed us to perform a public execution by the axe, this being the method of disposal of James, Duke of Monmouth, his claim to execution fame being that no fewer than five strokes of the axe were required to decapitate him, delivered by Jack Ketch, the executioner mentioned earlier, so we all drove to a football pitch where, in the centre circle, Rory was duly introduced to the gentle art of how to use the weapon; he was not particularly adept, so I advised him not to give up his day job – great fun! The final product appeared on the Discovery Channel in April 2004 and continues to be broadcast occasionally, as do most of the others in which I've appeared. I received an appreciative letter later on from Sam Grace, the producer, thanking me and adding, 'Your expert knowledge of the history of public executions, and especially the beheading of the Duke of Monmouth following the Monmouth Rebellion, was invaluable, and has helped to bring the history alive in the programme.'

Back to writing after that, and I realised that busy people travelling by public transport or aircraft like to dip into a book without necessarily getting involved in a lengthy plot-line. It was then that I wrote *A Macabre Miscellany* for Virgin Books, a paperback containing a thousand weird and wonderful facts – "While awaiting burial, Henry VIII's leaden coffin sprung a leak, and the blood which dripped on to the chapel pavement was licked up by dogs." So popular was that one, that in the following year, 2005 I managed to compile a further thousand bizarre facts; Virgin then publishing *More Macabre Miscellany* – "The Romanian Prince Vlad the Impaler (1431-1476) not only ate the flesh of his defeated foes, but rather than waste the blood, spread it on bread and ate it."

One watches various programmes on the television, content that they are all either fiction or about other people elsewhere in the country or the world. I occasionally watched *Who Do You Think You Are?* finding the lengthy tracking down of the subjects' ancestors fascinating, but never for a moment did I think that anything like that would ever happen to me until, one day in December 2004, I received a letter stating my name and asking whether I was he; was I born at 5 Carlton Street, Moss Side, Manchester, the son of Frank and Ada Abbott – the letter going on to say that if I was that person, I would be the half-brother of the writer, Helen Turnbull. It was creepy; I felt as if someone was looking through the window at me! The letter continued, saying that if I didn't wish to reply, she would understand, and also apologising if in fact I was not that person.

Of course out of sheer curiosity I wrote back to my newly-discovered half-sister, she providing me with much of the information she had discovered while climbing up the family tree. I already knew that my father had served in the trenches during the first World War and had been badly wounded by a sniper, and that he and my mother had separated some years after my birth, and had no doubt later divorced, but Helen filled in all the subsequent details – and now, after all these years, I suddenly had another family! More Christmas and birthday prezzies to buy! Seriously though, it was rather a wonderful experience, and she and her husband Andrew still keep in touch.

Lancaster, but twenty miles or so from Kendal, has always been one of my favourite cities, and on an earlier visit I entered the imposing court room in the Castle and stood in the dock, where the little stairway leads to the cells below, the words used today 'Take him down!' being the origin of those spoken by the judge after passing sentence on a guilty prisoner. While there I also handled a noose used by the 19th century hangman William Calcraft to hang Richard Pedder on 27th August 1853, Pedder having been found guilty of murdering his wife. On studying Calcraft's life I discovered that he held the record of being the longest serving executioner in

England, having performed hangings from 1829 to 1874, a total of 45 years. Nor was that all, for he had been the last executioner to officiate at a public hanging, that of Michael Barrett in 1868, the last one to carry out a multiple hanging: five pirates having suffered death at his hands in 1864; and the first hangman to operate in private, i.e. behind prison walls. He was also the one who used the shortest rope, three feet or less in length, so most of his victims died of slow strangulation. On discovering all that I decided that he, of all hangmen, surely deserved a book of his own, as it were, so I tracked down some of his living relatives and with the information they willingly provided, wrote *William Calcraft, Executioner Extraordinaire!*, it being brought out by Eric Dobby Publishing in 2004.

In preparation for the American television programme *The Body Snatchers*, filmed in 2000, as described earlier (The ankle bone's connected to the...!), I had researched the general subject of body-snatchers and now decided to dig deeper into the subject (how else?) with the result that by 2005 I had garnered sufficient material for a book about those shovel-wielding gentlemen, giving it the appropriate title of *Grave Disturbances,* and it was published in 2006 – "once the coffin had been opened it was then necessary to secure a rope around the corpse's neck. This ghastly task was usually performed by one body-snatcher who was suspended head-first by his companions and lowered into the cavity, there to grope in the darkness for the body. It was then hauled to the surface, taking care not to decapitate it, and it was found that this could be achieved by means of a gentle rhythmic action rather than a single violent pull.'

That wasn't the only output that year, for following the success of *A Macabre Miscellany* and its stable mate *More Macabre Miscellany*, I had found so many more odd facts while researching the bodysnatchers that I assembled a similar conglomeration, Eric Dobby publishing *It's A Weird World* in 2006 – "To pay for her son's education, American Kari Smith has sold space on her forehead by having the address of a gambling website tattooed there."

By now I had reached the stage where, should the phone ring, I didn't know whether it would be a guest-speaker-hunting secretary, a TV producer, or even another half-sister, but I was certainly not prepared when, in January 2007, I found myself being asked by a journalist of the *New York Times* for my opinion regarding the number of people who had reportedly crowded the scaffold during the execution of the deposed Iraqi leader Saddam Hussein on the previous 20th December. I explained that the regulation number of officials permitted to be present at hangings in the western world would include the chaplain, prison governor, chief warder, doctor, etc, but due to the notoriety of the condemned ex-dictator, no doubt many of his opponents wanted to gloat over his execution with their own eyes. My opinion was quoted in their newspaper, a copy of which the journalist sent to me: 'Is there an optimal way to execute a deposed ruler, then? If speed is paramount, "By far the best is the guillotine for despatching anyone," said Geoffrey Abbott, author of 'Execution: the Guillotine, the Pendulum, the Thousand Cuts, the Spanish Donkey and 66 Other Ways of Putting Someone to Death', and a former Yeoman Warder at the Tower of London. Mr. Abbott did not say which of the 70 ways might have suited Mr. Hussein, but if the idea is to 'pay the penalty untinged by revenge' then, "I would say firing squad," he said. "The thought of a military execution is more honourable than a crude hanging."'

Nor did it end there, for some months later, following the execution of Hussein's half-brother Barzan el-Tikriti – which went badly awry, those present noticing that after he had dropped out of sight, the empty noose jerked back upwards again, and on looking down into the pit they saw that his torso lay in one place and his severed head some distance away – I had a similar phone call, this time from a reporter on the *Associated Press* International News Agency, New York. He asked how the hanging could have resulted in decapitation (I explained, too long a length of rope, so too great a rate of descent). Considering that they could have asked any one of the considerable number of professional hangmen still employed in the USA, I took it as a compliment that they should instead have contacted me.

Execution was certainly the byword for that year; Summersdale Publishers, having bought the rights to my book *Execution* in 1995 and sold the US and Canadian rights to St Martin's Press, 5th Avenue, New York, informed me that they had also been successful in selling the rights to their opposite numbers in Australia and New Zealand. Nor was that all, for they had negotiated similar sales to Greek and Italian publishers – suitably translated, of course. A Greek newspaper reviewing the book also included a picture of me appropriately garbed. Fortunately I was not asked to proof-read them before publication.

In my browsing around sundry book fairs that year, I came across a book which virtually begged me to adopt and do something with it. Its title was *London's Burial Grounds*, written by an incredible Victorian lady Mrs Basil Holmes who, in 1901, while studying a map of London drawn in 1742, noticed a large number of plague pits, cemeteries and burial grounds, were no longer shown on her more modern maps. Determined to find out what had happened to them, she visited each site – a rare adventure for ladies of that time, their activities being mainly those of sewing, embroidery and cooking, and then she had her work published.

On reading the book I realised that even many of the burial grounds of *her* day now lay beneath new buildings or had been obliterated by the bombing raids of World War II, so I revised her findings, updated them as far as possible, and in 2007 had it published under my chosen title *Who's Buried Under Your Floor?* – "Pet owners taking their dogs for walkies across the playing fields of Vincent Square in London would be surprised, to say the least, if they knew that the turf was laid over what was the burial site of 1,200 Scottish prisoners and their wives, as would commuters waiting for trains in Cannon Street Station; they might complain about the lack of porters, but are completely unaware of the skeleton staff beneath the platforms on which they're standing, for the station was built on the site of the Cemetery of St. John's Church, Cloak Lane." Possibly the book led to house owners wondering what lay beneath the floors of *their* cellars, or what sort of bone the dog had just brought in, and I think it highly significant that within months of its publication there was a noticeable reduction in house prices in the London area!

Not having been on camera since 2004, I had come to the conclusion that my name had long since been confined to television's waste paper basket, so it came as a pleasant surprise when, in November 2008, I received a phone call from a staff member of the French television company SEP TV. He, having read my various books on the subject, asked me whether I would perform the role of executioner in a programme with the title *Secret d'Histoire*, to be broadcast on that country's Channel 2 in 2009. I accepted, and so the lights, sound, and camera crew, accompanied by Elodie, a charming young French presenter, arrived some days later, the filming taking place outdoors on my patio. Following the filming of my sets of handcuffs, leg-irons, ball and chain and similar grim items of medieval ironmongery, I donned my black mask and improvised black hood, and wielded my ancient axe energetically; as usual volunteers were singularly reluctant to come forward and kneel over the block, so I had to be content with 'beheading' the water melons they had brought with them. The filming continued for about three hours, Elodie eventually professing her satisfaction.

Three months later I was again judiciously employed, this time for Pulse Films of London, participating in a pilot programme for a series subsequently appearing on television with the title *History's Toughest Prison,* featuring the Marshalsea gaol which once housed London's debtors.

And then I came across a mention of the old London Bridge – no, not the one that was sold to the Americans and now spans Lake Havasu in Arizona, USA, but the one which, for more than six hundred years, was the only road-crossing into the City from the Continent and the south of England. Over the centuries it was traversed by royals and rogues, queens and convicts, lords and layabouts, not merely a roadway but a veritable village, being lined on both sides by houses and shops, even having its own chapel. Nowadays, villages vie for the title of 'Best Kept Village' or 'Village in Bloom', but the one on old London Bridge would have had few rivals for the title of 'Village with Most Heads', for between the thirteenth and seventeenth centuries more than eighty-six severed heads of traitors adorned its pinnacles – with a couple of dismembered quarters thrown in for good measure. The story of this simply cried out to be written, and so in 2009 *The Gruesome History of Old London Bridge* reached the shelves of all good bookshops – "The last of the total of eighty-six severed heads displayed on the Bridge over the centuries belonged to William Stayley who had been found guilty of plotting the assassination of Charles II. He was sentenced to be hanged, drawn and quartered, his remains then to be put on public display, but following appeals by his relatives, a Christian burial for the body parts was permitted instead. However at the funeral service held in St Paul's Cathedral, the mourners were unable to control their emotions, and when the King heard about the noisy uproar, he promptly reversed his decision, and poor Mr Stayley's dismembered quarters were exposed on the City gates and his head spiked on the Bridge, its sightless eyes gazing out over the City."

In November of that year I was once more in front of the cameras, this time by at the invitation of ITN producers working on a History Channel series called *Mudmen*, a mix of archaeology, torture and execution, the latter taking place in the Clink Prison, now a tourist attraction in South London. No black garb/mask this time, but my Yeoman Warder-badged blazer sufficed.

People not only love plots but more especially what happened to those who plotted, from Guy Fawkes onward. Well, lots of horrible things happened to them, so it was a case of 'back into history', and eventually my twenty-third book, *Plots and Punishments,* was published by Willow Bank in March 2010 – "A leading member of a conspiracy to poison Sir Thomas Overbury in the Tower was Mrs Anne Turner, known to be a herbalist skilled in the use of charms, these being written on parchments bound in the dried skin of a man. Such macabre bindings were not unusual; human skin is about one-sixth of an inch in thickness and can be increased by tanning, i.e. by soaking it in a mixture of alum, salt and Roman vitriol, then allowing it to dry. The lady in question was hanged at Tyburn in March 1615 watched by an immense crowd, many of the spectators being persons of quality, ladies as well as men having arrived in their coaches."

Two months later, fame beckoned once more when the BBC invited me to play the role of a Tudor executioner in a Blue Peter programme designed to illustrate the fate of those who, opposed to Henry VIII, went into plots headlong and left head short. The ruins of Kendal Castle atop 'my' town's hill again provided a superb backdrop – appropriately enough, as the Castle was reputedly once the residence of Queen Catherine Parr, His Majesty's sixth wife, who herself escaped the block due to the prior death of her royal husband – and I, menacingly masked and hooded, demonstrated the art of axe-wielding to the programme presenter Helen Skelton (see photo on page 198), more water-melons subsequently meeting an early (and thirst-quenching!) demise. By wearing a mask, I was admirably protected from any legal claims that might have been submitted by indignant parents demanding compensation for the subsequent nightmares suffered by their precious little kiddiwinks who had watched the programme – 'It wasn't me, Your Honour!' I now wear my personal Blue Peter badge with pride.

Taking advantage of the Royal Wedding year 2011, publisher Eric Dobby neatly combined *Crowning Disasters*, published in 2001, and *Regalia, Robbers and Royal Corpses*, published in 2002, into one, *Crowning Calamities and Royal Corpses*, purchasers of the book thereby being able to find out not only what happened during the Coronation of Edward *VII*: "The ceremony passed off without event, other than the moment when Dr Temple, Archbishop of Canterbury, placed the crown the wrong way round on the King's head! A further minor yet noisy contretemps occurred when one lady, seated in a balcony overlooking the altar, dropped her prayer book over the edge, and to her horror heard it clatter among the

Abbey plate spread out below", but also what followed the exhumation of Oliver Cromwell's body and those of his former cohorts, as described by Sir George Wharton in 1662: "The odious carcases of O. Cromwell, H. Ireton, and J. Bradshaw, were drawn on sledges to Tyburn on the anniversary of the execution of Charles I and, being pulled out of their coffins, there hanged at the several angles of the Triple Tree (gallows) till Sunset. Then taken down, beheaded and their loathsome Truncks thrown into a deep hole beneath the gallows. Their heads were afterwards set upon Poles on the top of Westminster Hall".

The 'magic' number of twenty TV appearances came up in April 2011, thanks to a company named Legasee. They were creating a website based on the subject of veterans' experiences for the benefit of colleges, students and the general public, and the fact that my 35 years RAF service was crowned by my years at the Tower of London was an added bonus for them. Appropriately enough, we filmed in the British Legion Headquarters in West London.

August 2011 found me, on camera deep, in a dungeon in Warwick Castle with a BBC crew, making a programme called *How God Made the English* in which, being classified in BBC records as a 'torture consultant', I was required to describe in detail how Guy Fawkes and others were half-hanged, then drawn and quartered – ugh! Then, in March of the following year, I was invited by those in charge of the York Dungeon to visit their exhibition and comment 'professionally' on the realistic scenes of torture and executions which attract thousands of shudder-loving visitors a year, an invitation which I accepted with pleasure! Coincidentally, a few months later I was contacted by a Los Angeles TV producer Laurel Parker tasked with researching for a programme on torture for the American networks. She, having read my books on the subject, was desperate to find a suitably equipped location, and upon my recommendation, we eventually got together in York Dungeon, where I was duly 'miked up', the camera rolled, and the sequence completed to her satisfaction.

Now, in 2014, my book *Execution*, published in 1994, is proving to be my bestseller, a new edition having just been published – whatever next, I wonder! I sometimes think 'what if' – what if I had accepted the attractive offer of becoming an officer back in the fifties? If I had, I would never have attained one of the ranks necessary to be a Yeoman Warder (Flight Sergeant or Warrant Officer). What if I hadn't become interested in windmills at High Wycombe then Holland? I wouldn't have posed in front of one, the picture then appearing in the copy of the *Air Force News* in which the vacancy at the Tower was advertised. What if the authorities there hadn't approached me a second time after my having had to back out first time because of the appendicitis? It's almost as if it had been my destiny to become a 'Beefeater', all the time!

When starting to write this autobiography, I was surprised by what my intensive memory-dredging brought up from the past; things long-forgotten emerged, some amazing (did I really do that?), others regretted (I should have known better!). Alas, it's much too late now! Having served for over sixty-five years in uniform – as Airman, Yeoman Warder, Mace and Sword Bearer – mine has been a hectic, sometimes scary, often uneventful life, but rarely boring, and, given the chance, I'd do it all again (well, most of it!) So in conclusion; to those of my readers who might be approaching maturity; the minute you find yourself saying, 'I shouldn't be doing this at my age' – I offer you my personal motto – *'Never allow yourself to be dictated to by your birth certificate!'*

EPILOGUE

During my transient way of life, I have of course made many friends. Being in the Armed Forces is akin to being a long-distance coach driver; as postings to different units and places are frequent, people enter one's life for one or two 'stops', then the coach moves on and they're gone and all but forgotten. Depending on Service exigencies, some stay on board a little longer, a few until the vehicle reaches the terminus.

At the Tower a new clutch of friends was made: Catherine Campbell, the Resident Governor's efficient and ever-helpful secretary, relic excavator Dr Geoff Parnell, great-mate Brian Harrison and his always-welcoming wife Mary, Dave and Mo Cope, and all the other Yeoman Warder colleagues too numerous to mention. Many, regrettably, are now but names on the memorial board in the Tower's Chapel Royal.

Settling in Civvy Street brought more permanent friends: the irreplaceable Jil and David Atkinson, writer and photographer Ed Geldard and the ever-charming Maggie Howard, best-ever neighbours such as Ray and Pat, and Jamie, Carol and family, not forgetting my creative artist friend Elaine Nelson, and Chris Holmes, who is not only responsible for the professional digital processing of the illustrations in this book but also taught me not to be scared of using a computer (I still am but don't tell him!). My frequent visits to Blackpool bring me into contact with additional friends, the helicopter-school staff of June, Graham, Annie (and their baby Millie!), Michelle, Joel and Karen also adding to my list of definitely more-than-just casual acquaintances. My 'step-family', Mary, Peter and Humphrey are in weekly contact, and Robert, now living with his wife, Catherine and son in Sydney, occasionally phones to remind me to eat plenty of vegetables! And of course I keep my reactions razor-sharp by strapping in beneath the whirling rotor blades as often as the weather permits.

MY TOWER OF LONDON 'FAMILY TREE'

This is a transcript of a chart listing my predecessors who, like me, have been number 37 in the Register of Yeoman Warders during the past 345 years, researched and compiled by my good friend Brian Harrison, author of the definitive work *The Tower of London Prisoner Book,* published by the Royal Armouries in 2004.

As described in Chapter 10, in earlier centuries the 'place' as a Yeoman Warder, guaranteeing as it did a position in a royal palace and exclusion from compulsory parish duties such as street cleaner, watchman, town constable, churchwarden, etc., (as itemised in my Yeoman Warder's Warrant) was 'bought' for approximately 250 guineas, this sum being recouped by the warder by selling it to his replacement on retirement. However, should the warder die 'in harness', one of the high ranking officers of the Tower was entitled to sell the vacancy and retain the cash for himself!

Ancient records of the Body of Yeoman Warders reveal that *Warder Edward Whitwell* purchased his place in the Tower of London in September 1664; the same position (ie Register Number 37) then passed to *James Walmesley* in November 1676. He died in the office of Warder and according to his ancient privileges, George Legge, Lord Dartmouth, as Constable of the Tower, then sold the vacancy to *John Wray* who, after only four years, decided to sell his place in

1682 to *John Sparrowhawke*. This gentleman died in 1691 and was buried in the Tower near his father of the same name. Once again the Constable sold his place, this time to *David Meredith* who, after more than twenty-two years of Yeoman Service, died in 1714. The position then passed successively to *William Stokes* who sold his place in 1720; *Robert Richardson* (sold 1721); *Anthony Adams* (sold November 1725); *John Ingall* (sold December 1737); *Charles Speed* (sold August 1745); *Roger Hainesworth* (died 1786); *Benjamin Fraser* (died October 1805) and *Isaac Bowne* (died December 1812). With so many deaths in harness having taken place, the officers who were Constables at the time must have reaped a rich financial harvest!

Next was *Gabriel Baker*, who sold his place in March 1826 to *John Kirby*, that gentleman being, in fact, the last person ever to purchase a place in the Tower, for later that year the Duke of Wellington, on becoming Constable, abolished the system in favour of presenting such vacancies as a reward to 'deserving, gallant and meritorious discharged NCOs of the Army'. But John Kirby continued to serve under the Iron Duke's command and died in the Tower in September 1861. (One wonders whether, following the change in the regulations, his family was subsequently reimbursed).

Under the new method of recruiting, the vacancy was filled by *John McVeagh*, an ex-Hospital Sergeant of the 4th Light Dragoons, known to have been a personal friend of Nurse Florence Nightingale. McVeagh had been awarded one of the earliest DCMs (Distinguished Conduct Medal) for his conduct during the Charge of the Light Brigade and also held the Crimea Medal with clasps for the Battles of Alma, Inkerman, Balaklava and Sebastopol. He died in his quarter in the Salt Tower on 3rd October 1882 and was buried at Nuneaton. His place then passed to *Charles Mills*, ex-Battery Sergeant Major of the 11th Brigade, Royal Artillery, of whom very little is known. He died at No. 8 Tower Green on 4th February 1898. The next day the resultant vacancy was filled by *Albert Gooderham*, a veteran of the 9th Foot Regiment (Norfolks) who had served in the Indian and Afghan campaigns of 1877-1879. After a Yeoman career spanning more than twenty-nine years Albert died in Guy's Hospital on 28 May 1927. His replacement as No. 37 in the Register reported for duty on 15th August that year, it being *Robert Henry Haysom*, late Company Sergeant Major of the Border Regiment and an old campaigner from the First World War. During his service as a Yeoman Warder he was awarded the Jubilee Medal 1933, Coronation Medal 1937, Defence Medal 1939-45 and the Meritorious Medal. He was transferred to the Supernumerary List on 3rd March 1951.

His replacement, *Gilbert Frederick Futter* DCM MM, ex-Regimental Sergeant Major of the Oxfordshire and Buckinghamshire Light Infantry, did not report until 21st May 1951. Before the Second World War he had seen service in India and during the War had served with the 8th Army in North Africa and Italy. On 10 December 1952 he was awarded his Meritorious Service Medal and in the following year the Coronation Medal of Queen Elizabeth II.

On his transferring to the Supernumerary List on 1st August 1970, there was a temporary reduction to the establishment of the Yeoman Body, but the post was filled on 25th November 1974 by Gerald 'Bud' Abbott, ex-Warrant Officer of the Royal Air Force, he having joined up in August 1939 and during his thirty-five years served in North and East Africa, Italian Somaliland (now Somalia), India, Iraq, the Hashemite Kingdom of Jordan, the Gulf States, the Suez Campaign, and with NATO in France, Germany and Holland. He and his wife Shelagh lived at No. 16 The Casemates in the Tower, until transferring to the Supernumerary List in October 1982.

Being a 'descendent' of such a distinguished and renowned membership of Register Number 37, makes me feel proud and somewhat – although not altogether – humble!

YEOMAN WARDER'S WARRANT

Field Marshal Sir Richard Hull GCB DSO MA LLD (Hon)
Exeter
Constable HM Tower of London

By virtue of the power and authority given unto me by *HER MAJESTY*, I do hereby and ordain, constitute, and appoint you, the said Yeoman Warder
GERALD ABBOTT
To be one of the Yeoman Warders of the said Tower, you behaving yourself as becometh a loyal and faithful subject and servant to *HER MAJESTY*, her heirs and successors, according to the trust reposed in you. To which end and purpose I do hereby signify and declare that you, the said
GERALD ABBOTT
have taken the usual and accustomed oath of a Yeoman Warder. You are to receive the wages and fees incident to the office or place of a Yeoman Warder, you are to enjoy all other duties, profits, emoluments and commodities together with all other ancient privileges of the same belonging or in anywise appertaining. Among divers others, you are superceded from arrest. You may not be restrained of your liberty or be detained as a prisoner without leave first being had and obtained from me. You are likewise exempted from bearing any parish office as churchwarden, collector (of rubbish and detritus), scavenger or the like, neither are you chargeable with any kind of taxes or payment except in court only as others of *HER MAJESTY'S* servants are. You are not to be empanelled on juries or give your attendance at assizes or sessions. Neither are you to watch or

ward or pay others for doing those duties, with divers other privileges not herein particularly mentioned, which, as *HER MAJESTY'S* servant, you may justly pretend to enjoy. Which said place of Yeoman Warder of the Tower, together with all profits, commodities, emoluments and privileges above specified and thereunto belonging to you, the said

GERALD ABBOTT

are to hold, possess and enjoy for and during the Royal will and pleasure of our *SOVEREIGN THE QUEEN* and I do and hereby require all persons whom these presents shall or may concern that they take notice hereof, and commit no act or thing whatsoever that may in any way infringe or violate the privileges of you, the said

GERALD ABBOTT

as they tender *HER MAJESTY'S* Service, and will answer the contrary at their peril.

Given under my hand and seal of the Tower this twenty-fifth day of November nineteen hundred and seventy four, in the twenty –second year of the Reign of
HER MOST EXCELLENT MAJESTY ELIZABETH THE SECOND
by the Grace of God of the United Kingdom of Great Britain and Northern Ireland and of her other Realms and Territories, *QUEEN*, Head of the Commonwealth, Defender of the Faith.

Signed   (R A Hull)   Field Marshal, Constable of HM Tower of London
(Note; this wording of a Yeoman Warder's Warrant originated in 1683, except for names and dates).

<u>**DECLARATION OF SPECIAL CONSTABLE**</u>
<u>**METROPOLITAN POLICE**</u>
<u>**LONDON**</u>

I, GERALD ABBOTT, solemnly and sincerely declare and affirm that I will well and truly serve our **Sovereign Lady and Queen** in the Office of **Special Constable**, without fear or affection, malice or ill-will; and that I will to the best of my power cause the peace to be kept and preserved, and prevent all offences against the persons and properties of **Her Majesty's** Subjects; and that while I continue to hold the said office I will, to the best of my skill and knowledge, discharge all the duties thereof, according to law.

Signed G. Abbott
Date 29.1.75

Yeoman Warder
Her Majesty's Royal Palace and Fortress
The Tower of London

SWEARING IN OATH

<u>AS A YEOMAN WARDER</u>
<u>OF HER MAJESTY'S ROYAL PALACE AND FORTRESS</u>
<u>THE TOWER OF LONDON</u>

I swear to serve *Her Majesty Queen Elizabeth the Second*, by the
Grace of God, of the United Kingdom and Northern Ireland,
Queen, Defender of the Faith, Her Heirs and Successors, Lawful
Kings and Queens of these Realms, both faithfully and truly in
the Office I am now called unto, that is, to be

A Yeoman Warder of the Tower of London

And in all things touching Her honour and safety I will neither do
nor procure or give my consent to be done by any other person,
anything that shall be prejudicial or hurtful to *Her Majesty's*
person, Crown or Dignity, or to any of the Royal Family, but if I
should hear of any such intended bodily hurt, prejudice or
dishonour, I will do as much as in me lyeth to prevent the same,
and speedily disclose it to *Her Majesty* or such of her Privy
Council as I may next come to, and by all ways and means in my
power, to cause the same to *Her Majesty* truly to be made known.

I do also swear to be obedient to the Constable of the Tower, my
Captain and all such Officers as are to have command over me
there. I will not depart from the Tower into the country without
the licence of the Constable. I will not suffer any person or
persons whomsoever to pass to and from the Tower after the
Watch is set, unless such person or persons have the Watchword.

And upon every needful and urgent occasion, if I shall hear or know of anything concerning the endangering of the Tower or attempting thereof, I will immediately disclose it, and use all possible means to make the same known.

I will keep the *Queen*'s peace myself in the Tower and all other places, as much as in me lyeth, and shall cause all others to do the same, to the utmost of my power.
All these things I will faithfully and truly perform,
so help me God.

(G. Abbott)
Sworn this 25 November 1974
At Her Majesty's Tower of London

SWEARING IN OATH

OF THE QUEEN'S BODY GUARD
OF THE YEOMEN OF THE GUARD

I, Gerald Abbott, sincerely promise and swear to serve *Her Most Sacred Majesty Elizabeth the Second*, by the Grace of God, of the United Kingdom and Northern Ireland, *Queen*, Defender of the Faith, Her Heirs and Successors, Lawful Kings and Queens of these Realms, both faithfully and truly in the Place and Office I am now called unto and to be placed in, namely, as one of the

YEOMEN OF THE GUARD EXTRAORDINARY
OF HER MAJESTY'S GUARD OF HER BODY IN
ORDINARY

And in all things touching her Honour and Safety, I shall neither myself do, or procure, or give consent to be done, by any other, any manner of thing that shall, or may be, prejudicial or harmful to *Her Majesty's* Person, Crown, or Dignity, or to any of the Royal Family. But if I shall hear of, or by any way understand any such, or that any manner of bodily hurt, dishonour or prejudice may be in agitation, contriving or likely to happen, I shall do as much as in me lyeth to prevent, stop, or hinder the same, and besides to disclose and discover (reveal) it with all speed to *Her Majesty*, or to such of *Her Majesty's* Privy Council as I can or may next come to, or to some or one of my Officers on duty, and by all ways and means I can possibly, to cause the same to be made known.
I swear to be obedient to my Captain and all other of my Officers of the said Guard, in all things concerning my office in *Her*

263

Majesty's Service. I shall keep the Queen's peace in my own person, both in the Court and in all other places, as much as in me lyeth, and shall cause all others to do the same, to the utmost of my power.

All these things I shall truly, faithfully and obediently keep and perform, so help me God.

(G. Abbott)
Sworn this day 24 January 1975
At St. James' Palace
London

TROOPSHIPS SAILED IN

HMT Staffordshire 11 January 1942 - 13 February 1942
Gourock – Freetown – Durban / South Africa
HMT Narkunda 2 March 1942 - 19 March 1942
Durban – Mombasa / East Africa – Bombay / India
HMT Felix Roussel 21 March 1942 - 30 March 1942
Bombay – Aden – Port Tewfik / Egypt
HMT Burma 17 June 1942 - 28 June 1942
Port Tewfik – Port Sudan – Berbera – Mombasa
HMT Ascania 21 December 1945 - 27 December 1945
Port Said / Egypt – Malta – Toulon / France

Total time spent at sea in troopships – three months

AIRCRAFT FLOWN IN

DH Tiger Moth – 2 seater basic trainer

Operational types;
Blackburn Skua – 2-seater dive-bomber
Boulton & Paul Defiant – 2-seater fighter
Fairey Fulmar – 2- seater fighter
Armstrong Whitworth Whitley – heavy bomber

Communication types
Hastings – 4 engined a/c
Valetta – twin engined a/c
Avro York – 4 engined a/c
Pembroke – twin engined a/c

DH Devon – twin engined a/c
Vickers Viking – twin engined a/c
Douglas Dakota – twin engined a/c
DH Rapide – 5 seater twin engined a/c
Avro Anson – twin engined, also bomber a/c
Lockheed Hudson – twin engined, also bomber a/c

Bell 206 helicopter – as passenger
Robinson R44 helicopter – as passenger
Schweitzer – 2 seater helicopter – as pilot
Robinson R22 – 2 seater helicopter – as pilot

SHELAGH'S VERSES

ON THE TOWER AS A PRISON

A box of draughts is this, the Tower of London.
A whistling cage of weather
Set on the City's edge.
But if you would find one chink, one slit
Through which a man may wedge his finger,
Then you have magic, sir, and there's an end of it.
For stick to stone
As skull to bone,
Tight is this prison bound.
And clever is he
Who to be free
Thinks he a path hath found.

A box of tricks is this, the Tower of London.
A deluder of men's senses.
Sly thief of sanity.
What random vanity it is therefore
To thrust the blunted dagger of thine hope
Between old England's stubborn lock and door.

ON THE YEOMAN WARDERS

Oh, I would a Yeoman Warder be
With tunic aflare from neck to knee.
Partizan held so straight and steady
That it could be said I was Ruff'd and Ready!

But only in jest I'd have ye know
For across my chest in manly row
Are strung the medals I won in defence
Of truth and right and common sense.
Oh, I would a Yeoman Warder be –
Say, who is the man who would stand with me?

If there would be a sight for all to look upon
And say "This, then, is Britain!"
For sensibility's sake let there be chosen
A Yeoman Warder.
Set him to stand athwart our heritage,
For none is more proud of it.
Approve his service,
For none is more honourable.
Place him in cloth of scarlet well-adorned with gold,
And ye shall have in him our very nation thus behold.

ON THOSE WHO YEARNED TO ESCAPE

A fig for sunshine!
I would have
The thickest fog
In manufacture
From the heavens,
Swirling and sniping
At my cloak,
And stealing
The raven's raucous croak
To render it a whisper.

As I have saved a penny gainst a rainy day,
And some sweet maid yet to be kiss't
I would cast these fine treasures full away,
To flee this prison in a kindly mist.

ON TOWER WHARF

Go walk on the Wharf and ye'll surely see
The world and his wife and children three.
Dogs in assortment, beggars leering,
Office boys fresh from a nearby beering,
Pink at the collar and daft at the knees,
All set for a wench or two to tease.

But go again in a silent hour
When the cobbles are wet from an evening shower,
Ye'll see how the silvery shaft of the moon
Glints on the tiny buckled shoon...
Of my lady who hurried, her Lord to see,
For a prisoner in the Tower is he.

ON THE RAVENS

An Echo of Ravens it should be
To describe this bird collectively.
For if one doth croak
Thou can swear on one's sword
That another stands
Across the sward,
Dipping and calling and gawkily hopping,

One wing outstretched – the other dropping.
Fashioned like this with a few feathers clipped
So our Sovereign shall rule
And her Crown ne'er be tipped.

ON THE GHOSTS

In the sunlight 'tis easy to swagger and strut
To push on a door that is carelessly shut.
But evening will bring just the hint of a query
Turning reason awry and producing an eerie
Domination of doubt where once certainty stood -
What lies just beyond that great portal of wood?
Is it fiercesome or gentle? – rapid or slow?
Wilt thou brazenly enter – or tarry – or go?
I'll not wait for thine answer
But meet thee below…!

ON GIVING GUIDED TOURS

'Tis a tale I relate of sorrow and strife
Of kingly desires and choices of wife.
Merriment surely when spirits were high,
And the telling of beads as the axe drew nigh.
Mirth I must show them in case they grow feared,
And smiles I shall exercise under my beard –
For these folks who come by to listen agape
To the Warder's fine stories of trial and escape.

ON THE SCOTTISH EARL OF NITHSDALE
(who escaped dressed as a woman)

Would ye ha'e me sneakit frae this place
Wi' neither soldier's stamp nor pace -
Bedaddled out in frills and lace?
Och, woman, find your senses.
In twenty days, full twenty ways
Ha'e come to mind and faded
And no douce wee wife
Shall save my life
In petticoats paraded
But och, the smell o' freedom's air,
The eagle's glance, the wildcat's lair,
Enough to render soft and sair
A Scotsman's grand defences.....
So sit awhile and tell me yet
How you and I shall slip this net!

(he did escape and with his wife, lived happily ever after!)

INDEX